Osip Mandelstam: Selected Essays

The Dan Danciger Publication Series

Osip Mandelstam: Selected Essays

Translated by Sidney Monas

University of Texas Press, Austin

Library of Congress Cataloging in Publication Data

Mandel'shtam, Osip Emil'evich, 1891–1938.
    Osip Mandelstam, selected essays.
    (The Dan Danciger publication series)
    Includes bibliographical references and index.
    1. Russian literature—History and criticism—
Addresses, essays, lectures. 2. Literature—Addresses,
essays, lectures. I. Monas, Sidney. II. Title.
PG2933.M2713   1977   809   76–22456
ISBN 978-0-292-74145-4

Contents

Preface

Osip Emilevich Mandelstam was a great poet, a great critic, and a profound humanist, perhaps even one of the last of the breed, though let us hope not. There is much interest in him now, if not exactly a "bandwagon." In any case, I am not a bandwagon man; my aim is to serve.

I thought Mandelstam better served by a careful, if broad, selection than by a complete volume of his prose. Inevitably a certain subjective element has entered into my choices of what to include. I have included all the essays that Mandelstam himself collected in the volume of literary essays published in his lifetime, *About Poetry*. In addition, I have tried to limit myself to the literary essays. I have excluded the journalistic pieces, though some of them, like the interview with Ho Chi Minh or the account of the Mensheviks in Georgia, are quite interesting. I feel I would have Mandelstam's approval here. The charming little radio play that he wrote in Voronezh about the early life of Goethe gave me more pain, as did the piece called "Sukharevka," but I decided finally they did not fit well into the "mix." Some of Mandelstam's reviews are interesting, especially his review of Huysmans; yet they do not really display Mandelstam at his best, nor do the two articles dealing with problems of translation.

On the other hand, the fragment "Pushkin and Scriabin," which Mandelstam himself seems to have rejected, seems to me so central to his thought, so full of the swelling of all his major themes, that in spite of its clearly fragmentary nature and its many obscurities it had to be included. "Fourth Prose," which might as easily have been included among Mandelstam's autobiographical writings, is nevertheless so important a commentary on his idea of his calling and his distinction between "poetry" and "Literature" that it similarly could not be left out. I must also confess that I could not resist the eloquence of its angry style; after a first, superficial impression of incoherence, the profundity and impersonality of its anger cannot but make a lasting impression on the reader. It should be more obvious that *Journey to Armenia* is not simply a travel piece. Even more than Andrei Biely's book about Armenia, to which it bears a previously unacknowledged kinship, it is an essay on culture, on literature, on life; and it is quite central to Mandelstam's thought.

A number, though by no means the greater number, of these essays have been previously translated by other hands. Of those I have seen, the only one that struck me as unimprovable upon was the "Conversation about Dante" in the version by Clarence Brown and Robert Hughes. With their permission, the essay is included in this volume in their translation. Other translations are my own; I have worked on them long and hard, and with English cadences as much on my mind as the Russian. I wish I could have done better; but I have done my best.

Although "Conversation about Dante" is the last of the essays included here in its date of composition, I have placed it first, because it seems to me the most comprehensive statement of Mandelstam's ideas about poetry and poetics. The essays that were included by Mandelstam in his volume *About Poetry* follow in the order in which he arranged them.

I have tried to keep scholarly apparatus to a minimum. Names and events presumably well known to every educated reader have been neither footnoted nor endnoted. I have had my Interlocutor in mind throughout; but he (or she) is at times, I must admit, a conveniently nebulous figure. He is an educated, intelligent reader, interested not only in Russian literature, but in *literature*. He is not a specialist. He may or may not know Russian. The idea that even "specialists" (i.e., graduate students in Russian literature) actually read Mandelstam in the original Russian, if they don't have to for a given seminar or assignment, is a kind of fond Cloudcuckooland that I have no wish to disrupt, though I don't believe in it for a moment. I hope this book will help them, as I hope the previous Mandelstam volume that I edited helped them, in spite of its regrettable mistakes (*Complete Poetry of Osip Emilevich Mandelstam*, translated by Burton Raffel and Alla Burago, edited by Sidney Monas [Albany: State University of New York Press, 1972]). But the book is not primarily, and certainly not exclusively, for them. Mandelstam is a world figure, and he should be known to anybody who cares at all about literature and has the sensitivity to respond to a major poet. I do not really know whether the Interlocutor will coincide with the actual readers of this book. He may be somewhere among them.

Most of the notes are endnotes, so that the reader may consult them or not as he sees fit. In some cases, where a brief and simple explanation seemed more immediately called for, I have used a footnote.

The system of transliteration used here is based on that of the Library of Congress, but it may be overstatement to call it a system. I have deferred to common usage: Tolstoy, and not Tolstoi; Biely, not Belyi; Scriabin and not Skriabin. In some cases, where the person involved seems to prefer a given usage, I have retained it: Filipoff, for instance, rather than Filippov. I have preferred to keep Russian names ending in -*skii* in the more familiar -*sky*. It isn't entirely satisfactory, but I tend to eschew fanatic spelling.

In the course of preparing this volume, I have had much help from a large number of individuals, and I hope, if I have not managed to acknowledge them all, none will be offended. Clearly, final responsibility is mine alone, and none of the good people mentioned here should be held to blame in any way for the book's shortcomings.

All students and readers of Mandelstam must first and foremost acknowledge their debt to his indefatigable widow, Nadezhda Iakovlevna. I have profited not only from her two books of memoirs and her interesting critical essay, but also from personal interviews and brief correspondence. The Struve-Filipoff edition of the Collected Works (*Sobranie Sochinenii*, 3 vols. [New York: Language Library Associates, 1972]), especially volume 2, which contains all the Russian essays translated here, is an indispensable source. I have not only used the Struve-Filipoff texts but have also taken information from many of their notes and have taken much light from the essays by various hands that are included in the three volumes. I wish to thank Clarence Brown and Robert Hughes for permission to include their translation of "Conversation about Dante." In addition, I have had much valuable help and advice from them both. Translations from the poems of Gumilev and Mandelstam are by Burton Raffel and Alla Burago, with some emendations by me. Translations from the French are by Carolyn Cates Wylie, who has also served as an exceptionally alert and conscientious copy editor. All other translations are mine. George Ivask has been unstinting of his time and deep knowledge of Russian literature, and I owe him a great deal. Two readers from a university press submitted criticisms of the translations that I at first could not help resenting but in the long run came very much to appreciate, along with the comments of two readers for the present press, one of them most helpfully detailed. I have had help and encouragement from many people: Rita and David Monas, Alla Burago, Elnora Carrino, and Louis Iribarne. William Arrowsmith gave me good cheer when I needed it. Carol Monas, my wife, was a stalwart support, a good critic. The person who seemed to identify with the work of getting Mandelstam into English almost as much as I did, who worked unstintingly and indefatigably, typing, correcting, criticizing, arranging was Gianna Kirtley, and I wish to thank her specially.

Introduction: Friends & Enemies of the Word

Osip Mandelstam was born in 1891 of middle-class Jewish parents, grew up in St. Petersburg, and received his formal education in part there, in part in France and Germany. He studied philology, and, though he never took an academic degree or acquired much erudition, his word-love was deep and very sure of itself and became in his imagination a kind of substitute for the warm and secure domesticity he was not otherwise to know. His first poems, published in 1909–1910, whatever traces they might show of his apprenticeship to Symbolism, were of a marked originality, and the sense of a stillness in them, the sense of a motion arrested and about to resume, the sense of *transition* now strike the attentive reader as the distinctive features of his early work. Crowded between two worlds, the nineteenth century dying, the twentieth in ominous labor, it is small wonder that Mandelstam's talent, like that of so many of his contemporaries, lent itself to apocalyptic expectations— to a vision of the end of the world that at the same time saw a terrible beauty stirring to be born out of that death—grass growing in the streets of St. Petersburg, paradoxically making of it "the most advanced city in the world."[1]

No doubt these apocalyptic expectations had been nourished by the mystical Marxism of his early years as well as by his later Christianity. Writing from Paris in 1908 to his former teacher, V. V. Gippius, Mandelstam affirmed: "My first religious experiences date from the period of my childish infatuation with Marxist dogma and can't be separated from that infatuation."[2] He saw a culture marked for death, and a new barbarism, terrifying yet perhaps potentially creative, waiting at the gates. Looking back on his youth through the acquired irony of maturity, Mandelstam wrote: "I perceived the entire world as an economy, a human economy—and . . . . I heard . . . the burgeoning and increase, not of the barley in its

Note: A previous version of this introductory essay appeared in *Texas Studies in Language and Literature* 17: 357–373 and was reprinted, with a few changes, in *Arion* 2, no. 4 (1976).

ear . . . but of the world, the capitalist world, that was ripening in order to fall!"[3]

Mandelstam was early associated with the journal *Apollon* and with Acmeism, a literary movement that had strong Classicist, Neo-Parnassian overtones. Its leader was Nikolai Gumilev, whose stance, given the Russian context, had strong analogies with that of the early Ezra Pound.

The Acmeists were at least as opposed as the Symbolists to the powerful Russian-intelligentsia tradition of a socially useful and up-lifting art. Like the Symbolists, they believed in the sacred nature of the word and the autonomy and integrity of the work of art— but not, like the Symbolists, in the priesthood of poets. And they rebelled against a certain excess, the decadence of Symbolism—its obscurity, its glorification of self-indulgent and self-pitying atti-tudes, its love of oblivion and the abyss, its compulsive obsession with "other worlds." The Acmeists tried to emphasize clarity, lucidity, forthrightness, and, above all, this-worldliness, a sense of being of the earth, earthy. At the same time they attempted to re-store a traditional, rational *formality,* and Gumilev, though certainly not Mandelstam, indulged a certain heroic, Hemingway-like, aristo-cratic athleticism, meant among other things to distinguish him from the mob. I think it fair to sum up the major thrust of the Acmeist revolt against Symbolism not in its aristocraticism but, on the contrary, in its emphasis on the poet as a man among men, its this-worldliness, its attempt to return to earth. Mandelstam's associa-tion with Acmeism was an important chapter in his life; yet, al-though his essay "About the Nature of the Word" was the most complete and the most eloquent expression of Acmeism and its rela-tion to Symbolism, he was never a "leader" or even much of a "member" of that or any other group. He did, however, participate in that will toward a new taste-formation in which he himself saw the historical significance of Acmeism.[4]

Like other poets of his generation, Mandelstam reacted to the Bol-shevik Revolution at first in terms of his apocalyptic expectations, welcoming it with some hope, not unmixed with dread and appre-hension. From the 1920's on, he saw that apprehension more and more insistently confirmed. It became increasingly clear that the revolution he had thought might produce a new universalizing human domesticity, the new "Social Gothic" he had hoped for, was not taking place. The barbarism at the gates was a repressive, not a creative barbarism. He found it increasingly difficult to survive in the Soviet context, though his spirit remained in general cheerful and indomitable. In 1934, the Soviet press ceased to publish his work; he was exiled, under very harsh circumstances, to the provincial town of Voronezh. In 1937, he was arrested and sent to the Far East, where, in a transit camp in Vladivostok, in the winter of 1938, he died. For almost two decades, his name disappeared from print in the USSR.

In 1973, a slender volume of Mandelstam's poems appeared in the *Biblioteka poeta* series, in a limited edition, more than half of which was exported abroad, and then by curious circumnavigations much of it reimported! From the introduction to this volume by the Socialist Realist critic Alexander Dymshits, in his own way trying, I suppose, to bring Mandelstam back, one might gather that Mandelstam "cut himself off" from literature in 1934 as an act of eccentric self-isolation and that he died in 1938 of some unnamed but probably self-inflicted and equally eccentric illness![5] Nevertheless, thanks very largely to the efforts of his widow and a number of devoted scholars and admirers both in the Soviet Union and abroad, Mandelstam is now commonly, even if still too often in the USSR only tacitly, acknowledged as one of the great Russian poets of the twentieth century.

Mandelstam's criticism has to this day been seriously underestimated. He does not provide us with a new methodology and in general tends to take a deflating view of the importance of methodologies. Nor is he quick to put on the judge's robes and consign his fellow poets to this or that circle of critical hell. There are poets he speaks of frowningly and with displeasure in one context who often appear with vibrantly positive force elsewhere in his work. In his essays, there is some sarcasm directed at poets like Akhmatova and Tsvetaeva, whom he was elsewhere to cherish. Andrei Biely appears as a kind of villain, yet became the inspiration later for a whole cycle of poems; and it is Biely who must be thought of as a kind of interlocutor for the essay on Dante. A number of figures who appear in these essays are particularly close to Mandelstam in an almost intimate, personal sense—Villon, Chaadaev, the historian Kliuchevsky—without his necessarily making universal claims for them. A number of poets whom he treats rather harshly—Mayakovsky, Kruchenykh, Balmont—at the same time clearly command his respect. He offers us neither the luxury of an imitable method nor that of an authoritative juridical decision, and so interest in him as critic in our age of luxurious criticism has been limited to the illumination his criticism provides his poetry.

This is of course no mean interest. He was a poet first, and no doubt his criticism must be approached from the perspective of his poetry and in relation to his poetic practice. At the same time, it becomes immediately apparent that the quality and gift of his criticism partake of the quality and gift of his poetry while remaining, properly, prose.

Just as T. S. Eliot's interest in Dante and the English metaphysical poets, Pound's in the troubadors and Confucius, Wallace Stevens' Symbolist essays in esthetics cannot be seen apart from their own poetry, so Mandelstam's "Conversation about Dante" has to be read, I think, as an incipient project for a new *Divine Comedy*, or at the very least as the ringing affirmation of a sense of poetic identity so closely and passionately held as to make mere mistakes of historical detail or social interpretation seem relatively insignificant.[6]

It is interesting to compare it with Eliot's essays on Dante. The poets attempt to rescue Dante from the Dante scholars. Each, while respectful of the need for knowledge about Dante's time and its cultural assumptions so very different from our own, makes a powerful effort to remain true to his own "amateur" reading of the poem. Each rejects the "antiquarian" Dante and seeks in his work what is potentially alive as poetry.

Yet Eliot's Dante is more like that of the scholars—a formidable and remote figure. Eliot's immediate involvement is with the *visual*, not far away from the conceptual. "Dante's," he writes, "is a visual imagination," adding that "it is visual in the sense that he lived in an age in which men still saw visions."[7] There follows a typically Eliotic distinction between "then" and "now." "Then," having been a religious age, turns out to have been better. Its visions were superior to the mere dreaming of "now." For vision, he writes, "was once a more significant, interesting and disciplined kind of dreaming." It might even be presumed to come from above, whereas we "take it for granted that our dreams spring from below." The essays on Dante by Eliot are permeated by a nostalgia for a remote, more integral, more spiritually grounded age.

Mandelstam's involvement is immediate and personal. For him, the essential question is "How many sandals did Alighieri wear out in the course of his poetic work, wandering about on the goatpaths of Italy?" For him, poetry is *movement*, the embodying, the incar-

nation, of movement. Elsewhere, Mandelstam repeatedly refers to
Verlaine's "Art poétique," and often he substitutes the word *mouvement* for Verlaine's *musique*.[8] His own synonym for poetry was
"moving lips," and composition was inseparable from physical
movement, from pacing and gesturing. Mandelstam *wrote* his
poems—that is, "fixed" them on paper; abstracted them—only after
they had already been composed.[9] The composition of a poem was
a physical process and "another poet" a physical presence.

Mandelstam tries to erase the impression left by Dante's face in
the well-known portraits; the aquiline profile, the haughty and superior gaze. Dante, he says, was an exile and a *raznochinets* (like
Mandelstam!), a man of uncertain social background, nervous about
his deportment in the presence of the mighty, all too capable of
swinging to extremes of self-abasement and self-assertion. It is clear
that Mandelstam knew little of the social history of Florence.
Dante's pride of lineage is not quite so easily dismissed. Nevertheless, Mandelstam finds his grounding in the text: Dante needed his
guide, to make his way properly among the mighty shades!

The visual is by no means absent from the "Conversation about
Dante," and even the musical "instruments" with which the essay
begins soon turn out to be "images." It is not the visual stasis of a
tableau. One senses the physical: incipient movement. In his obsession with architecture, Mandelstam sees the Goethean *erstarrte
Musik*, "frozen music"; and, in weaving, the flow of rivers. Music
is motion; words are motion. When he writes about Italian vowels,
he talks of their place in the mouth, the mode of their issuance, the
movement of the muscles. In his discussion of the "mineralogical"
nature of Dante's work—an image of stone borrowed from Novalis
—he sees the most solid thing in the world, a rock, as a product of
the motion of time and the weather.

It is not that Mandelstam has less than Eliot the sense of a "different" age. What he has is a physical confidence in the rightness
of his own presence there, and it is a confidence that survives anachronism and incongruity. To catch the motion—*there* he concentrated. Mandelstam was obsessed with birds and bird flight to the
degree that many of his contemporaries referred to him as "bird-
like," though he was in fact a tall, rather well-built and solid man.
He is not slow to pick up the images of flight in Dante. This gift of
physical sympathy, of susceptibility to motion, is apparent also in
his almost physical sense for the presence and movement of cultural
epochs. *Where does it come from? Where does it go?* These are

questions he is always asking. For Mandelstam, an epoch is also a presence in motion. And he has the sense that Dante's epoch, like his own, is transitional.

He does not in any case attempt to use his acquaintance with Dante as an occasion for feeling superior to his own time. He was of the earth, earthy; and, rightly or wrongly, Mandelstam believed that Dante was a *raznochinets* like himself. If the great French critic Gaston Bachelard is right, and a poet's work tends to be dominated metaphorically by one of the four medieval archetypal elements, Mandelstam's "dominant" was earth.[10] In his reading of Dante, he scarcely notices the fire; and, although air (ascent; flight) and water (rivers; the ocean) recur in powerful images, there is no doubt that the basic element for Mandelstam is *earth*. Other images acquire their significance fundamentally in their *relation* to the earth. There is no Nietzschean climbing into the stratosphere, no Zarathustran ascent, the aim of which is to leave earth behind, so that even the return to earth has as its purpose the telling of what is above the earth, what belongs to the heights. For Mandelstam, space is empty and takes on significance only insofar as it can be populated—"colonized," he wrote—with earthy images by the human imagination. Of the two aspects of earth, building and burial, Mandelstam emphasized the earth as material crying out to be built: stone as potential sculpture.

If earth and the materials of earth are his "ground bass," the poetic process of building out of the materials of earth is inextricably connected with the Christian music of redemption. Mandelstam's Christianity was by no means a decorative, that is to say, a purely esthetic phenomenon. Nor was it merely the form taken by his deep resistance to barbaric Stalinism. It was more fundamental and more complex.

"Christian art," he wrote, "is always an action based on the great idea of redemption." This is from the fragments of the unpublished essay "Pushkin and Scriabin." It was written, or at least begun, as early as 1915, on the occasion of Scriabin's death. The passage on Christian art seems to me central and deserves quotation at length:

> It [Christian art] is an "imitation of Christ" infinitely various in its manifestations, an eternal return to the single creative act that began our historical era. Christian art is free. It is, in the full meaning of the phrase, "Art for art's sake." No necessity of any kind, even the highest, clouds its bright inner freedom,

for its prototype, that which it imitates, is the very redemption
of the world by Christ. And so, not sacrifice, not redemption
in art, but the free and joyful imitation of Christ—that is the
keystone of Christian esthetics.[11]

It is a strange kind of estheticism—the imitation of Christ! Like
Jesus, the artist redeems the world—but in his art. We are close here
to Jakob Böhme, to the old mystic himself, without the intermediacy
of Schelling and the German Romantics:

> Art cannot be a sacrifice, for a sacrifice has already been made;
> cannot be redemption, for the world along with the artist has
> already been redeemed. What then is left? A joyful commerce
> with the divine, like a game played by the Father with his
> children, a hide-and-seek of the spirit! The divine illusion of
> redemption, which is Christian art, is explained precisely by
> this game Divinity plays with us, permitting us to stray along
> the byways of mystery so that we would as it were of ourselves
> come upon salvation, having experienced catharsis, redemption
> in art. Christian artists are as it were the freedmen of the idea
> of redemption, rather than slaves; and they are not preachers.[12]

What an extraordinary explication of "art for art's sake" and its
consequent "freedom of the artist"! As a kind of Christianity, it
places its emphasis not on the crucifixion, not on Golgotha, but on
resurrection and transfiguration. It conceives of art as play—the
play of a game in which the artist imitates Christ by redeeming the
world.

The poet and the architect imitate Christ by endowing the world
with meaning, by giving it a form and pattern in their works that
is analogous to the form and pattern God made out of the world.
The poet is a colonizer, a settler, a kind of Saint George, like the
intrepid Russian monks of the period of the Mongol Yoke that
Kliuchevsky wrote about; like Chaadaev with his need for form,
his vision of unity, his "West." Anticipating Heidegger, Mandelstam wrote: "To build means to fight against emptiness, to hypnotize space. The fine arrow of the Gothic belltower is angry, because
the whole idea of it is to stab the sky, to reproach it for being
empty."[13] Poets were the shepherds of being.

This freedom of the artist and the builder is therefore not the
empty liberty of the unimportant. His mission is to hypnotize space

and, like Joshua in the Old Testament or the priest in performance of the Eucharist, to make time stand still.

> Behold the chalice like a golden sun
> Suspended in the air—a splendid moment;
> Here must only Greek resound:
> To take the whole world in its hands, like a simple apple.
>
> Festive height of the service,
> Light in a rounded structure under the dome in July,
> That, beyond time, we might, full-chested, sigh
> For that meadow where time does not run.
>
> And like eternal noon the Eucharist endures—
> All take part, all play and sing,
> And in the sight of all, the holy vessel
> Flows with unending joy.*[14]

The poet may redeem the most recalcitrant materials: "There is nothing hungrier than the contemporary state, and a hungry state is more terrible than a hungry man. To show compassion for the state which denies the word is the contemporary poet's civic 'way,' the heroic feat that awaits him."[15] That is a long way from the mere "defense" of poetry, or from the notion, wearily conceded by Eliot, that poetry is probably little more than a superior form of amusement. For Mandelstam, too, it is a game—but a game to be played as seriously as children play games, that is, as a sacred and heroic calling.

For all his juxtaposing of Chinese junks and racers at Verona, Jesus and Joshua, Beethoven and Dante, Verlaine and Villon, incarnation and Ovidian metamorphosis, Mandelstam knows very well what time it is. He never asks, as does the lyrical voice in a Pasternak poem, "What millennium is it out there?"[16] His feeling for "the age" is one of the qualities of his gift. Not clock time (he disliked clocks and would never have one in his flat), time spatially conceived, but rather Bergsonian time, time as *durée*, a system of intuited inner connections. Like the lover in his essay, he "gets tangled up in tender names and suddenly remembers that all this

---

* Reprinted, with slight modifications, from *Complete Poetry of Osip Emilevich Mandelstam,* translated by Burton Raffel and Alla Burago, by permission of the State University of New York Press. Copyright © 1973 State University of New York.

has happened before."[17] Shaping form out of matter, life creates
pattern; and pattern is repetition.

It is dangerous, the time he lives in. He feels the ominous shift
of direction. The nineteenth century, weighed down by "the enormous wings" of its cognitive powers, cannot lift itself from the exhausted shore.[18] One feels the shadow of an oncoming night. Those
essays of the Civil War period, "The Word and Culture" and
"Humanism and Modern Life," still vibrate with a certain optimism,
still hold the early conjunction of his religious sensibility and his
unorthodox interpretation of Marxism. He *hopes* for a new "Social
Gothic," that universalized domesticity, an all-human family. But
he *sees* the other alternative: a new Assyrian age in which "captives
swarm like chickens under the feet of the immense king."[19]

It is a time of crisis and there is magic in it; the tree is about to
become a girl again. It is a time when

> Social distinctions and class antagonisms pale before the divi-
> sion of people into friends and enemies of the word. Literally,
> sheep and goats. I sense, almost physically, the unclean goat
> smell issuing from the enemies of the word.[20]

Who are these goat-smelling enemies of the word?

Those for whom the word had merely a denotative, a *utilitarian*
meaning. Those for whom its living nature is a secondary or subordinate quality. Propagandists of political parties, philosophers,
anthroposophists like Andrei Biely, who, in Mandelstam's view,
yoked his great poetic gift to a "Buddhist" worldview.[21] Those who
used the word as slave labor to support some other external structure—a church, a state, a party, a program.

"Friends" were those who believed in the sacred and redemptive
power and the psychic nature of the word.

Luther was a poor word-lover; he departed from verbal argument
to fling his inkpot at the devil. The literary critics whose response
to the anniversary of the death of the great poet Blok was mere lyrical effusion served the word badly, for a critic's minimal task is to
establish where the poet's words came from—that is, his poetic
genealogy—where he stood in relation to the larger pattern-form-
ing, historical energies of the word. The Moscow "poetesses" pay
only half-tribute to the word, for, of the constituent elements of
poetry, remembrance and invention, they honor remembrance alone;
they are *all* genealogy, mere traditionalists; while the Futurists
blaringly honor invention alone.[22]

"Culture has become a church," Mandelstam wrote in 1921, and he hailed the separation of this "church" from the state. It is in this time of transformation and transfiguration that culture assumes a sacred quality, a sacred mission. Within the state, those are friends of the word who acknowledge the statutory independence of culture, who "consult" it, as the princes of old Moscow used to consult the monasteries. But within these monasteries, there were monks and laymen; and Mandelstam identified himself as a layman. Monkish structure—whether Byzantine, or whether the new monasticism of the secularized Russian intelligentsia—was hostile to the word.

Even Literature, with a capital *L*, was hostile. Mandelstam was an Acmeist, but he did not like schools. Still less did he like the way these schools were organizing themselves in the 1920's—preparation for their own slaughter, in which the Stalinist organization of Socialist Realism would later use the rivalries and the acrimonies as well as the phrases and slogans of contending schools in order definitively to decimate them all. As the 1920's came to an end and Literature tightened the clamp on Mandelstam, invoking even antisemitism against him, Mandelstam increased the angle of the defiant tilt to his head. More and more he came to distinguish "poetry" from "Literature." Reading his poems at occasional "evenings," he intoned them, I suspect, rather in the manner we have heard from Joseph Brodsky, liturgically. One memoirist writes: "He sang them like a shaman."[23]

For friends of the word there was the blessing of the Russian language itself; its *Hellenic* nature. By "Hellenic," Mandelstam explains, he does not mean that Russian derives etymologically from the Greek. Still less does he refer to the Byzantine cultural heritage—which, in a certain slant of light, he tends to see as "monkish" and dead and hostile or confining to the word. He calls it "the gift of free imagination," or "free embodiment." Just as Aristophanes in *The Birds* creates a structure out of the rootword *eros*, the manifold play and stresses of the meaning of "desire" and "desiring," so Mandelstam sees the genius of the Russian language in the great depth and multiple branchings of its root meanings.[24] So, too, he sees the writer Rozanov looking for "church walls" and finding only Russian words; for Russia had produced no Acropolis, no lasting legal or political structure, and the Russian language *was* Russian history.[25] For that reason among others, history is a subject close to Mandelstam. When he listens, he hears it breathe.

A Hellenic language is one in which the word-psyche finds rich opportunity for embodiment, without the hindrance of authoritative utilitarian standards.

Mandelstam's Hellenism should not be confused with that program of classical studies that for so long dominated the higher education of Europe and Great Britain. It is not that aristocratic/priestly key to possession of a mystery that wielded power in a secularizing world still stunned by the sacred. For Mandelstam, "Hellenic" means "human." Perhaps it would be better to call it a kind of creative, procreative projection of the human onto the emptiness of the world. Crucial here is the conception of the *utvar'*, which one may translate as "utensil," except that it has at its root a sense that is not that of "use" but is rather closer to the notions of "creation" and "creature," something "creaturized." It is, he tells us, the insistence on a relatedness between the warmth in the stove and the warmth in the human body. "Christianity," in Mandelstam's definition, is "the Hellenization of death."[26]

Both Victor Terras and Clarence Brown have written eloquently of Mandelstam's "Classicism."[27] It should not be confused with a preference for "high style." There is, as Brown points out, a strong Flemish element, a transformation of the lowliest details of the everyday. Like Villon, Mandelstam has a keen sense of "roast duck," and the vow of which he speaks in his poetry "to the fourth estate," to his fellow *raznochintsy*, he took as a binding oath.

Yet his interest in Ovid is surely more than identification with a fellow exile, as Brown implies. He cares as much for the poet of the *Metamorphoses* and the *Amores* as for the exile of *Tristia* and *Ex Ponte*. One is reminded of Ovid's absorption into medieval Christian cosmology as "Saint Ovid the Martyr." It is possible that Mandelstam saw in metamorphosis a kind of resurrection: the creative process itself as death and rebirth, an arresting of the flow of time, "and then, after dwelling in the protracted moment wrested from it," a return, changed by contact with the external, to life.[28]

Nor is "the Classical" simply a matter of Greeks and Romans. "Classical poetry," Mandelstam tells us, "is the poetry of revolution."[29] He is not referring to David's historical tableaux or to eighteenth-century pseudo-Classical "tragedy." The Classical is that which is remembered when the mere piety of remembrance fails. It is remembrance energized by a powerful sense of the new, by a sense of what the new requires from the past. The trouble arises, Mandelstam writes, "when, instead of the real past with its deep roots, we get 'former times.' " This is a poetry that has not had to wrestle with its conventions: "easily assimilated poetry, a henhouse with a fence around it, a cosy little corner where the domestic fowl cluck and scratch about. This is not work done upon the word but rather a rest from the word."[30] The Classical is what is required to complete a mode of experience: its *necessity*. In that sense, Mandelstam refers to the "genuinely Classic" style of Racine and the Classical furies of André Chénier.

He does not see the Classical as mere translation. In spite of his real devotion to the craft of translating—though his efforts are uneven, they contain some examples of the highest skill—he tended to speak of translation in the pejorative, implying use of the ready-made phrase, the formula, the pat device, something mechanical and ready to hand. He did not see the task of the "Classicist" as releasing from the resources of the Russian language those qualities which might make it phonetically or syntactically resemble Latin or Greek, but rather as building out of Russian phonetic materials and the history of the Russian language (Hellenic only in its latent powers of incarnation) its own equivalents of Catullus, Ovid, Racine. It is not Latin or Greek that slumbers in Russian, Mandelstam insists, but the power of Russian itself. "Latin Russian" is therefore a pejorative, and even the commentary on Balmont, that he is the brilliant translator of a nonexistent original, is not praise.

Nor does he care much for Balmont's assumption of superiority to his audience, the fashionably lofty hauteur toward the reader. If the poet has a special relationship to the word-psyche, it is not one that gives him a place on any elevation above the rest of mankind. On the contrary, what distinguishes him from a "literary man" is that he speaks to other men on their own level. The professor, the critic, the litterateur require their elevation; the poet is the same as any other man, if perhaps "not so well made as most."[31] He has no need to be morally superior. Villon, for instance, was a criminal, a murderer, possibly morally inferior to even the average man of his time, and yet a great poet.

A man speaking to men, with no need to be morally or intellectually superior: yet the poet *speaks*, and that means he speaks to someone, an addressee, an interlocutor. With its quiet humor and exceptional charm, the essay called "About an Interlocutor" articulates the poet's reaching out past his beleaguered feeling of impending doom, to a very personal reader of some other time, a time beyond that "wing of oncoming night" he felt already encroaching upon him. The essay conveys, among other things, a remarkable

understanding of those commonly not too well understood poems
of Pushkin's about the poet, his publisher, his audience, the powers-
that-be. The poet's interlocutor must be someone not too close, not
too immediate. He must elicit surprises and carry about him and also
invite a certain mystery. But above all he must be *someone*. He must
have particularity. And that particularity must be respected.

The Classic has nothing to do with lofty attitudinizing, but rather
with the idea of a human potential fulfilled. In this sense Mandelstam speaks in his poems of the Classic *lands* of the Mediterranean,
of Italy and Greece, "those all-human hills" near Florence, and in
the same sense, of the lands of the Caucasus and the Crimea which
he associates with the Mediterranean, which for him are part of
that "all-human" Mediterranean world.[32]

In a recent impassioned essay, the novelist Arthur A. Cohen has
written well of Mandelstam. Like Nadezhda Iakovlevna, who has
insisted on it, he has been able to see how the poems of Mandelstam's last years, the "phases" and "cycles," gain from being published complete, all their variants included. He has grasped the
mutual implicativeness that joins poem to poem and makes each
repetition of a word, a phrase, an image, or an association an addition to the meaning of the cycle. He has gone beyond this to suggest
that the poems form a kind of eschatological epic, or that something like an eschatological epic is struggling to be born in them.[33]
I think one finds implications of this in the last great essays as well:
in "Fourth Prose," "Conversation about Dante," and *Journey to
Armenia*. Mandelstam's obsessive themes draw together in them.
They capture his sense of a civilization coming to an end, and, in
the shipwreck of that civilization, they constitute his letter-in-the-
bottle thrown overboard to find a distant interlocutor in future time.

While the Russian countryside was still being devastated by collectivization and the five-year plans for the forced, rapid industrialization of the Soviet Union were being launched, Mandelstam, who
dearly loved travel, went off on what was to be his last extended
voluntary journey. He had suffered a writing block for almost five
years. The organization and regimentation of the country that preceded and accompanied collectivization and industrialization, including the ever-increasing pressure on writers, editors, and pub-
lishers, oppressed his sensibility. Rescuing him from on high at this
crucial time, his "protector," Nikolai Bukharin, arranged for him
and his wife to go to Armenia. Whether in the long run his association with Bukharin may have precipitated his last arrest and his

death is a moot point, but, just then, it saved his creative life as a poet. The journey itself, his meeting with Andrei Biely, the therapeutic outburst of "Fourth Prose" set the juices flowing again and the lips moving. The essays are certainly overshadowed by the poems, but they partake of the same qualities and, indeed, the same themes as the poems.

If there is anything that *Journey to Armenia* is not about, it is not about either the joys of collectivization or the successes of industrialization in Armenia. Whatever expectations may have been aroused by the title—it was a time when writers were going on all kinds of trips and turning them into euphoric odes to the new order —Mandelstam clearly does not aim the essay for entry into the fat privileges of the new writers' elite. Collectivization and industrialization come up briefly in passing, and an occasional journalistic cliché is inserted for the irony with which it flavors the context. One has the impression that Armenia would probably survive the mechanical regulation imposed by the five-year plans.

He does not write only about Armenia, but about everything he carries with him to Armenia as well: his memories of Russia, his interest in Impressionist painting (now revived and revised), his obsession with biological theory, especially that of Lamarck, threaded through long dialogues with the chess-playing biologist, his friend, B. S. Kuzin; and, above all, his passion for language, his philology. As elsewhere, he tells his story by means of significant association rather than linear narrative. A chapter on the island of Sevan and its architectural "digs" is followed by a chapter on Zamoskvorech'e, the old merchants' section of Moscow, setting for so many of the plays of Ostrovsky, dramas of personal and cultural tyranny, and for the poems and essays of Apollon Grigoriev with their exaltation of the "seven-stringed guitar" and the home-soil aspects of Russian nationalism. The fullness of Armenia is contrasted in restrospect with the "watermelon-emptiness of Russia," with Zamoskvorech'e, where Mandelstam himself had lived, and its "cheery little houses" and "nasty little souls and timidly oriented windows." Armenia might survive the five-year plans with their hypostasization of nineteenth-century scientific rationalist "Buddhism"—but Zamoskvorech'e?

In connection with thoughts on evolutionary theory, Mandelstam uses the word "development" (*razvitie*), which, of course, also has many associations with the five-year plan. It is a word he dislikes: "A plant is a sound evoked by the wand of a termenvox,

pulsating in a sphere oversaturated with wave processes. It is the
envoy of a living storm that rages permanently in the universe—
akin in equal measure to stone and lightning! A plant in the world—
that is an event, a happening, an arrow; and not boring, bearded
'development'!"[34] The passage recalls Mandelstam's poem, no. 254,
on Lamarck, and carries as well the implicit comparison of "a plant"
with "a poem," an ineluctable resemblance to Mandelstam's theory
of composition as expressed in "Conversation about Dante" and
elsewhere. Even the adjective "bearded" as applied to "development" recalls the Italian idiom *Che barba!* and the expressive gesture that normally accompanies it. Mandelstam's biological is really
poetic theory:

> All of us, without suspecting it, are the carriers of an immense
> embryological experiment: for even the process of remember-
> ing, crowned with the victory of memory's effort, is amazingly
> like the phenomenon of growth. In one as well as the other,
> there is a sprout, an embryo, the rudiment of a face, half a
> character, half a sound, the ending of a name, something labial
> or palatal, a sweet legume on the tongue, that doesn't develop
> out of itself but only responds to an invitation, only stretches
> out *toward*, justifying one's expectation.[35]

That a Jew should identify closely with Armenia and Armenians
is of course not at all unusual or surprising, but an instance of the
natural kinship of gifted diasporic peoples, often persecuted, often
mistaken one for the other by "the heathen." What country, as
Nadezhda Mandelstam asked, could be more worthy of being called
"the younger sister of Judea"?[36] Since the mood is eschatological,
there is Mount Ararat, where the ark came to rest; and there are the
Gog and Magog of the long dark night of imperial oriental siege
and conquest. But Armenia resembles Greece and Italy as much as
Judea: it is a wine-growing region, with the culture habits that ac-
company the grape, and there are even traces of an ancient goat cult
in the mountains. Above all, Mandelstam is fascinated by the
jangling of the philological keys, with his discovery that the Japhetic verbs "to see," "to hear," and "to understand" once coalesced
into a single semantic bundle.[37]
    Armenia is the first Christian kingdom and the longest Christian
survivor as a cultural entity. It is the homeland of Christian architecture—both the Romanesque and the Gothic. Mandelstam sees it
as a place of renewal, whose language will be studied when the

phonetic ores of Europe and America are all used up, a place lifted
outside of time like the Eucharist. Armenians were a people

> whom you respect, with whom you sympathize, of whom you
> are, though a stranger, proud. The Armenians' fullness of life,
> their rough tenderness, their noble inclination for hard work,
> their inexplicable aversion to any kind of metaphysics, and
> their splendid intimacy with the world of real things—all this
> said to me: you're awake, don't be afraid of your own time,
> don't be sly.
>
> Wasn't this because I found myself among people, re-
> nowned for their teeming activity, who nevertheless told time
> not by the railroad station or the office clock, but by the sun-
> dial, such as the one I saw among the ruins of Zvartnots in
> the form of the zodiac or of a rose inscribed in stone?[38]

Mandelstam's farewell journey—the longer ones he was to make
were not of his own choosing—reinvigorated him and renewed his
gift. "Parting," he wrote, "is the younger sister of death," and his
departure from Armenia, "the younger sister of Judea," was a preparation for death.[39] The apocalyptic theme is unmistakable. Yet
Mandelstam's apocalypse is also an *apokothastasis*: he looks forward
not only to the end, but also to resurrection and renewal. Amidst
the crumbling of walls and exhaustion of phonetic ores, he counts
on "the complicity of those united in a conspiracy against emptiness
and nonbeing."[40]

A world come to an end; *the* world goes on.

Osip Mandelstam: Selected Essays

Conversation about Dante

Translated by Clarence Brown & Robert Hughes

Così gridai colla faccia levata.
  (*Inferno*, XVI, 76)

I.

Poetic speech is a crossbred process, and it consists of two sonorities. The first of these is the change that we hear and sense in the very instruments of poetic speech, which arise in the process of its impulse. The second sonority is the speech proper, that is, the intonational and phonetic work performed by the said instruments.

Understood thus, poetry is not a part of nature, not even the best or choicest part. Still less is it a reflection of nature, which would lead to a mockery of the law of identity; but it is something that, with astonishing independence, settles down in a new extraspatial field of action, not so much narrating nature as acting it out by means of its instruments, which are commonly called images.

It is only very conditionally possible to speak of poetic speech or thought as sonorous, for we hear in it only the crossing of two lines, and of these one, taken by itself, is absolutely mute, while the other, taken apart from its instrumental metamorphosis, is devoid of all significance and all interest and is subject to paraphrase, which is in my opinion the truest sign of the absence of poetry. For where one finds commensurability with paraphrase, there the sheets have not been rumpled; there poetry has not, so to speak, spent the night.

Dante is a master of the instruments of poetry and not a manufacturer of images. He is a strategist of transformations and crossbreedings, and least of all is he a poet in the "All-European" and outwardly cultural sense of this word.

Note: This translation was originally published as "Talking about Dante" in *Delos*, no. 6 (1971): 65–107. A few minor editorial changes have been made in the interest of conformity with the other essays in this volume, and endnotes have been added.

The wrestlers winding themselves into a tangle in the arena may be regarded as an example of a transformation of instruments and a harmony.

> These naked and glistening wrestlers who walk about pluming themselves on their physical prowess before grappling in the decisive fight. . . .[1]

The modern cinema, meanwhile, with its metamorphosis of the tapeworm, turns into a malicious parody on the function of instruments in poetic speech, since its frames move without any conflict and merely succeed one another.

Imagine something understood, grasped, torn out of obscurity, in a language voluntarily and willingly forgotten immediately upon the completion of the act of understanding and execution.

In poetry only the executory understanding has any importance, and not the passive, the reproducing, the paraphrasing understanding. Semantic satisfaction is equivalent to the feeling of having carried out a command.

The wave signals of meaning disappear once they have done their work: the more powerful they are, the more yielding, and the less prone to linger.

Otherwise one cannot escape the rote drilling, the hammering in of those prepared nails called "cultural-poetic" images.

External, explanatory imagery is incompatible with the presence of instruments.

The quality of poetry is determined by the rapidity and decisiveness with which it instills its command, its plan of action, into the instrumentless, dictionary, purely qualitative nature of word formation. One has to run across the whole width of the river, jammed with mobile Chinese junks sailing in various directions. This is how the meaning of poetic speech is created. Its route cannot be reconstructed by interrogating the boatmen: they will not tell how and why we were leaping from junk to junk.[2]

Poetic speech is a carpet fabric with a multitude of textile warps which differ one from the other only in the coloring of the performance, only in the musical score of the constantly changing directives of the instrumental code of signals.

It is a most durable carpet, woven out of water: a carpet in which the currents of the Ganges (taken as a textile theme) do not mix with the samples of the Nile and the Euphrates, but remain many-hued, in braids, figures, and ornaments—but not in regular patterns, for a pattern is that very paraphrase of which we were speaking. Ornament is good by virtue of the fact that it preserves the traces of its origin as a performed piece of nature—animal, vegetable, steppe, Scythian, Egyptian, what you will, national or barbarian, it is always speaking, seeing, active.

Ornament is stanzaic.

Pattern is a matter of lines.

The poetic hunger of the old Italians is magnificent, their animal, youthful appetite for harmony, their sensual lust after rhyme— *il disio.*

The mouth works, the smile moves the verse line, the lips are cleverly and merrily crimson, the tongue presses itself trustfully to the roof of the mouth.

The inner image of the verse is inseparable from the numberless changes of expression which flit across the face of the teller of tales as he talks excitedly.

For that is exactly what the act of speech does: it distorts our face, explodes its calm, destroys its mask.

When I began to study Italian and had only just become slightly acquainted with its phonetics and prosody, I suddenly understood that the center of gravity of the speech movements had been shifted closer to the lips, to the external mouth. The tip of the tongue suddenly acquired a place of honor. The sound rushed toward the canal lock of the teeth. Another observation that struck me was the infantile quality of Italian phonetics, its beautiful childlike quality, its closeness to infant babbling, a sort of immemorial Dadaism:[3]

> e, consolando, usava l'idioma
> che prima i padri e le madri trastulla:
>
> .   .   .   .
>
> favoleggiava con la sua famiglia
> de' Troiani, di Fiesole e di Roma.[4]
> (*Paradiso,* XV, 122–123, 125–126)

Would you like to become acquainted with the lexicon of Italian rhymes? Take the entire Italian dictionary and leaf through as you please. Here everything rhymes. Every word cries out to enter into *concordanza.*

There is a marvelous abundance of endings that are wed to each other. The Italian verb gains force as it approaches its end and only in the ending does it live. Every word hastens to burst forth, to fly from the lips, go away, and clear a place for the others.

When it became necessary to trace the circumference of a time for which a millennium was less than the wink of an eyelash, Dante introduced an infantile "transsense"[5] language into his astronomical, *concertante*, deeply public, pulpit lexicon.

The creation of Dante is above all the emergence into the world arena of the Italian language of his day, its emergence as a whole, as a system.

The most Dadaist of all the Romance languages moved into first place internationally.

II.

It is essential to demonstrate some bits and pieces of Dante's rhythms. This is an unexplored area, but one that must become known. Whoever says, "Dante is sculptural," is enslaved by beggarly definitions of a magnificent European. Dante's poetry is characterized by all the forms of energy known to modern science. Unity of light, sound, and matter constitutes its inner nature. The labor of reading Dante is above all endless, and the more we succeed at it the farther we are from our goal. If the first reading results only in shortness of breath and wholesome fatigue, then equip yourself for subsequent readings with a pair of indestructible Swiss boots with hobnails. The question occurs to me—and quite seriously— how many sandals did Alighieri wear out in the course of his poetic work, wandering about on the goat paths of Italy?

The *Inferno* and especially the *Purgatorio* glorify the human gait, the measure and rhythm of walking, the foot and its shape.

The step, linked to the breathing and saturated with thought: this Dante understands as the beginning of prosody. In order to indicate walking he uses a multitude of varied and charming turns of phrase.

In Dante philosophy and poetry are forever on the move, forever on their feet. Even standing still is a variety of accumulated motion; making a space for people to stand and talk takes as much trouble as scaling an alp. The metrical foot of his poetry is the inhalation;

the exhalation is the step. The step draws a conclusion, invigorates, syllogizes.

A good education is a school of the most rapid associations: you grasp things on the wing, you are sensitive to allusions—this is Dante's favorite form of praise.

As Dante understands it, the teacher is younger than the pupil, because he "runs faster."

> He [Brunetto Latini] turned aside and seemed to me like one of those who run races through the green meadows in the environs of Verona, and his whole bearing bespoke his belonging to the number of winners, not the vanquished.[6]
>
> (*Inferno*, XV, 121–124)

The rejuvenating force of metaphor returns to us the educated old man Brunetto Latini in the guise of a youthful victor in a track race in Verona.

What is Dantean erudition?

Aristotle, like a downy butterfly, is fringed with the Arabian border of Averroës.

> Averroìs, che il gran comento feo.[7]
> (*Inferno*, IV, 144)

In the present case the Arab Averroës accompanies the Greek Aristotle. They are the components of the same drawing. There is room for them on the membrane of one wing.

The end of Canto IV of the *Inferno* is a genuine orgy of quotations. I find here a pure and unalloyed demonstration of Dante's keyboard of allusions.

It is a keyboard promenade around the entire mental horizon of antiquity. A kind of Chopin polonaise in which an armed Caesar with the blood-red eyes of a griffin appears alongside Democritus, who took matter apart into atoms.

A quotation is not an excerpt. A quotation is a cicada. It is part of its nature never to quiet down. Once having got hold of the air, it does not release it. Erudition is far from being the same thing as the keyboard of allusions, which is the main essence of an education.

I mean to say that a composition is formed not from heaping up of particulars but in consequence of the fact that one detail after another is torn away from the object, leaves it, flutters out, is hacked away from the system, and goes off into its own functional space or dimension, but each time at a strictly specified moment and provided the general situation is sufficiently mature and unique.

Things themselves we do not know; on the other hand, we are highly sensitive to their location. And so, when we read the cantos of Dante, we receive as it were communiqués from a military field of operations and from them we can very well surmise how the sounds of the symphony of war are struggling with each other, even though each bulletin taken separately brings the news of some slight shift here or there of the flags showing strategic positions or indicates some change or other in the timbre of the cannonade.

Thus, the thing arises as an integral whole as a result of the one differentiating impulse which runs all through it. It does not continue looking like itself for the space of a single minute. If a physicist should conceive the desire, after taking apart the nucleus of an atom, to put it back together again, he would be like the partisans of descriptive and explanatory poetry, for whom Dante represents, for all time, a plague and a threat.

If we were to learn to hear Dante, we should hear the ripening of the clarinet and the trombone, we should hear the viola transformed into the violin and the lengthening of the valve of the French horn. And we should see forming around the lute and the theorbo the hazy nucleus of the homophonic three-part orchestra of the future.

Further, if we were to hear Dante, we should be unexpectedly plunged into a power flow which is sometimes, as a whole, called "composition," sometimes, in particular, "metaphor," and sometimes, because of its evasive quality, "simile," and which gives birth to attributes in order that they might return into it, increase it by their melting and, having scarcely achieved the first joy of coming into existence, immediately lose their primogeniture in attaching themselves to the matter that is straining in among the thoughts and washing against them.

The beginning of Canto X of the *Inferno*. Dante shoves us into the inner blindness of the compositional clot: "We now entered upon a narrow path between the wall of the cliff and those in torment—my teacher and I at his back." Every effort is directed toward the struggle against the density and gloom of the place. Lighted shapes break through like teeth. Conversation is as necessary here as torches in a cave.

Dante never enters upon single-handed combat with his material unless he has prepared an organ with which to apprehend it, unless he has equipped himself with some measuring instrument for calculating concrete time, dripping or melting. In poetry, where everything is measure and everything proceeds out of measure and turns around it and for its sake, measuring instruments are tools of a special quality, performing a special, active function. Here the trembling hand of the compass not only humors the magnetic storm, but produces it.

And thus we see that the dialogue of Canto X of the *Inferno* is magnetized by the tense forms of the verbs. The past imperfect and perfect, the past subjunctive, the present itself and the future are, in the tenth canto, given categorically, authoritatively.

The entire canto is built on several verbal thrusts, which leap boldly out of the text. Here the table of conjunctions has an air of fencing about it, and we literally hear how the verbs kill time. First lunge:

> La gente che per li sepolcri giace
> *potrebessi* veder? . . .
>   (*Inferno*, X, 7–8)

> These people, laid in open graves,
>   may I be permitted to see?

Second lunge: "Volgiti: che fai?"[8] [line 31]. This contains the horror of the present tense, a kind of *terror praesentis.* Here the unalloyed present is taken as a charm to ward off evil. In complete isolation from the future and the past, the present tense is conjugated like pure fear, like danger.

Three nuances of the past tense, washing its hands of any responsibility for what has already taken place, are given in this tercet:

> I [had] fixed my gaze upon him
>   And he drew himself up to his full height
>   As though [he were] insulting Hell with his immense
>   disdain.[9]
>   (*Inferno*, X, 34–36)

And then, like a powerful tube, the past breaks upon us in the question of Farinata: "Who were your ancestors?" (*Chi fur li maggior tui?*) [line 42]. How the copula, the little truncated form *fur* instead of *furon*, is stretched out here! Was this not the manner in which the French horn was formed, by lengthening the valve?

Later there is a slip of the tongue in the form of the past definite. This slip of the tongue was the final blow to the elder Cavalcanti: he heard Alighieri, one of the contemporaries and comrades of his son, Guido Cavalcanti, the poet, still living at the time, say something—it does not matter what—with the fatal past definite form *ebbe*.

And how remarkable that it is precisely this slip which opens the way for the main stream of the dialogue. Cavalcanti fades out like an oboe or clarinet that had played its part, and Farinata, like a deliberate chess player, continues the interrupted move and renews the attack:

> e sè continuando al primo detto,
>   "s'elli han quell'arte," diesse "male appresa,
>   ciò mi tormenta più che questo letto."[10]
>   (*Inferno*, X, 76–78)

The dialogue in the tenth canto of the *Inferno* is an unexpected clarifier of the situation. It flows all by itself from the space between the two rivers of speech.

All useful information of an encyclopedic nature turns out to have been already furnished in the opening lines. The amplitude of the conversation slowly, steadily grows wider; mass scenes and throng images are introduced obliquely.

When Farinata stands up in his contempt for Hell like a great nobleman who has landed in prison, the pendulum of the conversation is already measuring the full diameter of the gloomy plain, broken by flames.

The notion of scandal in literature is much older than Dostoevsky, but in the thirteenth century and in Dante's work it was far more powerful.

Dante runs up against Farinata, collides with him, in an undesired and dangerous encounter exactly as the rogues in Dostoevsky are always blundering into their tormentors in the most inopportune places. From the opposite direction comes a voice—whose it is, is so far not known. It becomes harder and harder for the reader to conduct the expanding canto. This voice—the first theme of Farinata—is the minor Dantean *arioso* of the suppliant type, extremely typical of the *Inferno*.

> O Tuscan who travels alive through this city of fire and speaks so eloquently, do not refuse my request to stop for a moment.

By your speech I recognize in you a citizen of that noble region
to which I—alas!—was too great a burden.[11]

Dante is a poor man. Dante is an internal *raznochinets* [an intellectual, not of noble birth][12] of an ancient Roman line. Not courtesy but something completely opposite is characteristic of him. One
has to be a blind mole not to notice that throughout the *Divina
Commedia* Dante does not know how to behave, he does not know
how to act, what to say, how to make a bow. This is not something
I have imagined; I take it from the many admissions which Alighieri
himself has strewn about in the *Divina Commedia*. The inner anxi-
ety and the heavy, troubled awkwardness which attend every step
of the unself-confident man, the man whose upbringing is inade-
quate, who does not know what application to make of his inner
experience or how to objectify it in etiquette, the tortured and outcast man—it is these qualities which give the poem all its charm, all
its drama, and they create its background, its psychological ground.

If Dante were to be sent out alone, without his *dolce padre*,
without Vergil, a scandal would inevitably erupt in the very beginning, and we should not have a journey among torments and remarkable sights but the most grotesque buffoonery.

The gaucheries averted by Vergil systematically correct and
straighten the course of the poem. The *Divina Commedia* takes us
into the inner laboratory of Dante's spiritual qualities. What for us
are an unimpeachable capuche and a so-called aquiline profile were,
from the inside, an awkwardness overcome with torturous difficulty,
a purely Pushkinian, Kammerjunker struggle[13] for the social dignity
and social position of the poet. The shade that frightens old women
and children was itself afraid, and Alighieri underwent fever and
chills all the way from marvelous fits of self-esteem to feelings of
utter worthlessness.

Up to now Dante's fame has been the greatest obstacle to understanding him and to the deeper study of him and it will for a long
time continue to be so. His lapidary quality is nothing other than a
product of the huge inner imbalance which found its outlet in the
dream executions, the imagined encounters, the exquisite retorts,
prepared in advance and nurtured by biliousness, calculated to de-
stroy utterly his enemy, to bring about the final triumph.

How many times did the loving father, preceptor, sensible man,
and guardian silence the internal *raznochinets* of the fourteenth
century, who was so troubled at finding himself in a social hierarchy

at the same time that Boccaccio, practically his contemporary, delighted in the same social system, plunged into it, sported about in it?

Che fai?—"What are you doing?"—sounds literally like the shout of a teacher: "You've gone crazy!" Then one is rescued by the playing of the organ pipes, which drown out shame and cover embarrassment.

It is absolutely incorrect to conceive of Dante's poem as a single narration extended in one line or even as a voice. Long before Bach and at a time when large monumental organs were not yet being built, and there existed only the modest embryonic prototypes of the future marvel, when the chief instrument was still the zither, accompanying the voice, Alighieri constructed in verbal space an infinitely powerful organ and was already delighting in all of its imaginable stops and inflating its bellows and roaring and cooing in all its pipes.

Com'avesse l'inferno in gran dispitto.[14]
(*Inferno*, X, 36)

—the line that gave rise to all of European demonism and Byronism. Meanwhile, instead of elevating his figure on a pedestal, as Hugo, for example, would have done, Dante envelops it in muted tones, wraps it about in grey half-light, hides it away at the very bottom of a dim sack of sound.

This figure is rendered in the diminuendo stop; it falls down out of the dormer window of the hearing.

In other words, the phonetic light has been switched off. The grey shadows have been blended.

The *Divina Commedia* does not so much take up the reader's time as intensify it, as in the performance of a musical piece.

In lengthening, the poem moves further away from its end, and the end itself arrives unexpectedly and sounds like a beginning.

The structure of the Dantean monologue, built on a system of organ stops, can be well understood with the help of an analogy to rocks whose purity has been violated by the intrusion of foreign bodies. Granular admixtures and veins of lava point to one earth fault or catastrophe as the source of the formation. Dante's lines are formed and colored in just such a geological way. Their material structure is infinitely more important than the famous sculptural quality. Let us imagine a monument of granite or marble the symbolic function of which is not to represent a horse or a rider but to disclose the inner structure of the very marble or granite itself. In other words, imagine a monument of granite which has been erected in honor of granite and as though for the revelation of its idea. You will then receive a rather clear notion of how form and content are related in Dante.

Every unit of poetic speech—be it a line, a stanza, or an entire composition—must be regarded as a single word. When we pronounce, for example, the word "sun," we are not throwing out an already prepared meaning—that would be a semantic abortion—we are living through a peculiar cycle.

Every word is a bundle and the meaning sticks out of it in various directions, not striving toward any one official point. When we pronounce "sun" we are, as it were, making an immense journey which has become so familiar to us that we move along in our sleep. What distinguishes poetry from automatic speech is that it rouses us and shakes us awake in the middle of a word. Then the word turns out to be far longer than we thought, and we remember that to speak means to be forever on the road.

The semantic cycles of Dante's cantos are so constructed that what begins with *mёd* "honey," for instance, ends with *medʾ* "bronze," and what begins with *lai*, "bark of a dog," ends with *lёd*, "ice."

Dante, when he has to, calls the eyelids "the lips of the eye." That is when the icy crystals of frozen tears hang from the lashes and form a covering which prevents weeping.

> li occhi lor, ch'eran pria pur dentro molli,
>   gocciar su per le labbra ...[15]
>   (*Inferno*, XXXII, 46–47)

Thus, suffering crosses the organs of sense, creates hybrids, produces the labial eye.

There is not one form in Dante—there is a multitude of forms. One is driven out of another and it is only by convention that they can be inserted one into the other.

He himself says: "Io premerei di mio concetto il suco" (*Inferno*, XXXII, 4), "I would squeeze the juice out of my idea, out of my conception." That is, form is conceived of by him as something wrung out, not as something that envelops. Thus, strange as it may be, form is pressed out of the content—the conception—which, as it were, envelops the form. Such is Dante's clear thought.

But only if a sponge or rag is wet can anything, no matter what, be wrung from it. We may twist the conception into a veritable plait but we will not squeeze from it any form unless it is in itself a form. In other words, any process of creating a form in poetry presupposes lines, periods, or cycles of form on the level of sound, just as is the case with a unit of meaning that can be uttered separately.

A scientific description of Dante's *Comedy*—taken as a flow, a current—would inevitably take on the aspect of a treatise on metamorphoses, and would strive to penetrate the multitudinous states of the poetic matter just as a physician making a diagnosis listens to the multitudinous unity of the organism. Literary criticism would approach the method of live medicine.

III.

Penetrating as best I can into the structure of the *Divina Commedia*, I come to the conclusion that the entire poem is one single unified and indivisible stanza. Or, to be more exact, not a stanza but a crystallographic shape, that is, a body. There is an unceasing drive toward the creation of form that penetrates the entire poem. The poem is a strictly stereometric body, one integral development of a crystallographic theme. It is unthinkable that one might encompass with the eye or visually imagine to oneself this shape of thirteen thousand facets with its monstrous exactitude. My lack of even the vaguest notion about crystallography—an ignorance in this field, as in many others, that is customary in my circle—deprives me of the pleasure of grasping the true structure of the *Divina Commedia*. But such is the astonishing, stimulating power of Dante that he has awakened in me a concrete interest in crystallography, and as a grateful reader—*lettore*—I shall endeavor to satisfy him.

The formation of this poem transcends our notions of invention and composition. It would be much more correct to acknowledge instinct as its guiding principle. The approximate definitions offered here have been intended as anything but a parade of my metaphoric inventiveness. This is a struggle to make the whole conceivable as an entity, to render in graphic terms what is conceivable. Only with the aid of metaphor is it possible to find a concrete sign for the forming instinct with which Dante accumulated his terza rima to the point of overflowing.

Thus, one has to imagine how it would be if bees had worked at the creation of this thirteen-thousand-faceted shape, bees endowed with instinctive stereometric genius, who attracted more and still more bees as they were needed. The work of these bees, who always keep an eye on the whole, is not equally difficult at the various stages of the process. Their cooperation broadens and becomes more complex as they proceed with the formation of the combs, by means of which space virtually arises out of itself.

The analogy with bees, by the way, is suggested by Dante himself. Here are the three lines which open Canto XVI of the *Inferno*:

> Già era in loco, onde s'udia il rimbombo
> dell'acqua che cadea nell'altro giro,
> simile a quel che l'arnie fanno rombo.[16]
> (*Inferno*, XVI, 1–3)

Dante's similes are never descriptive, that is, purely representational. They always pursue the concrete goal of giving the inner image of the structure or the force. Let us take the very large group of bird similes—all those long caravans now of cranes, now of crows, and now the classical military phalanxes of swallows, now the anarchically disorderly ravens, unsuited to Latin military formations—this group of extended similes always corresponds to the instinct of pilgrimage, travel, colonization, migration. Or let us take, for example, the equally extensive group of river similes, portraying the rise in the Apennines of the river Arno, which irrigates the Tuscan plain, or the descent into the plain of Lombardy of its alpine wet nurse, the river Po. This group of similes, marked by an extraordinary liberality and a step-by-step descent from tercet to tercet, always leads to a complex of culture, homeland, and unsettled civic life, to a political and national complex, so conditioned by water boundaries and also by the power and direction of rivers.

The force of Dante's simile, strange as it may seem, is directly proportional to our ability to get along without it. It is never dictated by some beggarly logical necessity. What, pray tell, could have been the logical necessity for comparing the poem as it neared its end to an article of attire—*gonna*, what we would today call "skirt" but in early Italian meant, rather, a "cloak" or "dress" in general— and himself to a tailor who, forgive the expression, had run out of stuff?

IV.

As Dante began to be more and more beyond the powers of readers in succeeding generations and even of artists themselves, he was more and more shrouded in mystery. The author himself was striving for clear and exact knowledge. For his contemporaries he was difficult, he was exhausting, but in return he bestowed the award of knowledge. Later on, things got much worse. There was the elaborate development of the ignorant cult of Dantean mysticism, devoid, like the very idea of mysticism, of any concrete substance. There appeared the "mysterious" Dante of the French etchings,[17] consisting of a monk's hood, an aquiline nose, and some sort of occupation among mountain crags. In Russia this voluptuous ignorance on the part of the ecstatic adepts of Dante, who did not read him, claimed as its victim none other than Alexander Blok:

> The shade of Dante with his aquiline profile
> Sings to me of the New Life . . .[18]

The inner illumination of Dante's space by light—light derived from nothing more than the structural elements of his work—was of absolutely no interest to anyone.

I shall now show how little concern the early readers of Dante felt for his so-called mysteriousness. I have in front of me a photograph of a miniature from one of the very earliest copies of Dante, made in the mid-fourteenth century (from the collection in the library of Perugia). Beatrice is showing Dante the Holy Trinity. A brilliant background with peacock designs, like a gay calico print, the Holy Trinity in a willow frame—ruddy, rosy-cheeked, round as merchants. Dante Alighieri is depicted as an extremely dashing young man and Beatrice as a lively, round-faced girl. Two absolutely ordinary little figures—a scholar, exuding health, is courting a no less flourishing girl.

Spengler, who devoted some superlative pages to Dante, nevertheless saw him from his loge in a German *Staatsoper*, and when he says "Dante" one must nearly always understand "Wagner, as staged in Munich."

The purely historical approach to Dante is just as unsatisfactory as the political or theological. Future commentary on Dante belongs to the natural sciences, when they shall have been brought to a sufficient degree of refinement and their capacity for thinking in images sufficiently developed.

I have an overwhelming desire to refute the disgusting legend
that Dante's coloring is inevitably dim or marked by the notorious
Spenglerian brownness. To begin with, I shall refer to the testimony
of one of his contemporaries, an illuminator. A miniature by him
is from the same collection in the museum at Perugia. It belongs to
Canto I: "I saw a beast and turned back." Here is a description of
the coloring of this remarkable miniature, which is of a higher type
than the preceding one, and completely adequate to the text.

Dante's clothing is *bright blue* (*adzura chiara*). Vergil's beard is
long and his hair is *grey*. His toga is also *grey*. His short cloak is
rose. The hills are bare, *grey*.

Thus we see here bright azure and rose flecks in the smoky grey
rock.

In Canto XVII of the *Inferno* there is a monster of transportation
named Geryon, something like a super-tank, and with wings into
the bargain. He offers his services to Dante and Vergil, having received from the sovereign hierarchy an appropriate order for the
transportation of two passengers to the lower, eighth circle:

> due branche avea pilose infin l'ascelle;
> lo dosso e 'l petto ed ambedue le coste
> dipinte avea di nodi e di rotelle:
> con più color, sommesse e sopraposte
> non fer mai drappi Tartari nè Turchi,
> nè fur tai tele per Aragne imposte.[19]
> (*Inferno*, XVII, 13–18)

The subject here is the color of Geryon's skin. His back, chest,
and sides are gaily colored with decorations consisting of little knots
and shields. A more brilliant coloration, Dante explains, is not to
be found among the carpets of either Turkish or Tatar weavers.

The textile brilliance of this comparison is blinding, and nothing
could be more unexpected than the drapery-trade perspectives which
are disclosed in it.

In its subject, Canto XVII of the *Inferno*, devoted to usury, is
very close to commercial goods assortments and banking turnover.
Usury, which made up for a deficiency in the banking system, where
an insistent demand was already being felt, was the crying evil of
that time, but it was also a necessity which facilitated the circulation
of goods in the Mediterranean world. Usurers were vilified in the

church and in literature, but they were still resorted to. Usury was practiced even by noble families—odd bankers whose base was farming and ownership of land—and this especially annoyed Dante.

The landscape of Canto XVII is composed of hot sands—that is, something related to Arabian caravan routes. Sitting on the sand are the most aristocratic usurers: the Gianfigliazzi, the Ubbriachi from Florence, the Scrovigni from Padua. Around the neck of each there hangs a little sack or amulet, or purse embroidered with the family arms on a colored background: one has an azure lion on a golden background, a second has a goose whiter than freshly churned butter against a blood-red background, and a third has a blue pig against a white ground.

Before embarking on Geryon and gliding off into the abyss, Dante inspects this strange exhibit of family crests. I call your attention to the fact that the bags of the usurers are given as samples of color. The energy of the color epithets and the way they are placed in the line muffle the heraldry. The colors are named with a sort of professional brusqueness. In other words, the colors are given at the stage when they are still located on the artist's palette in his studio. And why should this be surprising? Dante knew his way around in painting, was the friend of Giotto, and closely followed the struggle of artistic schools and fashionable tendencies.

Credette Cimabue nella pintura[20]
(*Purgatorio*, XI, 94)

Having looked their fill at the usurers, they take their seats on Geryon. Vergil puts his arm around Dante's neck and says to the official dragon: "Descend in wide, flowing circles, and remember your new burden."

The craving to fly tormented and exhausted the men of Dante's time no less than alchemy. It was a hunger for cleaving space. Disoriented. Nothing visible. Ahead—only that Tatar back, the terrifying silk dressing gown of Geryon's skin. One can judge the speed and direction only by the torrent of air in one's face. The flying machine has not yet been invented, Leonardo's designs do not yet exist, but the problem of gliding to a landing is already solved.

And finally, falconry breaks in. The maneuvers of Geryon as he slows the rate of descent are likened to the return of a falcon who has had no success and who after his vain flight is slow to return at the call of the falconer. Once having landed, he flies off in an offended way and perches at an aloof distance.

Let us now try to grasp all of Canto XVII as a whole, but from the point of view of the organic chemistry of the Dantean imagery, which has nothing to do with allegory. Instead of retelling the so-called contents, we shall look at this link in Dante's work as a continuous transformation of the substratum of poetic material, which preserves its unity and strives to penetrate into its own interior.

As in all true poetry, Dante's thinking in images is accomplished with the help of a characteristic of poetic material which I propose to call its transformability or convertibility. It is only by convention that the development of an image can be called development. Indeed, imagine to yourself an airplane (forgetting the technical impossibility) which in full flight constructs and launches another machine. In just the same way, this second flying machine, completely absorbed in its own flight, still manages to assemble and launch a third. In order to make this suggestive and helpful comparison more precise, I will add that the assembly and launching of these technically unthinkable machines that are sent flying off in the midst of flight do not constitute a secondary or peripheral function of the plane that is in flight; they form a most essential attribute and part of the flight itself, and they contribute no less to its feasibility and safety than the proper functioning of the steering gear or the uninterrupted working of the engine.

It is of course only by greatly straining the meaning of "development" that one can apply that term to this series of projectiles that are built in flight and flit away one after the other for the sake of preserving the integrity of the movement itself.

The seventeenth canto of the *Inferno* is a brilliant confirmation of the transformability of poetic material in the above sense of the term. The figures of this transformability may be drawn more or less as follows. the little flourishes and shields on the varicolored Tatar skin of Geryon—silk, ornamented carpet fabrics, spread out on a shop-counter on the shore of the Mediterranean—maritime commerce, perspective of banking and piracy—usury—the return to Florence via the heraldic bags with samples of colors that had never before been in use—the craving for flight, suggested by the oriental ornamentation, which turns the material of the canto in the direction of the Arabian fairy tale with its device of the flying carpet—and, finally, the second return to Florence with the aid of the falcon, irreplaceable precisely on account of his being unnecessary.

Not satisfied with this truly miraculous demonstration of the transformability of poetic material, which leaves all the associative process of modern European poetry simply nowhere, and as if in mockery of his slow-witted reader, Dante, when everything has already been unloaded, used up, given away, brings Geryon down to earth and benevolently fits him out for new wanderings as the nock of an arrow sent flying from a bowstring.

v.

Dante's drafts have of course not come down to us. There is no possibility of our working on the history of his text. But it does not follow from this, of course, that there were no rough copies full of erasures and blotted lines and that the text hatched full grown, like Leda's brood from the egg or Pallas Athene from the brow of Zeus. But the unfortunate gap of six centuries, and also the quite forgivable fact of the nonextant original, have played us a dirty trick. For how many centuries now has Dante been talked and written of as if he had put down his thoughts directly on the finest legal parchment? Dante's laboratory—with this we are not concerned. What has ignorant piety to do with that? Dante is discussed as if he had had the completed whole before his eyes even before he began to work and had busied himself with the technique of moulage—first casting in plaster, then in bronze. At the very best, he is handed a chisel and allowed to carve or, as they love to say, "sculpt." Here they forget one small detail: the chisel very precisely removes all excess, and the sculptor's draft leaves no material traces behind, something of which the public is very fond. The very fact that a sculptor's work proceeds in stages corresponds to a series of draft versions.

Draft versions are never destroyed.

In poetry, in the plastic arts, and in art generally there are no ready-made things.

We are hindered from understanding this by our habit of grammatical thinking—putting the concept "art" in the nominative case. We subordinate the process of creation itself to the purposeful prepositional case, and our thinking is something like a little manikin with a lead heart who, having wavered about in various directions as he should and having undergone various jolts as he went through the questionnaire of the declension—about what? about whom? by whom? and by what?—is at the end established in the Buddhist, schoolboy tranquillity of the nominative case. A finished thing, meanwhile, is just as subject to the oblique cases as to the nominative case. Furthermore, our whole doctrine of syntax is a very powerful survival of scholasticism, and when it is put into its proper subordinate position in philosophy, in the theory of cognition, then it is completely overcome by mathematics, which has its own independent, original syntax. In the study of art this syntactic scholasticism has the upper hand and hour by hour it causes the most colossal damage. In European poetry those who are furthest away from Dante's method and, to put it bluntly, in polar opposition to him, are precisely the ones who are called Parnassians: namely, Heredia, Leconte de Lisle. Baudelaire is much closer to him. Still closer is Verlaine, and the closest of all French poets is Arthur Rimbaud. By his very nature Dante shakes the sense and violates the integrity of the image. The composition of his cantos resembles the schedule of the air transport network or the indefatigable circulation of carrier pigeons.

Thus the conversation of the draft version is a law of the energetics of the literary work. In order to arrive at the target one has to accept and take account of the wind blowing in a different direction. This is also the rule for tacking in a sailing vessel.

Let us remember that Dante Alighieri lived at the time when navigation by sail was flourishing and the art of sailing was highly developed. Let us not disdain to keep in mind the fact that he contemplated models of tacking and maneuvering. Dante had the highest respect for the art of navigation of his day. He was a student of this supremely evasive and plastic sport, known to man from the earliest times.

Here I should like to call attention to one of the remarkable peculiarities of Dante's psyche: his dread of direct answers, occasioned perhaps by the political situation in that most dangerous, intricate, and criminal century.

While the whole *Divina Commedia*, as we have already shown, is a series of questions and answers, every direct utterance of Dante's is literally squeezed out of him through the midwifery of Vergil or with the help of the nursemaid Beatrice, and so on.

Inferno, Canto XVI. The conversation is carried on with that impassioned haste known only to prisons: to make use at all costs of the tiny moment of meeting. The questions are put by a trio of eminent Florentines. About what? About Florence, of course. Their knees tremble with impatience and they dread to hear the truth. The answer, lapidary and cruel, comes in the form of a cry. At this, even though he has made a desperate effort to control himself, even Dante's chin quivers and he tosses back his head, and all this is conveyed in nothing more nor less than the author's stage direction:

> Così gridai colla faccia levata.[21]
> (*Inferno*, XVI, 76)

Dante is sometimes able to describe a phenomenon in such a way that there is absolutely nothing left of it. To do this he makes use of a device which I should like to call the Heraclitean metaphor, with which he so strongly emphasizes the fluidity of the phenomenon and with such a flourish cancels it altogether that direct contemplation, once the metaphor has done its work, is really left with nothing to live on. Several times already I have had occasion to remark that the metaphoric devices of Dante surpass our notions of composition, since our critical doctrines, fettered by the syntactic mode of thinking, are powerless before him.

> When the peasant, climbing to the top of a hill
> At that time of the year when the being who lights the world
> Least conceals his face from us
> And the watery swarm of midges yields its place to the
>   mosquitos,
> See the dancing fireflies in the hollow,
> The same one where he, perhaps, labored as a reaper and as a
>   plowman;
> So with little tongues of flame gleamed the eighth circle,
> All of which could be surveyed from the height where I had
>   climbed;
> And as with that one who revenged himself with the help of
>   bears,
> Seeing the departing chariot of Elijah,
> When the team of horses tore headlong into the sky,
> Looked with all his might but saw nothing
> Save one single flame
> Fading away like a little cloud rising into the sky
> So the tongue-like flame filled the crevices of the graves
> Stealing away the property of the graves, their profit,
> And wrapped in every flame there lay hidden a sinner.[22]
> (*Inferno*, XXVI, 25–42)

If you do not feel dizzy from this miraculous ascent, worthy of the organ of Sebastian Bach, then try to show what is here the second and what the first member of the comparison. What is compared with what? Where is the primary and where is the secondary, clarifying element?

In a number of Dante's cantos we encounter impressionistic prolegomena. The purpose of these is to present in the form of a scattered alphabet, in the form of a leaping, glistening, splashed alphabet the very same elements which, according to the rule of the transformability of lyric poetry, are later to be united into the formulas of sense.

Thus, in this introduction we see the infinitely light, brilliant Heraclitean dance of the swarm of summer midges, which prepares us to hear the solemn and tragic speech of Odysseus.

Canto XXVI of the *Inferno* is the most saillike of all the compositions of Dante, the most given to tacking, the best at maneuvering. For resourcefulness, evasiveness, Florentine diplomacy, and a kind of Greek wiliness, it has no equals.

We can clearly discern two basic parts of the canto: the luminous, impressionistic preparatory passage and the balanced, dramatic account by Odysseus of his last voyage, how he sailed out over the deeps of the Atlantic and perished terribly under the stars of another hemisphere.

In the free flowing of its thought this canto is very close to improvisation. But if you listen attentively, it will become clear that the poet is inwardly improvising in his beloved, cherished Greek, for which nothing more than the phonetics, the fabric, is furnished by his native Italian idiom.

If you give a child a thousand rubles and then leave him the choice of keeping either the small change or the notes, he will of course choose the coins, and by this means you can take the entire amount away from him by giving him a ten-kopeck piece. Precisely the same thing has befallen European Dante criticism, which has nailed him to the landscape of Hell as depicted in the etchings. No one has yet approached Dante with a geologist's hammer, in order to ascertain the crystalline structure of his rock, in order to study the particles of other minerals in it, to study its smoky color, its garish patterning, to judge it as a mineral crystal which has been subjected to the most varied series of accidents.

Our criticism says: distance the phenomenon from me and I can handle it, I can cope with it. For our criticism, what is "a longish way off" (Lomonosov's[23] expression) and what is knowable are practically the same thing.

In Dante the images depart and say farewell. It is difficult to make one's way down through the breaks of his verse with its multitude of leave-takings.

We have scarcely managed to free ourselves from that Tuscan peasant admiring the phosphorescent dance of the fireflies nor rid our eyes of the impressionistic dazzling from Elijah's chariot as it fades away into a little cloud, before the pyre of Eteocles has already been mentioned, Penelope named, the Trojan horse has slipped past, Demosthenes has lent Odysseus his republican eloquence, and the ship of old age is already being fitted out. Old age, in Dante's understanding of that term, is first of all breadth of mental horizon, heightened capacity, the globe itself as a frame of reference. In the Odyssean canto the world is already round.

It is a canto which deals with the composition of the human blood, which contains within itself the salt of the ocean. The beginning of the voyage is in the system of blood vessels. Blood is planetary, solar, salty . . .

With every fiber of his being Odysseus despises sclerosis just as Farinata despised Hell.

> Surely we are not born for security like a cow, it cannot be that we will shrink from devoting the last handful of our fading senses to the bold venture of sailing westward, beyond the Gates of Hercules, there where the world, unpeopled, goes on?[24]

The metabolism of the planet itself takes place in the blood, and the Atlantic absorbs Odysseus and sucks down his wooden ship.

It is unthinkable to read the cantos of Dante without aiming them in the direction of the present day. They were made for that. They are missiles for capturing the future. They demand commentary in the *futurum*.

Time, for Dante, is the content of history, understood as a single, synchronic act. And conversely: the content is the joint containing of time with one's associates, competitors, codiscoverers.

Dante is an antimodernist. His contemporaneity is inexhaustible, measureless, and unending.

That is why the speech of Odysseus, bulging like the lens of a magnifying glass, may be applied to the war of the Greeks and the

Persians as well as to the discovery of America by Columbus, the bold experiments of Paracelsus, and the world empire of Charles V.

Canto XXVI, devoted to Odysseus and Diomed, is a splendid introduction to the anatomy of Dante's eye, so naturally adjusted for one thing only: the revelation of the structure of the future. Dante had the visual accommodation of birds of prey, unsuited to focusing at short range: too large was the field in which he hunted.

To Dante himself may be applied the words of the proud Farinata:

> "Noi veggiam, come quei c'ha mala luce."[25]
> (*Inferno*, X, 100)

We, that is, the souls of sinners, are capable of seeing and distinguishing only the distant future, for which we have a special gift. The moment the doors into the future are slammed in front of us, we become totally blind. In this regard we are like one who struggles with the twilight and, able to make out distant objects, cannot discern what is near him.

The dance basis is strongly expressed in the rhythms of the terza rima of Canto XXVI. One is struck here by the high lightheartedness of the rhythm. The feet are arranged in the movement of the waltz:

> E se già fosse, non saria per tempo.
>   così foss' ei, da che pur esser dee!
>   chè più mi graverà, com'più m'attempo.[26]
> (*Inferno*, XXVI, 10–12)

For us as foreigners it is difficult to penetrate to the ultimate secret of an alien poetry. It is not for us to judge; the last word cannot be ours. But in my opinion it is precisely here that we find that captivating pliability of the Italian language, which only the ear of a native Italian can fully grasp. Here I am quoting Marina Tsvetaeva, who once mentioned "the pliability of Russian speech."[27]

If you pay close attention to the mouth movements of a person who recites poetry distinctly, it will seem as if he were giving a lesson to deaf-mutes; that is, he works as if he were counting on being understood even without the sound, articulating each vowel with a pedagogic obviousness. And it is enough to see how Canto XXVI sounds in order to hear it. I should say that in this canto the vowels are agitated, throbbing.

The waltz is essentially a wavy dance. Nothing even faintly resembling it was possible in Hellenic or Egyptian culture, but it could
conceivably be found in Chinese culture, and it is absolutely normal
in modern European culture. (For this juxtaposition I am indebted
to Spengler.) At the basis of the waltz there lies the purely European passion for periodic wavering movements, that same intent
listening to the wave which runs through all our theory of light and
sound, all our theory of matter, all our poetry and all our music.

VI.

Envy, O Poetry, the science of crystallography, bite your nails in
wrath and impotence: for it is recognized that the mathematical
combinations needed to describe the process of crystal formation
are not derivable from three-dimensional space. You, however, are
denied that elementary respect enjoyed by any piece of mineral
crystal.

Dante and his contemporaries did not know geological time.
The paleontological clock was unknown to them: the clock of coal,
the clock of infusorial limestone, granular, gritty, stratified clocks.
They whirled around in the calendar, dividing the twenty-four hours
into quarters. The Middle Ages, however, did not fit into the
Ptolemaic system: they took refuge there.

To biblical genetics they added the physics of Aristotle. The two
poorly matched things were reluctant to knit together. The huge ex-
plosive power of the Book of Genesis (the idea of spontaneous
generation) assailed the tiny little island of the Sorbonne from all
quarters, and it would be no mistake to say that Dante's people lived
in an antiquity completely awash in the present, like the earthly
globe embraced by Tiutchev's ocean. It is difficult for us to imagine
how it could be that things which were known to absolutely everyone—cribbed schoolboy's notes, things which formed part of the
required program of elementary education—how it could be that
the entire biblical cosmogony with its Christian supplements could
have been read by the educated men of that time quite literally as if
it were today's newspaper, a veritable special edition.

And if we approach Dante from this point of view, it will appear
that he saw in tradition not so much its dazzling sacred aspects as an

object which, with the aid of zealous reporting and passionate experimentation, could be used to good effect.

In Canto XXVI of the *Paradiso* Dante goes so far as to have a personal conversation with Adam—an actual interview. He is assisted by Saint John the Divine, author of the Apocalypse.

I maintain that every element of the modern method of conducting experiments is present in Dante's approach to tradition. These are: the deliberate creation of special conditions for the experiment, the use of instruments of unimpeachable accuracy, the demand that the result be verifiable and demonstrable.

The situation in Canto XXVI of the *Paradiso* can be described as a solemn examination in the surrounding of a concert and optical instruments. Music and optics constitute the heart of the matter.

The fundamental antinomy of Dante's "experiment" consists of the fact that he rushes back and forth between example and experiment. Example is drawn out of the patriarchal bag of ancient consciousness only to be returned to it as soon as it is no longer required. Experiment, pulling one or another needed fact out of the purse of experience, does not return them as the promissory note requires, but puts them into circulation.

The parables of the Gospel and the little scholastic examples of the science taught in school—these are cereals eaten and done away with. But the experimental sciences, taking facts out of coherent reality, make of them a kind of seed-fund which is reserved, inviolable, and which constitutes, as it were, the property of a time that is unborn but must come. The position of the experimenter as regards factology is, insofar as he strives to be joined with it in truth, unstable by its very nature, agitated and awry. It resembles the figure of the waltz that has already been mentioned, for, after every half-turn on the extended toe of the shoe, the heels of the dancer may be brought together, but they are always brought together on a new square of the parquet and in a way that is different in kind. The dizzying Mephisto Waltz of experimentation was conceived in the *trecento* or perhaps even long before that, and it was conceived in the process of poetic formation, the undulating proceduralness, the transformability of the poetic matter—the most precise of all matter, the most prophetic and indomitable.

Because of the theological terminology, the scholastic grammar, and our ignorance of the allegory, we overlooked the experimental dances of Dante's *Comedy*; to suit the ways of a dead scholarship, we made Dante look more presentable, while his theology was a vessel of dynamics.

A sensitive palm touching the neck of a heated pitcher identifies its form because it is warm. Warmth in this case has priority over form and it is that which fulfills the sculptural function. In a cold state, forcibly divorced from its incandescence, Dante's *Comedy* is suitable only for analysis with mechanistic tweezers, but not for reading, not for performing.

> Come quando dall'acqua o dallo specchio
> salta lo raggio all'opposita parte,
> salendo su per lo modo parecchio
> a quel che scende, e tanto si diparte
> dal cader della pietra in igual tratta,
> sì come mostra esperienza ed arte.
> <div align="center">(<i>Purgatorio</i>, XV, 16–21)</div>

"As a ray of sunlight that strikes the surface of water or a mirror reflects back at an angle corresponding to the angle of its fall, which differentiates it from a falling stone that bounces back perpendicularly from the ground—which is confirmed by experience and by art."

At the moment when the necessity of an empirical verification of the legend's data first dawned on Dante, when he first developed a taste for what I propose to call a sacred—in inverted commas—induction, the conception of the *Divina Commedia* had already been formed and its success intrinsically secured.

The poem in its most densely foliated aspect is oriented toward authority, it is most resonantly rustling, most *concertante* just when it is caressed by dogma, by canon, by the firm chrysostomatic word. But the whole trouble is that in authority—or, to put it more precisely, in authoritarianism—we see only insurance against error, and we fail to perceive anything in that grandiose music of trustfulness, of trust, in the nuances— delicate as an alpine rainbow—of probability and conviction, which Dante has at his command.

> Col quale il fantolin corre alla mamma—[28]
> <div align="center">(<i>Purgatorio</i>, XXX, 44)</div>

thus does Dante fawn upon authority.

Many cantos of the *Paradiso* are encased in the hard capsule of an examination. In some passages one can even hear clearly the examiner's hoarse bass and the candidate's quavering voice. The embedding-in of a grotesque and a genre picture (the examination of a baccalaureate candidate) constitutes a necessary attribute of the elevated and *concertante* compositions of the third part. And the first sample of it is given as early as in the second canto of the *Paradiso* (in Beatrice's discussion of the origin of the moon's dark patches).

To grasp the very nature of Dante's intercourse with authoritative sources, that is, the form and methods of his cognition, it is necessary to take into account both the concertolike setting of the *Comedy*'s scholastic cantos and the conditioning of the very organs of perception. Let alone the really remarkably staged experiment with the candle and the three mirrors, where it is demonstrated that the return path of light has as its source the refraction of the ray, I cannot fail to note the conditioning of vision for the apperception of new things.

This conditioning is developed into a genuine dissection: Dante divines the layered structure of the retina: *di gonna in gonna* . . .[29]

Music here is not a guest invited in from without, but a participant in the argument; or, to be more precise, it facilitates the exchange of opinions, coordinates it, encourages syllogistic digestion, extends premises, and compresses conclusions. Its role is both absorptive and resolvent—its role is a purely chemical one.

When you plunge into Dante and read with complete conviction, when you transplant yourself entirely onto the poetic material's field of action, when you join in and harmonize your own intonations with the echoings of the orchestral and thematic groups which arise incessantly on the pocked and shaken semantic surface, when you begin to perceive through the smoky-crystalline matter of sound-form the glimmerings embedded within, that is, the extra sounds and thoughts conferred on it not by a poetic but by a geologic intelligence, then the purely vocal, intonational and rhythmic work gives way to a more powerful coordinating activity—to conducting —and, assuming control over the area of polyphony and jutting out from the voice like a more complex mathematical dimension out of a three-dimensional state, the hegemony of the conductor's baton is established.

Which has primacy, listening or conducting? If conducting is only a prodding of music which anyway rolls on of its own accord, what use is it, provided the orchestra is good in and of itself and displays an irreproachable *ensemble*? An orchestra without a conductor, that cherished dream, belongs to the same category of "ideals" of pan-European banality as the universal Esperanto language that symbolizes the linguistic *ensemble* of all mankind.

Let us consider how the conductor's baton appeared and we shall see that it arrived neither too late nor too soon, but exactly when it should have, as a new, original mode of activity, creating in the air its own new domain.

Let us hear about the birth or, rather, the hatching of the modern conductor's baton from the orchestra.

1732: Time (tempo or beat)—once beaten with the foot, now usually with the hand. Conductor—*conducteur—der Anführer* (Walther, *Musical Dictionary*).

1753: Baron Grimm calls the conductor of the Paris Opera a woodchopper because of his habit of beating time aloud, a habit which has reigned in French opera since the day of Lully (Schünemann, *Geschichte des Dirigierens*, 1913).

1810: At the Frankenhausen music festival, Spohr conducted with a baton rolled up out of paper, without any noise, without any grimacing (Spohr, *Selbstbiographie*).*

The birth of the conductor's baton was considerably delayed— the chemically reactive orchestra had preceded it. The usefulness of a conductor's baton is far from being its whole justification. The chemical nature of orchestral sonorities finds its expression in the dance of the conductor, who has his back to the audience. And this baton is far from being an external, administrative accessory or a *sui generis* symphonic police which could be abolished in an ideal state. It is nothing other than a dancing chemical formula that integrates reactions comprehensible to the ear. I also ask that it not be regarded a supplementary, mute instrument invented for greater clarity and to provide additional pleasure. In a sense, this invulnerable baton contains within itself qualitatively all the elements of the orchestra. But how does it contain them? It is not redolent of them, nor could it be. It is not redolent in the same way the chemical symbol of chlorine is not redolent of chlorine or the formula of ammonia or ammonium chloride is not redolent of ammonium chloride or of ammonia.

Dante was chosen as the theme of this talk not because I intended to concentrate on him as a means of learning from the classics and to seat him together with Shakespeare and Leo Tolstoy at a kind of

---

*A. Kars, *Istorija orkestrovki* [History of orchestration] (Muzgiz, 1932). (Brown and Hughes' note.)

table d'hôte in Kirpotin's manner, but because he is the greatest, the incontestible proprietor of convertible and currently circulating poetic material, the earliest and at the same time most powerful chemical conductor of a poetic composition that exists only in swells and waves, in upsurges and maneuverings.

VII.

Dante's cantos are scores for a special chemical orchestra in which, for the external ear, the most easily discernible comparisons are those identical with the outbursts, and the solo roles, that is, the arias and ariosos, are varieties of self-confessions, self-flagellations or autobiographies, sometimes brief and compact, sometimes lapidary, like a tombstone inscription; sometimes extended like a testimonial from a medieval university; sometimes powerfully developed, articulated, and reaching a dramatic operatic maturity, such as, for example, Francesca's famous cantilena.

Canto XXXIII of the *Inferno*, which contains Ugolino's account of how he and his three sons were starved to death in a prison tower by Archbishop Ruggieri of Pisa, is encased in a cello timbre, dense and heavy, like rancid, poisoned honey.

The density of the cello timbre is best suited to convey a sense of expectation and of agonizing impatience. There exists no power on earth which could hasten the movement of honey flowing from a tilted glass jar. Therefore the cello could come about and be given form only when the European analysis of time had made sufficient progress, when the thoughtless sundial had been transcended and the one-time observer of the shade stick moving across Roman numerals on the sand had been transformed into a passionate participant of a differential torture and into a martyr of the infinitesimal. A cello delays sound, hurry how it may. Ask Brahms—he knows it. Ask Dante—he has heard it.

Ugolino's narrative is one of Dante's most significant arias, one of those instances when a man, who has been given a unique, never-to-be-repeated chance to be heard out, is completely transformed under the eyes of his audience, plays like a virtuoso on his unhappiness, draws out of his misfortune a timbre never before heard and unknown even to himself.

It must be remembered that timbre is a structural principle, like the alkalinity or the acidity of this or that chemical compound. The retort is not the space in which the chemical reaction occurs. This would be much too simple.

The cello voice of Ugolino, overgrown with a prison beard, starving and confined with his three fledgling sons, one of whom bears a sharp, violin name, Anselmuccio, pours out of the narrow slit:

> Breve pertugio dentro dalla muda,[30]
> (*Inferno*, XXXIII, 22)

—it ripens in the box of the prison resonator—here the cello's fraternization with the prison is no joking matter.

Il carcere—the prison supplements and acoustically conditions the verbalizing work of the autobiographic cello.

Prison has played an outstanding role in the subconscious of the Italian people. Nightmares of prison were imbibed with the mother's milk. The *trecento* threw men into prison with an amazing unconcern. Common prisons were open to the public, like churches or our museums. The interest in prisons was exploited by the jailers themselves as well as by the fear-instilling apparatus of the small states. Between the prison and the free world outside there existed a lively intercourse, resembling diffusion—the process of osmosis.

Hence the story of Ugolino is one of the migratory anecdotes, a bugaboo with which mothers frighten children—one of those amusing horrors which are pleasurably mumbled through the night as a remedy for insomnia, as one tosses and turns in bed. By way of ballad it is a well-known type, like Bürger's *Lenore*, the *Lorelei*, or the *Erlkönig*.

In such a guise, it corresponds to the glass retort, so accessible and comprehensible irrespective of the quality of the chemical process taking place within.

But the largo for cello, proffered by Dante on behalf of Ugolino, has its own space and its own structure, which are revealed in the timbre. The ballad-retort, along with the general knowledge of it, is smashed to bits. Chemistry takes over with its architectonic drama.

> "Io non so chi tu se', nè per che modo
> venuto se 'qua giù; ma fiorentino
> mi sembri veramente quand' io t'odo.

Tu dei saper ch'i 'fui conte Ugolino."
(*Inferno*, XXXIII, 10–13)

"I do not know who you are or how you came down here, but by
your speech you seem to me a real Florentine. You ought to know
that I was Ugolino."

"You ought to know"—*tu dei saper*—the first stroke on the cello,
the first out-thrusting of the theme.

The second stroke: "If you do not burst out weeping now, I
know not what can wring tears from your eyes."

Here are opened up the truly limitless horizons of compassion.
What is more, the compassionate one is invited in as a new partner,
and already his vibrating voice is heard from the distant future.

However, it wasn't by chance I mentioned the ballad: Ugolino's
narrative is precisely a ballad in its chemical make-up, even though
it is confined in a prison retort. Present are the following elements
of the ballad: the conversation between father and sons (recall the
Erlkönig), the pursuit of a swiftness that slips away, that is—continuing the parallel with the *Erlkönig*—in one instance a mad dash
with his trembling son in arms, in the other, the situation in prison,
that is, the counting of trickling tempi, which bring the father and
his three sons closer to the threshold of death by starvation, mathematically imaginable, but to the father's mind unthinkable. It is the
same rhythm of the race in disguise—in the dampened wailing of
the cello, which is struggling with all its might to break out of the
situation and which presents an auditory picture of a still more terrible, slow pursuit, decomposing the swiftness into the most delicate
fibers.

Finally, in just the way the cello eccentrically converses with itself
and wrings from itself questions and answers, Ugolino's story is
interpolated with his sons' touching and helpless interjections:

... ed Anselmuccio mio
disse: "Tu guardi sì, padre: che hai?"
(*Inferno*, XXXIII, 50–51)

... and my Anselmuccio said:
"Father, why do you look so? What is the matter?"

That is, the timbre is not at all sought out and forced onto the
story as onto a shoemaker's last, but rather the dramatic structure
of the narrative arises out of the timbre.

VIII.

It seems to me that Dante has carefully studied all speech defects, that he has listened to stutterers and lispers, to whiners and mispronouncers, and that he has learned a good deal from them.

So I should like to speak about the auditory coloring in Canto XXXII of the *Inferno*.

A peculiar labial music: *abbo, gabbo, babbo, Tebe, plebe, zebe, converrebbe*. As if a wet-nurse were taking part in the creation of the phonetics. Lips now protrude like a child's, now are distended into a proboscis.

The labials form a kind of "enciphered bass"—*basso continuo*, that is, the chordal basis of harmonization. They are joined by smacking, sucking, whistling dentals as well as by clicking and hissing ones.

At random, I pull out a single strand: *cagnazzi, riprezzo, quazzi, mezzo, gravezza . . .*

Not for a second do the tweakings, the smacking, and the labial explosions cease.

The canto is sprinkled with a vocabulary that I would describe as an assortment of seminary ragging or of the blood thirsty taunting-rhymes of schoolboys: *cuticagna* ("nape"); *dischiomi* ("pull out hair, locks of hair"); *sonar con le mascella* ("to yell," "to bark"); *pigliare a gabbo* ("to brag," "to loaf"). With the aid of this deliberately shameless, intentionally infantile orchestration, Dante forms the crystals for the auditory landscape of Giudecca (Judas' circle) and Caina (Cain's circle).

> Non fece al corso suo sì grosso velo
> d'inverno la Danoia in Osteric,
> nè Tanaì là sotto il freddo cielo,
> com'era quivi: chè, se Tambernic
> vi fosse su caduto, o Pietrapana,
> non avrìa pur dall'orlo fatto cric.[31]
> (*Inferno*, XXXII, 25–30)

All of a sudden, for no reason at all, a Slavonic duck sets up a squawk: *Osteric, Tambernic, cric* (an onomatopoeic little word—"crackle").

Ice produces a phonetic explosion and it crumbles into the names of the Danube and the Don. The cold-producing draught of Canto XXXII resulted from the entry of physics into a moral idea: from betrayal to frozen conscience to the ataraxy of shame to absolute zero.

In tempo, Canto XXXII is a modern scherzo. But what kind? An anatomic scherzo that uses the onomatopoeic infantile material to study the degeneration of speech.

A new link is revealed here: between feeding and speaking. Shameful speaking can be turned back, is turned back to champing, biting, gurgling, to chewing.

The articulation of feeding and speaking almost coincide. A strange, locust phonetics is created.

> Mettendo i denti in nota di cicogna—
> (*Inferno*, XXXII, 36)

—using their teeth like grasshoppers' mandibles.

Finally, it is necessary to note that Canto XXXII is overflowing with anatomical lustfulness.

"That same famous blow which simultaneously destroyed the wholeness of the body and injured its shadow." There, too, with a purely surgical pleasure: "He whose jugular vertebra was chopped through by Florence."

> Di cui segò Fiorenza la gorgiera.
> (*Inferno*, XXXII, 120)

And further: "Like a hungry man who greedily falls on bread, one of them fell on another and sank his teeth into the place where the neck and the nape join."

> Là 've 'l cervel s'aggiugne colla nuca.
> (*Inferno*, XXXII, 129)

All this jigs like a Dürer skeleton on hinges and takes us to German anatomy.

After all, a murderer is a bit of an anatomist.

After all, for the Middle Ages an executioner was a little like a scientific researcher.

The art of war and the trade of execution are a bit like a dissection amphitheater's antechamber.

IX.

The *Inferno* is a pawnshop where all the countries and towns known to Dante lie unredeemed. There is a framework for the very powerful structure of the infernal circles. It cannot be conveyed in the form of a funnel. It cannot be represented on a relief map. Hell is suspended on the iron wires of urban egoism.

It is wrong to conceive of the *Inferno* as something volumetric, as some combination of enormous circuses, deserts with burning sands, stinking swamps, Babylonian capitals and mosques heated to red-hot incandescence. Hell contains nothing, and it has no volume, the way an epidemic, an infectious disease, or the plague has none; it is like any contagion, which spreads even though it is not spatial.

Love of the city, passion for the city, hatred of the city—these are the material of the *Inferno*. The circles of hell are nothing but the Saturn rings of exile. For the exile his sole, forbidden, and forever-lost city is scattered everywhere—he is surrounded by it. I *should* say that the *Inferno* is surrounded by Florence. The Italian cities in Dante—Pisa, Florence, Lucca, Verona—these dear civic planets—are stretched out into monstrous circles, extended into belts, restored to a nebulous, gaseous state.

The antilandscape character of the *Inferno* constitutes as it were the condition of its graphic quality.

Imagine that grandiose experiment of Foucault's carried out not with a single pendulum, but with a multitude of crisscrossing pendulums. Here space exists only insofar as it is a receptacle for amplitudes. To make specific Dante's images is as unthinkable as to enumerate the names of those who took part in the migration of peoples.

> As the Flemish between Wissant and Bruges, fearing the sea's flood tide, erect dikes to force back the sea, and as the Paduans construct embankments along the quays of the Brenta out of concern for the safety of their cities and bays, and in expectation of spring which melts the snows of the Chiarentana (a part of the snowclad Alps)—such were these dams, albeit not so monumental, whoever the engineer who built them.
>
> (*Inferno*, XV, 4–12)

The moons of the polynomial pendulum swing here from Bruges to Padua, teach a course in European geography, give a lecture on the art of engineering, on the techniques of city safety, on the organization of public works, and on the significance of the alpine watershed for national interests.

Crawling as we do on our knees before a line of verse, what

have we retained from these riches? Where are its godfathers, where its zealots? What are we to do about our poetry, which lags so shamefully behind science?

It is frightening to think that the blinding explosions of present-day physics and kinetics were put to use six hundred years before their thunder sounded: there are no words to brand the shameful, barbaric indifference to them on the part of the sad compositors of ready-made meaning.

Poetic speech creates its tools on the move and in the same breath does away with them.

Of all our arts only painting, and at that only modern French painting, still has an ear for Dante. This is the painting which elongates the bodies of the horses approaching the finish line at the race track.

Whenever a metaphor raises the vegetable colors of existence to an articulate impulse, I remember Dante with gratitude.

We describe just what cannot be described, that is, nature's text brought to a standstill; and we have forgotten how to describe the only thing which by its structure yields to poetic representation, namely the impulses, intentions, and amplitudes of oscillation.

Ptolemy has returned by the back door! . . . Giordano Bruno was burned in vain!

While still in the womb, our creations are known to each and every one, but Dante's polynomial, multi-sailed and kinetically incandescent comparisons still retain the charm of that which has been told to no one.

Amazing is his "reflexology of speech"—the science, still not well established, of the spontaneous psycho-physiological influence of the word on the discussants, the audience, and the speaker himself, and also on the means by which he conveys the impulse to speech, that is, signals by light a sudden desire to express himself.

Here he approaches closest of all the wave theory of sound and light, he establishes their relationship.

> As a beast, covered with a cloth, is nervous and shudders, and only the moving folds of the material betray its dissatisfaction, thus did the first created soul [Adam's] express to me through the covering [of light] how pleasant and joyous it was to answer my question.
>
> (Paradiso, XXVI, 97–102)

In the third part of the *Comedy* (the *Paradiso*) I see a genuine kinetic ballet. Here we have all possible kinds of luminous figures and dances, all the way up to the clacking of heels at a wedding feast.

> Before me four torches burned and the nearest suddenly came to life and became as rosy as if Jupiter and Mars were suddenly to become birds and exchange their plumage.
> (Paradiso, XXVII, 10–15)

It's odd, isn't it: a man, who intends to speak, arms himself with a taut bow, lays up a supply of bearded arrows, prepares mirrors and convex lenses, and squints at the stars like a tailor threading a needle . . .

I have devised this composite quotation, which is drawn from various passages in the *Comedy*, to bring into more emphatic relief the speech-preparatory strategies of Dante's poetry.

The preparation of speech is even more his sphere than the articulation, that is, than speech itself.

Recall the marvelous supplication which Vergil addresses to the wiliest of Greeks.

It is all arippling with the softness of the Italian diphthongs.

Those curly, ingratiating and sputtering flame-tongues of unprotected lamps, muttering about the oiled wick . . .

> O voi, che siete due dentro ad un foco,
>   s'io meritai di voi mentre ch'io vissi,
>   s'io meritai di voi assai o poco.[32]
> (Inferno, XXVI, 79–81)

Dante determines the origin, fate and character of a man by his voice, just as medical science of his time made diagnoses by the color of urine.

X.

He is brimming over with a sense of ineffable gratitude toward the copious richness which is falling into his hands. He has a lot to do: space must be prepared for the influx, the cataract must be removed from rigid vision, care must be taken that the abundance of outpouring poetic material does not trickle through his fingers, that it does not disappear into an empty sieve.

> Tutti dicean: "Benedictus qui venis,"
>   e fior gittando di sopra e dintorno,
> "Manibus o date lilia plenis."[33]
>   (*Purgatorio*, XXX, 19–21)

The secret of his scope is that not a single word of his own is introduced. He is set in motion by everything except fabrication, except inventiveness. Dante and fantasy—why this is incompatible! For shame, French romantics, you miserable *incroyables* in red vests, slanderers of Alighieri! What fantasy is there in him? He writes to dictation, he is a copyist, a translator. He is bent double in the posture of a scribe who squints in fright at the illuminated original lent him from the prior's library.

I think I forgot to say that a hypnotist's seance was a sort of precondition to the *Comedy*. This is true, but perhaps overstated. If one takes this amazing work from the viewpoint of written language, from the viewpoint of the independent art of writing, which in 1300 enjoyed equal rights with painting and music and was among the most venerated professions, then to all the earlier suggested analogies a new one can be added—writing down dictation, copying, transcribing.

Sometimes, very seldom, he shows us his writing tools: A pen is called *penna*, that is, it participates in a bird's flight; ink is *inchiostro*, that is, belonging to a cloister; lines of verse are also called *inchiostri*, or are designated by the Latin scholastic *versi* or, still more modestly, *carte*, that is, an amazing substitution, pages instead of lines of verse.

And when it is written down and ready, there is still no full stop, for it must be taken somewhere, it must be shown to someone to be checked and praised.

To say "copying" is not enough—rather it is calligraphy at the most terrible and impatient dictation. The dictator, the taskmaster, is far more important than the so-called poet.

. . . I will labor a little more, and then I must show my notebook, drenched with the tears of a bearded schoolboy, to a most strict Beatrice, who radiates not only glory but literacy too.

Long before Arthur Rimbaud's alphabet of colors, Dante conjoined color with the full vocalization of articulate speech. But he

is a dyer, a textile worker. His ABC is an alphabet of fluttering
fabrics tinted with colored powders, with vegetable dyes.

> Sovra candido vel cinta d'uliva
>   donna m'apparve, sotto verde manto,
>   vestita di color di fiamma viva.[34]
>   (*Purgatorio*, XXX, 31–33)

His impulses toward colors can be more readily called textile impulses than alphabetic ones. Color for him is displayed only in the
fabric. For Dante the highest concentration of material nature, as a
substance determined by its coloration, is in textiles. And weaving is
the occupation closest to qualitativeness, to quality.

Now I shall attempt to describe one of the innumerable conductorial flights of Dante's baton. We shall take this flight as it is, embedded in the actual setting of precious and instantaneous labor.

Let us begin with the writing. The pen draws calligraphic letters,
it traces out proper and common nouns. A pen is a small piece of
bird's flesh. Of course Dante, who never forgets the origin of things,
remembers this. His technique of writing in broad strokes and
curves grows into the figured flight of flocks of birds.

> E come augelli surti di riviera,
>   quasi congratulando a lor pasture,
>   fanno di sè or tonda or altra schiera,
> si dentro ai lumi sante creature
>   volitando cantavano, e faciensi
>   or D, or I, or L, in sue figure.[35]
>   (*Paradiso*, XVIII, 73–78)

Just as the letters under the hand of the scribe, who is obedient
to the one who dictates and stands outside literature, as a finished
product, are lured to the decoy of meaning, as to an inviting forage,
so exactly do birds, magnetized by green grass—now separately,
now together—peck at what they find, now forming a circle, now
stretching out into a line.

Writing and speech are incommensurate. Letters correspond to
intervals. Old Italian grammar—just as our Russian one—is always
that same fluttering flock of birds, that same motley Tuscan *schiera*,
that is, the Florentine mob, which changes laws like gloves, which
forgets by evening the decrees promulgated that same morning for
the public welfare.

There is no syntax: there is a magnetized impulse, a longing for the stern of a ship, a longing for a forage of worms, a longing for an unpromulgated law, a longing for Florence.

XI.

Let us turn again to the question of Dantean coloring.

The interior of a mountain crystal, Aladdin's expanse concealed within it, the lanternlike, lamplike, the candelabralike suspension of the piscine rooms implicit within it—this is the best of keys to a comprehension of the *Comedy*'s coloring.

A mineralogical collection is a most excellent organic commentary to Dante.

I permit myself a little autobiographical confession. Black Sea pebbles, tossed up by the surf, were of great help to me when the conception of this talk was ripening. I consulted frankly with the chalcedony, the cornelian, crystallized gypsum, spar, quartz, etc. I understood then that a stone is a kind of diary of the weather, a meteorological concentrate as it were. A stone is nothing but weather excluded from atmospheric space and put away in functional space. In order to understand this, it is necessary to imagine that all geological changes and displacements can be resolved completely into elements of the weather. In this sense, meteorology is more basic than mineralogy: it encompasses it, washes over it, it ages and gives meaning to it.

The delightful pages which Novalis[36] devotes to miners and mining make specific the interconnection of stone and culture and, by causing culture to grow like a rock formation, illumine it out of the stone-weather.

A stone is an impressionistic diary of weather, accumulated by millions of years of disasters, but it is not only the past, it is also the future: there is periodicity in it. It is Aladdin's lamp penetrating into the geologic murk of future times.

In combining the uncombinable, Dante altered the structure of time or, perhaps, the other way around: he was forced to resort to a glossolalia of facts, to a synchronism of events, names, and traditions separated by centuries, precisely because he heard the overtones of time.

The method chosen by Dante is one of anachronism, and Homer, who appears with a sword at his side, in company with Vergil,

Horace, and Lucan, from the dim shadow of the pleasant Orphic choirs, where the four together while away a tearless eternity in literary discussion, is its best expression.

Evidences of the standing-still of time in Dante are not only the round astronomical bodies, but absolutely all things and all persons' characters. Anything automatic is alien to him. He is disdainful of causality: such prophecies are fit for bedding down swine.

> Faccian le bestie fiesolane strame
>   di lor medesme, e non tocchin la pianta,
>   s'alcuna surge ancor nel lor letame.[37]
>   (*Inferno*, XV, 73–75)

If I were asked bluntly, "What is a Dantean metaphor?" I would answer, "I don't know," for a metaphor can be defined only metaphorically—and this can be substantiated scientifically. But it seems to me that Dante's metaphor designates the standing-still of time. Its root is not in the little word *how*, but in the word *when*. His *quando* sounds like *come*. Ovid's rumbling is closer to him than the French eloquence of Vergil.

Again and again I turn to the reader and ask him to "imagine" something, that is, I resort to analogy, which has a single goal: to fill up the insufficiency of our system of definition.

So, imagine that the patriarch Abraham and King David, and all of Israel, including Isaac, Jacob, and all their kinsmen, and Rachel, for whom Jacob endured so much, have entered into a singing and roaring organ, as into a house with the door ajar, and have disappeared within.

And our forefather Adam with his son Abel, and old Noah, and Moses the giver and obeyer of the law had entered into it even earlier.

> Trasseci l'ombra del primo parente,
>   d'Abèl suo figlio, e quella di Noè,
>   di Moisè legista e obediente;
> Abraàm patriarca, e Davìd re,
>   Israèl con lo padre, e co' suoi nati,
>   e con Rachele, per cui tanto fè.[38]
>   (*Inferno*, IV, 55–60)

And after this the organ acquires the ability to move—all its pipes and bellows become extraordinarily agitated and, raging and storming, it suddenly begins to back away.

If the halls of the Hermitage should suddenly go mad, if the paintings of all schools and masters should suddenly break loose from the nails, should fuse, intermingle, and fill the air of the rooms with futuristic howling and colors in violent agitation, the result then would be something like Dante's *Comedy*.

To wrench Dante away from scholastic rhetoric is to render the whole of European civilization a service of no small importance. I hope centuries of labor will not be required for this, but only joint international efforts will succeed in creating a true anticommentary to the work of many generations of scholiasts, creeping philologues, and pseudobiographers. Lack of respect for the poetic material— which can be comprehended only through the performance of it, only by a conductorial flight—was precisely the reason for the general blindness to Dante, to the greatest master-manager of this material, to European art's greatest conductor, who by many centuries anticipated the formation of an orchestra adequate—to what?—to the integral of the conductor's baton.

Calligraphic composition realized by means of improvisation: such is the approximate formula of a Dantean impulse, taken simultaneously both as a flight and as something finished. His comparisons are articulated impulses.

The most complex structural passages of the poem are performed on the fife, on a birdcall. Almost always the fife is sent out ahead.

Here I have in mind Dante's introductions, released by him as if they were trial balloons.

> Quando si parte il giuoco della zara,
>   colui che perde si riman dolente,
>   ripetendo le volte, e tristo impara:
> con l'altro se ne va tutta la gente:
>   qual va dinanzi, e qual di retro il prende,
>   e qual da lato li si reca a mente.
> El non s'arresta, e questo e quello intende;
>   a cui porge la man, più non fa pressa;
>   e così dalla calca si difende.
>   (*Purgatorio*, VI, 1–9)

When the dice game is finished, the loser in sad solitude replays the game, dejectedly throwing the dice. The whole crowd dogs the footsteps of the lucky gambler: one runs out ahead, one plucks at him from behind, one curries favor asking to be remembered; but fortune's favorite continues on, he listens to all alike, and by shaking hands, he frees himself from the importunate hangers-on.

And thus the "street" song of the *Purgatorio*—with its crush of importunate Florentine souls who desire gossip first, intercession second, and then gossip again—proceeds in the birdcall of genre, on the typical Flemish fife that became painting only three hundred years later.

Another curious consideration suggests itself: the commentary (explanatory) is an integral structural part of the *Comedy* itself. The miracle ship left the shipyard with barnacles sticking to it. The commentary is derived from the hubbub of the streets, from rumor, from hundred-mouthed Florentine slander. It is unavoidable, like the halcyon hovering behind Batiushkov's ship.[89]

There, there, look: old Marzzuco—how well he bore himself at his son's burial! A remarkably courageous old man. . . . And do you know, they were quite wrong to chop off the head of Pietro de la Broccia—they had nothing on him. . . . A woman's evil hand is implicated here. . . . By the way, there he is himself—Let's go up and ask.

Poetic material has no voice. It does not paint and it does not express itself in words. It knows no form, and by the same token it is devoid of content for the simple reason that it exists only in performance. The finished work is nothing but a calligraphic product, the inevitable result of the performing impulse. If a pen is dipped into an inkwell, the work created, stopped in its tracks, is nothing but a stock of letters, fully commensurate with the inkwell.

In talking of Dante, it is more proper to have in mind the generation of impulses and not the generation of forms: impulses to textiles, to sails, to scholastics, to meteorology, to engineering, to municipalities, to artisans and craftsmen, a list that could be continued ad infinitum.

In other words, the syntax confuses us. All nominative cases should be replaced by datives of direction. This is the law of reversible and convertible poetic material, which exists only in the performing impulse.

—Everything is here turned inside out: the substantive is the goal, and not the subject of the sentence. It is my hope that the object of Dante scholarship will become the coordination of the impulse and the text.

About Poetry

FROM THE AUTHOR

The sketches that form the present collection were written at various times, between 1910 and 1923. They are linked by a certain kinship of thought.

Not one of these excerpts attempts definitive literary characterization; literary themes and patterns serve only as graphic examples. Those of my incidental essays that do not share this common bond have not been included in this collection.

O. M.
1928

The Word & Culture

There is grass in the streets of Petersburg, the first runner-sprouts of the virgin forest that will cover the space of contemporary cities. This bright, tender greenery, with its astonishing freshness, belongs to a new, inspired nature. Petersburg is really the most advanced city in the world. The race to modernity isn't measured by subways or skyscrapers; but by the speed with which the sprightly grass pushes its way out from under the city stones.

Our blood, our music, our political life—all this will find its continuity in the tender being of a new nature, a nature-Psyche. In this kingdom of the spirit without man every tree will be a dryad, and every phenomenon will speak of its own metamorphosis.

Bring it to a stop? But why? Who will stop the sun as he sweeps in summer harness to his paternal home, seized by a passion for returning? Rather than beg alms from him, isn't it better to favor him with a dithyramb?

> He understood nothing
> And he was weak and shy as children are,
> Strangers trapped wild animals
> And caught fish for him . . .[1]

Thanks to you, "strangers," for such touching concern, for such tender care of the old world, which is no longer "of this world," which has withdrawn into itself in expectation of and preparation for the coming metamorphosis:

> Cum subit illius tristissima noctis imago,
> Quae mihi supremum tempus in urbe fuit,
> Cum repeto noctem, qua tot mihi cara reliquit,
> Labitur ex oculis nunc quoque gutta meis.[2]

Yes, the old world is "not of this world," yet it is more alive than it has ever been. Culture has become the Church. There has been a separation of Church (i.e., culture) and State. Secular life no longer concerns us; we no longer eat a meal, we take a sacrament; we do

Note: This translation was originally published in *Arion* 2, no. 4 (1976).

not live in a room but a cell; we do not dress, we attire ourselves in
garments. At last we have found our inner freedom, real inner joy.
We drink water in clay jugs as if it were wine, and the sun likes a
refectory better than a restaurant. Apples, bread, the potato—from
now on they will appease not merely physical but spiritual hunger
as well. The Christian—and every cultivated man is a Christian
now—knows not a merely physical hunger or a merely spiritual
nourishment. For him, the word is also flesh, and simple bread is
happiness and mystery.

Social distinctions and class antagonisms pale before the division
of people into friends and enemies of the word. Literally, sheep
and goats. I sense, almost physically, the unclean goat smell issuing
from the enemies of the word. Here, the argument that arrives last
in the course of any serious disagreement is fully appropriate: my
opponent smells bad.

The separation of culture from the state is the most significant
event of our revolution. The process of the secularization of our
political life has not stopped with the separation of church and state
as the French Revolution understood it. Our social upheaval has
brought a deeper secularization. The state now displays to culture
that curious attitude we might best call tolerance. But at the same
time, there is a new kind of organic connection binding the state to
culture as the appanage princes used to be linked to the monasteries.
The princes would support the monasteries for the sake of their
counsel. That says all. The state's exclusion from cultural values
places it in full dependence on culture. Cultural values ornament
political life, endow it with color, form, and, if you will, even with
sex. Inscriptions on government buildings, tombs, gates safeguard
the state from the ravages of time.

Poetry is the plow that turns up time so that the deep layers of
time, the black soil, appear on top. There are epochs, however, when
mankind, not content with the present, longing for time's deeper
layers, like the plowman, thirsts for the virgin soil of time. Revolution in art inevitably tends to Classicism. Not because David[3] reaped
Robespierre's harvest, but because that is how the earth would have
it.

One often hears: that might be good, but it belongs to yesterday.
But I say: yesterday hasn't been born yet. It has not yet really come
to pass. I want Ovid, Pushkin, Catullus afresh, and I will not be
satisfied with the historical Ovid, Pushkin, Catullus.

In fact, it's amazing how everybody keeps fussing over the poets and can't seem to have done with them. You might think, once they'd been read, that was that. Superseded, as they say now. Nothing of the sort. The silver horn of Catullus—"Ad claras Asiae volemus urbes"[4]—frets and excites more powerfully than any futuristic mystification. It doesn't exist in Russian; and yet it must. I picked a Latin line so the Russian reader would see that it obviously belongs to the category of Duty; the imperative rings more resonantly in it. Yet this is characteristic of any poetry that is Classical. Classical poetry is perceived as that which must be, not as that which has already been.

Not a single poet has yet appeared. We are free of the weight of memories. For all that, how many rare presentiments: Pushkin, Ovid, Homer. When in the silence a lover gets tangled up in tender names and suddenly remembers that all this has happened before, the words and the hair, and the rooster that crowed outside the window had been crowing in Ovid's *Tristia*,[5] a deep joy of repetition seizes him, a head-spinning joy—

> Like dark water I drink the dimmed air,
> Time upturned by the plow; that rose was once the earth.

So that poet, too, has no fear of repetition and gets easily drunk on Classical wine.

What is true of a single poet is true of all. There's no point forming schools of any kind. There's no point inventing one's own poetics.

The analytic method, applied to style, movement, form, is altogether a legitimate and ingenious approach. Lately, demolition has become a purely formal artistic premise. Disintegration, decay, rot —all this is still *décadence*. But the Decadents were *Christian* artists; in their own way, the last Christian martyrs. For them, the music of decay was the music of resurrection. Baudelaire's "Charogne" is a sublime example of Christian despair. Deliberate demolition of form is quite another matter. Painless suprematism. A denial of the shape of appearances. Calculated suicide, for the sake of mere curiosity. You can take it apart, or you can put it together: it might seem as though form were being tested, but in fact it's the spirit rotting and disintegrating. (Incidentally, having mentioned Baudelaire, I would like to recall his significance, as an ascetic hero, in the most authentic Christian sense of the word, a *martyr*.)

A heroic era has begun in the life of the word. The word is flesh
and bread. It shares the fate of bread and flesh: suffering. People
are hungry. Still hungrier is the state. But there is something even
hungrier: time. Time wants to devour the state. Like a trumpet-voice
sounds the threat scratched by Derzhavin on his slate board.[6] Whoever will raise high the word and show it to time, as the priest does
the Eucharist, will be a second Joshua, son of Nun. There is nothing
hungrier than the contemporary state, and a hungry state is more terrible than a hungry man. To show compassion for the state which
denies the word is the contemporary poet's civic "way," the heroic
feat that awaits him.

> Let us praise the fateful burden
> Which the people's leader tearfully bears.
> Let us praise the twilight burden of power,
> Its intolerable weight.
> Whoever has a heart, he must hear, O time,
> How your boat goes to the bottom . . .[7]

One shouldn't demand of poetry any special quiddity, concrete-
ness, materiality. It's that very same revolutionary hunger. The
doubt of Thomas. Why should one have to touch it with the fingers?
But the main point is, why should the word be identified with the
thing, with the grass, with the object that it signifies?

Is the thing master of the word? The word is a Psyche. The living
word does not signify an object, but freely chooses, as though for a
dwelling place, this or that objective significance, materiality, some
beloved body. And around the thing the word hovers freely, like a
soul around a body that has been abandoned but not forgotten.

What's been said of materiality sounds somewhat different applied to imagery: "Prends l'éloquence et tords-lui son cou!"[8]

Write imageless poems if you can, if you know how. A blind man
will recognize a beloved face by just barely having touched it with
his seeing fingers; and tears of joy, the authentic joy of recognition,
will spurt from his eyes after a long separation. The poem is alive
through an inner image, that resounding mold of form, which an-
ticipates the written poem. Not a single word has appeared, but the
poem already resounds. What resounds is the inner image; what
touches it is the poet's aural sense.

"And the flash of recognition alone is sweet to us!"[9]

These days, something like glossolalia manifests itself. In sacred frenzy, poets speak in the language of all times, all cultures. Nothing is impossible. Just as a room where a man is dying is opened to all, so the door of the old world is flung wide before the crowd. Suddenly everything has become common property. Come in and help yourself. Everything's available: all the labyrinths, all the hiding places, all the forbidden paths. The word has become, not a seven-stop, but a thousand-stop reed, instantly animated by the breathing of all the ages. In glossolalia the most striking thing is that the speaker does not know the language in which he speaks. He speaks in a totally obscure tongue. And to everyone, and to him, too, it seems he's talking Greek or Babylonian. It is something quite the reverse of erudition. Contemporary poetry, for all its complexity and its inner violence, is naïve: "Ecoutez la chanson grise . . ."[10]

A synthetic poet of modern life would seem to me to be not a Verhaeren, but a kind of Verlaine of culture. For him the whole complexity of the old world would be like that same old Pushkinian reed. In him, ideas, scientific systems, political theories would sing, just as nightingales and roses used to sing in his predecessors. They say the cause of revolution is hunger in the interplanetary spaces. One has to sow wheat in the ether.

Classical poetry is the poetry of revolution.

Attack

What poetry needs is Classicism, what poetry needs is Hellenism, what poetry needs is a heightened sense of imagery, the rhythm of the machine, urban collectivism, peasant folklore . . . Poor poetry! Under the muzzle of these unmitigated demands now being leveled at her, she shies. What should poetry be like? Well, maybe poetry shouldn't be like anything, maybe poetry doesn't owe anybody anything, and maybe these creditors of hers are all fraudulent! Nothing comes easier than talk about what art needs: first of all, it's always arbitrary and commits nobody to anything; second, it provides an inexhaustible theme for philosophizing; third, it relieves people of a rather unpleasant obligation that not everybody is up to—gratitude for what is. It relieves them from the most commonplace gratitude for what a given time has to offer as poetry.

O monstrous ingratitude: to Kuzmin, to Mayakovsky, to Khlebnikov, Aseev, Viacheslav Ivanov, Sologub, Akhmatova, Pasternak, Gumilev, Khodasevich[1]—quite different as they are, made of different clay. They aren't, after all, simply the Russian poets of yesterday or today; they are for all time. God wasn't humiliating us when he gave us the likes of these. A people does not choose its poets, just as no one ever chooses his own parents. A people that does not know how to honor its poets deserves . . . Well, it deserves nothing. You might just say it is irrelevant. Yet what a difference between the pure ignorance of the people and the half-knowledge of the ignorant fop. The Hottentots, to test their old men, would make them climb a tree. Then they would shake the tree: if the old man had grown so weak he fell out of the tree, that meant he had to be killed. The snob imitates the Hottentots; his favored method recalls the ritual I have just described. To this, I think the proper response is contempt. We must distinguish between those who are interested in poetry and those who are interested in a Hottentot amusement.

Nothing favors the contagion of snobbery more than frequent change in the generations of poets, given one and the same generation of readers. The reader gets used to feeling himself an observer in the parterre. Before him file the changing schools. He frowns, grimaces, acts capriciously. Finally, he begins to feel an altogether unfounded sense of his own superiority—of the constant before the ephemeral, of the immobile before the mobile. The rapid change of poetic schools in Russia has sent one and the same reader reeling.

The reading generation of the nineties turned out to be insubstantial, utterly incompetent in poetry. For this reason, the Symbolists long awaited their readers and, by strength of circumstances, by their intellect, their education and maturity, seemed much older than the callow youth to whom they turned. The first decade of the twentieth century, judging by the decadence of public taste, was not much higher than the nineties, and along with *The Scales*,[2] that militant citadel of the new school, we had the illiterate tradition of the "Wild Rose" group [Shipovniki], the monstrous almanac literature, with its coarse and ignorant pretentiousness.

As individual and highly polished poems appeared out of the great womb of Symbolism, as the tribe disintegrated and a kingdom of the poetic person ensued, the reader who'd been educated on tribal poetry of the Symbolist sort—that womb of all new Russian poetry—grew distraught in a world of blossoming diversity where everything would no longer fit under the tribal hat, where every person stood bareheaded and apart. After this tribal period, which infused new blood and proclaimed an exceptionally capacious canon, after a dense medley that triumphed in the rich, deep bell-ringing of Viacheslav Ivanov, came the time of the person, of personality. Yet all of contemporary Russian poetry came out of the tribal Symbolist womb. The reader has a short memory, and is unwilling to acknowledge this. O acorns, acorns! who needs an oak when we have acorns."

II.

Somebody once managed to photograph the eye of a fish. The picture showed a railroad bridge and several details of the landscape, but the optical law of fish-vision showed all this in an improbably distorted manner. If somebody managed to photograph the poetic eye of Academician Ovsianiko-Kulikovsky[4] or of the average member of the Russian intelligentsia, how for example he sees his Pushkin, the result would be a picture no less unexpected than the world seen by the fish.

Distortion of the poetic work in the perception of the reader is an inevitable social phenomenon, difficult and useless to combat: easier to bring electrification to Russia than to teach all literate readers to read Pushkin as he is written, rather than as their emotional needs require and their intellectual capacities permit.

As distinct from musical notation, for example, poetic notation leaves a fairly big gap, the absence of a large number of signs, indications, pointers, implications, which alone make the text comprehensible and coherent. Yet all these nonexistent signs are no less precise than musical notes or dance-hieroglyphs; the poetically literate reader supplies them on his own, eliciting them from the text itself, so speak.

Poetic literacy does not in any case coincide with ordinary literacy, with reading the alphabet, or even with literary erudition. If the percentage of ordinary and literary illiteracy is very high in Russia, poetic illiteracy is absolutely abysmal, and all the worse for being confused with ordinary illiteracy, so that anyone who knows how to read is considered poetically literate. The above has a special relevance to the half-educated mass of our intelligentsia, infected by snobbism, having lost their native feeling for the language, essentially rendered languageless, amorphous in relation to language, tickling their long-dulled language-nerves with cheap and easy stimuli, dubious lyricisms and neologisms, often alien and hostile to the essence of Russian speech.

It is the demands of this milieu, declassed in the linguistic sense, that current Russian poetry is *obliged* to satisfy.

The word, born in the most profound layers of speech-consciousness, has to serve the deaf-mutes and tongue-tied, the cretins and degenerates of the word.

Symbolism's great merit, the correct stance it took with regard to the Russian reading public, was in its pedagogy, in its inborn sense of authority, the patriarchal weightiness and legislative gravity with which it educated the reader.

One needs to put the reader in his place, and along with him the critic he has reared. Criticism should not consist of the arbitrary interpretation of poetry; this should give way to objective, scholarly research, to the scholarship of poetry.

Perhaps the most comforting thing in the whole situation of

Russian poetry is the deep and pure ignorance, the unknowingness of the people about their own poetry.

The masses, who have preserved a healthy philological sense, those layers where the morphology of language begins to sprout, strengthen, and develop, have quite simply not yet entered into contact with individualist Russian poetry. The Russian lyric has not yet found its readers. Perhaps it will find them only after the extinction of those poetic luminaries that have already sent out their rays of light to this distant and as yet unattained destination.

About an Interlocutor

What is there about a madman, tell me, that produces the most frightening impression of madness? The distended pupils—because they are unseeing, because they focus on nothing in particular, because they are empty. Or his mad speeches, because, even while turning to you, the madman does not take you into account, does not consider your existence, as if he did not wish to acknowledge it, because he is absolutely uninterested in you. In the madman, we fear for the most part that uncanny, absolute indifference that he turns toward us. Nothing frightens a man more than another man who has no concern for him. There is deep significance in that cultivated pretense, that politeness, we continually use in order to emphasize a certain interest in each other.

When a man has something to say, he usually goes to people, seeks out listeners. But a poet does the opposite. He runs "to shores of desert waves, to deep-sounding groves." The abnormality is obvious . . . A suspicion of madness falls on the poet. And people are right when they call him mad, who addresses inanimate objects, nature, and not his living brothers. And they would be in the right to recoil from the poet as from a madman if his word were not really addressed to anyone. But this is not the case.

The view of the poet as "God's creature" is very dangerous and basically incorrect. There is no reason to think that Pushkin, for instance, in his little song about the bird,[1] had the poet in mind. But even with regard to Pushkin's bird, the case isn't really so simple. Before it can sing forth, it "heeds the voice of God." Obviously he who orders the bird to sing listens to it. The bird "shook its wings and sang" because it was bound by a "natural contract" with God— an honor to which even a poet of the greatest genius dares not aspire . . . To whom then does the poet speak? It's a disturbing question, and very contemporary, because to this very day the Symbolists have avoided posing it sharply. Symbolism completely neglected the, as it were, contractual relationship, the mutuality that accompanies an act of speech. (I speak, and that means I am listened to, and not for nothing, not out of kindness, but because there is an obligation.) The Symbolist poets turned their attention exclusively to acoustics. They hurled sound into the architecture of the soul and, with that self-absorption characteristic of them, followed the sound's meanderings through the archways of another person's psychology. They would reckon up the sonic increment issuing from good acoustics and call this computation magic. In this regard Symbolism recalls "Prestre Martin" of the medieval French proverb, who himself serves Mass and listens to it. The Symbolist poet is not only a musician, he's a Stradivarius at the same time, the great artisan of the violin, preoccupied with estimating the proportion of the "box" in relation to the psychology of the listener. It is precisely depending on these proportions that the stroke of the bow either acquires a regal fullness or tends to sound squalid and unconvincing. Yet, gentlemen, a piece of music nevertheless exists independently of the player or the instrument or the place! Why then should the poet be so anxiety-ridden about the future? Where finally is that supplier of living violins for the poet's needs—those listeners whose psychic apparatus is up to Stradivarius' "helix"? We don't know, we never know where such listeners might turn up . . . François Villon wrote for the Parisian rabble of the mid-fifteenth century, yet we find in his poems a living charm . . .

Everybody has friends. Why doesn't the poet turn to his friends, to those people who are naturally close to him? The shipwrecked sailor throws a sealed bottle into the sea at a critical moment, and it has his name in it and what happened to him. Many years later, walking along the dunes, I find it in the sand, I read the letter, I learn when it happened, the testament of the deceased. I had a right to do this. I did not unseal someone else's letter. The letter sealed in the bottle was addressed to its finder. I found it. That means, then, that I am its secret addressee.

> My gift is poor, nor loudly rings my voice
> And yet I live—and on the earth, my being
> Means something dear to someone:
> My distant heir will find it
> In my verses; who can tell? my soul
> Will turn out to be bound with his in tie
> And as in my generation I found a friend
> So will I find a reader in posterity.

Reading Boratynsky's[2] poem I have the same feeling I would have if such a bottle had come into my hands. The ocean in all its vastness has risen to help it fulfill its designation, and the finder cannot escape a certain feeling of providentiality. In the sailor's flinging a bottle into the flow of the sea and in Boratynsky's poem there is a certain common bond. Like the poem, the letter isn't addressed to anyone in particular. Nevertheless, both have an addressee: the letter's is the person who will accidentally notice the bottle in the sand; the poem's is "a reader in posterity." What reader, I wonder, could look on these lines of Boratynsky without a sudden start and an uncanny shiver of joy, as happens sometimes when one is called unexpectedly by name?

Balmont[3] declares:

> I do not know a wisdom fit for others,
> What I carve in verse is only transience.
> In everything transient I see whole worlds,
> Changing with the play of rainbows.
> Do not curse me, wise men, what am I to you?
> Why I'm only a cloud full of fire,
> Why I'm only a cloud—see, I float
> And I call to dreamers—it's not you I call.

The unpleasant obsequious tone of these lines presents a curious contrast to the deep and modest dignity of Boratynsky's verses. Balmont justifies himself, apologizing as it were. Unforgivable! Intolerable for a poet! The only thing that cannot be forgiven! For poetry is the consciousness of one's own rightness. In the given instance, Balmont lacks such a consciousness. He has clearly lost his foothold. The first line kills the whole poem. Right off the poet emphatically declares that we are of no interest to him: "I do not know a wisdom fit for others . . ."

To his surprise, we pay him back in the same coin: if we are not interesting to you, you do not interest us. Who cares about your cloud; a lot of clouds float by . . . Real clouds have this advantage: they don't jeer at people. Rejection of an "interlocutor" passes like a red thread through all of Balmont's poetry and greatly diminishes its value. In his poems, Balmont is always slighting somebody, looking down his nose at him, contemptuously. This "somebody" is the secret interlocutor. Neither understood nor acknowledged by Balmont, he in turn takes a cruel revenge on the poet. When we speak, we search our interlocutor's face for a sanction, for a confirmation of our rightness. A poet does it even more so. In Balmont the precious consciousness of poetic rightness is often missing, because he does not have a constant interlocutor. From this lack spring two un-pleasant extremes in Balmont's poetry: his obsequiousness and his insolence. Balmont's insolence is unreal, inauthentic. His need for self-assertion is quite pathological. He cannot say "I" sotto voce. He screams "I." "I am"—an abrupt pause,—"I who play thunder." In Balmont's poetry, the "I" has definitely and unfairly tipped the scales against the "non-I" as if it were so much fluff. Balmont's shrill individualism is unpleasant. This is not the quiet solipsism of Sologub, offensive to nobody, but individualism at the expense of someone else's "I." Note how Balmont loves to catch you by sur-prise with his direct and harsh "thou": in these passages he is like a bad hypnotist. Balmont's "thou" never finds an addressee, whiz-zing past like an arrow that has burst loose from a too tight bow-string.

> And as in my generation I found a friend
> So will I find a reader in posterity.

Boratynsky's penetrating gaze goes beyond his generation—though he has friends in his generation—in order to pause at some unknown yet definite "reader." And anyone who happens to come across Boratynsky's poems feels himself to be such a "reader," chosen, called to by name . . . Why not a living, concrete interlocu-tor, why not a "representative of the epoch," why not a "friend in my generation"? I answer: addressing a concrete interlocutor takes the wings off the verse, deprives it of air, of flight. The air of a poem is the unexpected. Addressing someone known, we can say only what is known. It's a solid, authoritative psychological law. One cannot emphasize too strongly its significance for poetry.

Fear of a concrete interlocutor, a listener from the same "epoch," that very "friend in my generation," has persistently pursued poets at all times. The more genius a poet had, the more acutely the form in which he suffered this fear. Hence the cursed hostility of artist and society. What is true with regard to the litterateur, the man of letters, is absolutely inapplicable to the poet. The difference between literature and poetry is the following: the litterateur always ad-dresses a concrete listener, a living representative of the epoch. Even if he prophesies, he has in view the contemporary of a future time. What the litterateur has to say, he pours out to his contemporaries on the basis of the physical law of unequal levels. Consequently, the litterateur is obliged to be "above," "better" than society. Instruc-tion is the central nerve of literature. For that reason, the litterateur has to have a pedestal. Poetry is another matter. The poet is bound only to his providential interlocutor. He's not obliged to be above his epoch or better than his society. That same François Villon stands much lower than the average moral and intellectual level of the culture of the fifteenth century.

Pushkin's quarrel with the rabble can be regarded as a manifestation of that same antagonism between the poet and his concrete listener to which I am trying to call attention. With amazing dispassion, Pushkin allows the rabble to vindicate itself. It turns out that the rabble is not so very terribly savage and unenlightened. In what way was this rabble, so delicate as Pushkin describes it and so infused with the best intentions, guilty before the poet? As the rabble justifies itself, it gives vent to a certain incautious expression; and this is what causes the poet's cup of tolerance to overflow and inflames his hatred: "And we will listen to you"—that's the tactless expression. The obtuse vulgarity of these seemingly innocent words is apparent. It's not for nothing the indignant poet interrupts the rabble at just this point . . . The sight of a hand held out to receive charity is disgusting, and an ear primed to listen may dispose whom you will to inspiration—the orator, the tribune, the litterateur—but not the poet . . . The people of whom this rabble is concretely composed, the "philistines of poetry," would permit him "to give them bold lessons," and would in general be ready to hear out almost anything, so long as the poet's message had the precise address: "such-and-such rabble." In this way children and simple people feel themselves flattered when they read their own name on the envelope of a letter. There have been whole epochs when the charm and essence of poetry was brought as a sacrifice to this far from harmless demand. Such were the pseudo-civic poetry and the tedious lyric of the eighties. The civic orientation or the tendentiousness is fine in and of itself:

> You need not be a poet,
> But a citizen you're obliged to be—[4]

is an excellent verse, flying on powerful wings to its providential interlocutor. But put in his place the Russian philistine of this-or-that decade, thoroughly familiar, known ahead of time, and immediately it will turn into something trite.

Yes, when I speak to somebody, I do not know with whom I speak, and I do not wish, I cannot wish to know him. There is no lyric without dialogue. Yet the only thing that pushes us into the arms of the interlocutor is the desire to be surprised by our own words, to be captivated by their novelty and unexpectedness. The logic is ineluctable. If I know to whom I speak, I know ahead of time how he will regard what I say, whatever I might say, and consequently I shall manage not to be astonished by his astonishment, to be overjoyed by his joy, or to love through his love. The distance of separation wipes away the features of a beloved person. Only then does the desire arise in me to say to him that important thing I could not have said to him when I had his image before me in the fullness of its reality. I permit myself to formulate this observation thus: the sense of communication is inversely proportional to our real knowledge of the interlocutor and directly proportional to the felt need to interest him in ourselves. It isn't about acoustics one should concern oneself: that will come of itself. More likely, about distance. It's boring to be whispering to a neighbor. It's infinitely tedious to pressure-drill one's own soul (Nadson).[5] But to exchange signals with Mars—without fantasizing, of course—that is a task worthy of a lyric poet. Here we've come right up against Fedor Sologub. In many ways Sologub is a most interesting antipode to Balmont. Several qualities that Balmont lacks are found in abundance in Sologub: to wit, love and respect for the interlocutor and a consciousness of his own poetic rightness. These two excellent qualities of Sologub's poetry are closely connected with "the distance of enormous space," which he places between himself and his ideal friend-interlocutor.

> My secret friend, my distant friend,
> Look.
> I am the cold and sad
> Light of dawn . . .
> And cold and sad
> In the morning,
> My secret friend, my distant friend,
> I will die.

Maybe, for these lines to reach their address, it will take the same hundreds of years that it does for the light of a planet to reach another planet. As a result, Sologub's lines continue to live after they have been written, as events, not merely as tokens of emotional experience.

And so, if individual poems (in the form of missive or dedication) can actually address concrete persons, poetry as a whole is always directed at a more or less distant, unknown addressee, in whose existence the poet may not doubt without doubting himself. Metaphysics has nothing to do with it. Only reality can call to life another reality. A poet is not a homunculus and there is no reason why one should ascribe to him the characteristics of spontaneous generation.

The matter may be put very simply: if we had no acquaintances, we would not write them letters and would not take pleasure at the psychological freshness and novelty that is characteristic of this occupation.

About the Nature of the Word

But we worry about things, *and forget*
that only the word *glows and shines,*
and the Gospel of John
tells us this word is God.

We've surrounded it with a wall,
with the narrow borders of this world,
and like bees in a deserted hive
the dead words rot and stink.

N. Gumilev*

The only question I want to ask is whether Russian literature constitutes a unity. Is contemporary Russian literature really the same as the literature of Nekrasov, Pushkin, Derzhavin, or Simeon Polotsky?[1] If continuity has been preserved, then how far back does it go? If Russian literature has always been one and the same, then what determines its unity, what is its essential principle, its so-called criterion?

The question I have put acquires a special edge, thanks to acceleration of the historical process. No doubt it would be an exaggeration to consider each year of our present history an entire century, yet something in the nature of a geometric progression, a consistent quickening, may be noted in the stormy discharge of this accumulated historical energy. Thanks to such change in our time, the conception of the unity of time has been shaken, and it is not by accident that contemporary mathematical science has advanced the principle of relativity.

In order to rescue the principle of unity in the whirlpool of change and the ceaseless current of events, contemporary philosophy

Note: This translation was originally published in *Arion* 2, no. 4 (1976).

* Reprinted, with slight modifications, from *Selected Works of Nikolai S. Gumilev*, translated by Burton Raffel and Alla Burago, by permission of the State University of New York Press. Copyright © 1972 State University of New York.

in the person of Bergson, whose profoundly Judaic mind, obsessed
by the urgent practical need of sustaining monotheism, proposes to
us a doctrine of the systematization of phenomena. Bergson examines phenomena not through the logic of their subordination to
the law of temporal sequence, but, as it were, through the logic of
their distribution through space. It is exclusively the inner bond of
phenomena that interests him. This bond he liberates from time
and examines separately. In this way, interconnected phenomena
form a kind of fan, the folds of which may develop in time, while
at the same time the fan may be collapsed in a way that allows the
mind to grasp it.

Comparing phenomena united in time to such a fan merely
emphasizes their inner bond, and instead of the problem of causality,
bound so slavishly to thinking in time, which for long held the
minds of European logicians in thrall, it advances the problem of
connection, without any flavor of metaphysics and, for precisely that
reason, more fruitful in producing scientific discoveries and hy-
potheses.

A science built on the principle of connection rather than causality exempts us from the "foolish infinity" of evolutionary theory,
not to mention its vulgar appendage, the theory of progress.

The movement of an infinite chain of phenomena, without beginning and end, is really a foolish infinity that says nothing to the
mind seeking unity and connection. It hypnotizes scientific thought
with this easy and accessible evolutionism that gives, to be sure, an
appearance of scientific generalization, but at the price of rejecting
any synthesis or inner structure.

The diffuseness, the unstructured nature of nineteenth-century
European scientific thought, by the time of the turn of the present
century, had completely demoralized scientific thought. Intellect,
which does not consist of a mere aggregate of knowledge, but rather
of "grasp," technique, method, abandoned science, since intellect
can exist independently and can find its own nourishment where
convenient. Searching for intellect in precisely this sense in European
scientific life would be futile. The free intellect of man had removed
itself from science. It turned up everywhere, but not there: in poetry,
in mysticism, in politics, in theology. As for scientific evolutionism
and its concern with the theory of progress (insofar as it did not
wring its own neck as the new European science had), it puffed
along in the same direction and flung itself on the shores of theosophy, like an exhausted swimmer who had achieved a joyless shore.

Theosophy is the direct heir of that old European science which had
theosophy as its inevitable destination: the same foolish infinity, the
same absence of backbone in the doctrine of reincarnation (karma),
the same coarse and naïve materialism in the vulgar understanding
of a supersensate world, the same absence of will, the same taste for
the *cognition* of activity, and a certain lazy omnivorousness, an enormous, ponderous chewing of the cud, intended for thousands of
stomachs, an interest in everything that at the same time verges on
apathy, an omniscience that resembles know-nothingness.

Applied to literature, evolutionary theory is especially dangerous,
and the theory of progress is downright lethal. Listen to the evolu-
tionist literary historians and it might seem that writers think only
of how to clear the road for those who are to go ahead of them, and
not at all about how to finish their own job of work; or that they all
take part in some inventors' contest for the improvement of some
sort of literary machine, while it isn't at all clear where the jury is
hiding, or what purpose this machine serves.

The theory of progress in literary studies is the coarsest, most repulsive façade of academic ignorance. Literary forms change, some
forms give way to others. But every change, every such innovation,
is accompanied by bereavement, by a loss. There can be no "better,"
no progress of any kind in literature, simply because there is no
literature-machine of any kind, and there's no finish line to which
you have to rush to get ahead of anybody else. This senseless theory
of betterment is not even applicable to the manner and form of
individual writers—here every innovation is similarly accompanied
by bereavement and loss. Where does the Tolstoy who in *Anna
Karenina* mastered the psychological power and the highly struc-
tured quality of the Flaubertian novel show the animallike sensitivity and the physiological intuition of *War and Peace?* Where does
the author of *War and Peace* show the transparency of form, the
"Clarism"[2] of *Childhood and Boyhood?* Even if he had wanted to,
the author of *Boris Godunov* could not have repeated the lyceum
poems, and similarly no one now could write a Derzhavin ode.
Who likes what better is another matter. Just as there are two geo-
metries, Euclid's and Lobachevsky's, there may be two histories of
literature, written in two different keys: one that speaks only of
acquisitions, another only of losses, and both would be speaking of
one and the same thing.

Returning to the question of whether Russian literature is a unity
and, if it is, what the principle of that unity might be, let us cast

aside the amelioration theory from the very beginning. Let us speak only of the inner connections of phenomena, and above all let us try to seek out a criterion of possible unity, the core which allows the various dispersed phenomena of literature to unfold in time.

The only criterion that can serve to indicate the unity (conditional, to be sure) of the literature of a given people is that people's language, to which all other criteria are secondary. The language, although it changes from period to period, although it does not stand still and congeal, retains a certain common constant that to the philologist's mind at least is blindingly clear. An inner unity remains. Any philologist grasps when a language retains and when it changes its personality. When Latin speech, which had spread to all the Romanic lands, brought forth new bloom and began sprouting the future Romance languages, a new literature began, childish and impoverished compared with Latin, but already "Romance."

When the vibrant and graphic speech of *The Tale of Igor's Men*[3] resounded, thoroughly worldly, secular, and Russian in its every turn of phrase, Russian literature began. And while Velemir Khlebnikov, the contemporary Russian writer, immerses us in the very thick of Russian root words, in the etymological night dear to the mind and heart of the clever reader, that very same Russian literature is still alive, the literature of *The Tale of Igor's Men*. The Russian language, like the Russian national identity itself, was formed out of endless mixtures, crossings, graftings, and foreign influences. Yet in one thing it will remain true to itself, until our own kitchen Latin resounds for us, too, and on that powerful body which is language, the pale young runner-shoots of our life come up, as in the Old French song about Saint Eulalia.[4]

The Russian language is a Hellenic language. Due to a whole complex of historical conditions, the vital forces of Hellenic culture, which had abandoned the West to Latin influences, and which found scant nourishment to prompt them to linger long in childless Byzantium, rushed to the bosom of Russian speech and communicated to it the self-confident secret of the Hellenic world view, the secret of free incarnation, *and so the Russian language became indeed sounding and speaking flesh.*

While Western cultures and histories tend to lock language in from the outside, hem it in with walls of church and state and become saturated with it in order that they might slowly decay and slowly come into bloom as the language in due course disintegrates, Russian culture and history are washed and girdled on all sides by the awesome and boundless element of the Russian language, which does not fit into church or state forms of any kind.

The life of language in Russian history outweighs all other factors through the ubiquity of its manifestations, its plenitude of being, a kind of high goal that all other aspects of Russian life strive to attain without succeeding. One can identify the Hellenic nature of the Russian language with its capacity for achieving concrete modalities of existence. The word in the Hellenic conception is active flesh that resolves itself in an event. Therefore, the Russian language is historical even in and of itself, the incessant incarnation and activity of intelligent and breathing flesh. There is not a single other language that stands more squarely opposed than the Russian to merely denotative or practical prescription. Russian nominalism, that is, a doctrine of the reality of the word as such, animates the spirit of our language and links it with Hellenic philological culture, not etymologically and not literarily, but through a principle of inner freedom that is equally inherent in them both.

Utilitarianism of any sort is a mortal sin against Hellenic nature, against the Russian language, quite regardless of whether it be a tendency toward a telegraphic or stenographic code, whether for reasons of economy or simplified expediency, or even whether it be utilitarianism of a higher order, offering language in sacrifice to mystical intuition, anthroposophy, or word-hungry, omnivorous thinking of any kind.

Andrei Biely,[5] now, turns out to be a painful and negative phenomenon in the life of the Russian language. This is only because he pursues the word so single-mindedly and yet is guided in this pursuit exclusively by the fervor of his own speculative thought. He gasps, with a kind of refined garrulity. He cannot bring himself to sacrifice a single shading, a single fragment of his capricious thought, and he blows up the bridges he is too lazy to cross. As a result, we have, after momentary fireworks, instead of a fullness of life, an organic wholeness, and a moving balance, a heap of paving-stones, a dismal picture of ruin. The basic sin of writers like Andrei Biely is their lack of respect for the Hellenic nature of the word, their merciless exploitation of it for their own intuitive goals.

Russian poetry more than any other brings up as a motif again and again that ancient doubt of the word's capacity to express feeling:

How can the heart express itself?

> How can another understand you?
> (Tiutchev)[6]

—Thus our language secures itself from unceremonious encroachments.

The rate at which language develops is not the same as that of life itself. Any attempt to adapt language mechanically to the requirements of life is doomed in advance to failure. Futurism, as it is called, is a conception created by illiterate critics that lacks any real content or scope; it is, however, more than a curiosity of philistine literary psychology. Futurism acquires an exact sense if one understands by it precisely this attempt at a forced, mechanical adaptation, this lack of faith in our language itself which is at one and the same time Achilles and the turtle.

Khlebnikov busies himself with words, like a mole, and he provides for the future by burrowing enough passageways in the earth to last for a whole century. The representatives of the Moscow metaphorical school who call themselves Imaginists, on the other hand, exhaust themselves adapting our language to modern life. They have remained far behind language, and it is their fate to be swept away like litter.

Chaadaev,[7] when he wrote that Russia had no history, that is, that Russia belonged to no organized cultural system, omitted one circumstance—and that is language. Such a highly organized, such an organic language is not merely a door into history, it is history itself. For Russia, a defection from our language would be a defection from history, excommunication from the kingdom of historical necessity and sequence, from freedom and expediency. The "muteness" of two or three generations could bring Russia to its historical death. Excommunication from language has for us a force equal to that of excommunication from history. Therefore it is absolutely true that Russian history walks on tiptoes along the edge, along the bank, over the abyss, and is ready at any moment to fall into nihilism; that is, into excommunication from the word.

Of contemporary Russian writers, Rozanov[8] has felt this danger more keenly than any other, and he spent his whole life struggling to preserve a link with the word, on behalf of a philological culture, which would base itself firmly on the Hellenic nature of Russian speech. My attitude to just about everything may be anarchic, my world view a complete muddle, catch-as-catch-can; yet there is one thing I cannot do—live wordlessly; I cannot bear excommunication from the word. That was more or less Rozanov's spiritual makeup. This anarchic and nihilistic spirit acknowledged only one authority —the magic of language, the authority of the word. And this, mind you, not while being a poet, a collector and threader of words beyond any concern for style, but while being simply a babbler or a grumbler.

One of Rozanov's books is called *By the Church Walls*. It seems to me that all his life Rozanov rummaged about in a swampy wasteland, trying to grope his way to the walls of Russian culture. Like several other Russian thinkers, like Chaadaev, Leontiev, Gershenzon, he could not live without walls, without an Acropolis. The environment yields; everything is mellow, soft, and pliable. Yet we want to live historically; we have within us an ineluctable need to find the firm hard kernel of a Kremlin, an Acropolis, no matter what this nucleus might be called, whether we name it "state" or "society." The need for this nucleus and for whatever walls might serve as a symbol for this nucleus determined Rozanov's whole fate, and it definitely acquits him of the accusation of anarchic tendencies or lack of principle.

"It's hard for a man to be a whole generation. All there is left for him to do is to die. It's time for me to decay, for you to blossom." And Rozanov did not *live*; rather, he went on dying a clever, intellectual death, as generations die. Rozanov's life was the death of philology, the dessication, the withering of letters, and that bitter struggle for the life that glimmers in colloquialisms and small talk, in quotation marks and citations, and yet all the same remains philology and only philology.

Rozanov's attitude to Russian literature was as "unliterary" as it could be. Literature is a social phenomenon; philology is a domestic phenomenon, of the study. Literature is a public lecture, the street; philology is a university seminar, the family. Yes, just so, a university seminar where five students who know each other and call each other by first name and patronymic listen to the professor, while the branches of familiar campus trees stretch toward the window. Philology: it is a family because every family sustains itself by intonation and by citation, by quotation marks. In a family, the most lazily spoken word has its special shading. And an infinite, unique, purely philological literary nuancing forms the background of family life. This is why I deduce Rozanov's inclination to domesticity, which so powerfully determined the whole tenor of his literary activity, from the philological nature of his spirit, which, in inces-

sant search of the kernel, cracked and husked his words and colloquialisms, leaving us only the husk. No wonder that Rozanov turned
out to be an inutile and unproductive writer.

How awful it is that man (the eternal philologue) found a word
for it—"death." Can it be named at all? Does it really have a name?
A name is already a definition, already a "we-know-something."
Rozanov defines the essence of his nominalism in such an original
way; a perpetual cognitive motion, a perpetual unshelling of the
kernel, ending with nothing, because there is no way to crack it.
But what kind of a literary critic *is* this Rozanov? He's always only
plucking at everything, he's a casual, chancy reader, a lost sheep,
neither here nor there.

A critic has to know how to devour his way through volumes,
picking out what he needs, making generalizations: but Rozanov
plunges in over his head into the line of almost any Russian poet, as
he got stuck in that line of Nekrasov's: "If I ride at night along the
dark street," the first thing that came to mind one night in a cab.
The Rozanovian commentary: one could scarcely find another verse
like that in the whole of Russian poetry. Rozanov loved the church
for that very same philology for which he loved the family. Here is
what he says: "The church pronounced such amazing words over
the deceased, as we ourselves would scarcely know how to utter over
a father, a son, a wife, a dead mistress; that is, she has felt that any
man dying or dead was so close, so 'near her spirit' as only a mother
can feel her own dead child. How can we not leave her everything
in return for this . . . ?"

The antiphilological spirit with which Rozanov wrestled had
burst loose from the very depths of history; in its own way, it was
just as much an inextinguishable flame as the philological fire.

There are on earth just such eternal oil-fed fires; a place catches
fire accidentally and burns dozens of years. There is absolutely no
way to snuff them out. Luther showed himself to be a bad philologue
because, instead of an argument, he let fly an inkwell. The antiphilological fire ulcerates Europe's body, growing dense with flaming volcanoes in the land of the West, making an everlasting cultural
wasteland out of that soil on which it had burst forth. There is no
way to put out the hungry fire. We must let it burn, while avoiding
the cursed places, where no one really needs to go, toward which no
one will hurry.

Europe without philology isn't even America; it's a civilized
Sahara, cursed by God, an abomination of desolation. The European

castles and Acropolises, the Gothic cities, the cathedrals like forests, and the dome-topped basilicas would stand as before, but people would look at them without understanding them, and even more likely they would grow frightened of them, not understanding what force raised them up, or what blood it is that flows in the veins of the mighty architecture surrounding them.

What an understatement! America has outdone this Europe that for the time being is still comprehensible. America, having exhausted the philological supply it had carried over from Europe, somehow panicked, then took some thought and suddenly started growing its own personal philology, dug Whitman up from someplace or other; and he, like a new Adam, began to give names to things, provided a standard for a primitive, nomenclatural poetry to match that of Homer himself. Russia is not America; we have no philological import trade; an out-of-the-way poet like Edgar Poe wouldn't germinate here, like a tree growing from a date pit that had crossed the ocean in a steamer. Except maybe for Balmont, the most un-Russian of poets, alien translator of the Aeolian harp, of a sort never found in the West; a translator by calling, by birth, even in the most original of his works.

Balmont's position in Russia is that of being the foreign representative of a nonexistent phonetic power, the rare instance of a typical translation without an original. Although Balmont is actually a Muscovite, between him and Russia there lies an ocean. This is a poet completely alien to Russian poetry; he will leave less of a trace in it than the Edgar Poe or the Shelley who were translated by him, although his own poems lead one to assume a very interesting original.

We have no Acropolis. Our culture has been wandering until now and has not found its walls. But to make up for it, every word of Dal's dictionary is a kernel of Acropolis, a small castle, a winged fortress of nominalism, equipped with the Hellenic spirit for incessant struggle with the formless element, with the nonbeing that threatens our history on all sides.

Just as Rozanov is the representative in our literature of a domestic Hellenism that plays the holy fool and the beggar, so Annensky[9] is the representative of heroic Hellenism, philology militant. The poems and tragedies of Annensky can be compared to the wooden fortifications, the stockades, which were set up deep in the steppe by the appanage princes for defense against the Pechenegs as the time of the Khazar night came on.

Against my dark fate I no longer feel injury;
Stripped and unpowered was Ovid once, too.

Annensky's incapacity to submit himself to any kind of influence, to be a go-between, a translator, is immediately striking. With a most original swoop he seizes the foreign in his claws, and still in the air, at a great height, he haughtily lets his prey drop, allowing it to fall by its own weight. And so the eagle of his poetry, that had entaloned Euripides, Mallarmé, and Leconte de Lisle, never brought us anything in its clutch but some tufts of dry grass—

Hark, a madman is knocking at your door
God knows where and with whom he spent the past night,
His gaze wanders and his speech is wild,
And his hand is full of pebbles.
Before you know it, he empties the other hand.
He showers you with dry leaves.

Gumilev called Annensky a great European poet. It seems to me that when the Europeans come to know him, having humbly instructed their future generations in the study of the Russian language as former generations had been instructed in the ancient languages and classical poetry, they will take fright at the audacity of this regal predator, who has seized from them their dove Eurydice and carried her off to the Russian snows; who has torn the classical shawl from the shoulders of Phaedra, and has placed with tenderness, as becomes a Russian poet, an animal hide on the still-shivering Ovid. How amazing Annensky's fate is! He fingered universal riches, yet saved for himself only a miserable pittance; or rather, he lifted a handful of dust and flung it back into the blazing treasure house of the West. Everyone slept while Annensky kept vigil. The realist moral chroniclers [*bytoviki*] were snoring. The journal *The Scales* did not yet exist. The young student Viacheslav Ivanovich Ivanov was studying with Mommsen and writing a Latin monograph on Roman taxes. And at this time the headmaster of the Tsarskoe Selo lyceum was wrestling long nights with Euripides, assimilating the snake poison of crafty Hellenic speech, preparing an infusion of such strong, bitter-as-wormwood poems as no one had written before or would write after him. For Annensky, too, poetry was a domestic affair, and Euripides a domestic writer, just one continuous citation and set of quotation marks. Annensky perceived all of world poetry as a shaft of light thrown off by Hellas. He had a

sense of what distance means, felt its pathos and cold; and he never
tried to bring together externally the Russian and the Hellenic
world. The lesson Annensky's creative work taught Russian poetry
was not Hellenization but an inner Hellenism adequate to the spirit
of the Russian language, a domestic Hellenism so to speak. Hellenism is a baking dish, a pair of tongs, an earthenware jug with milk;
it is domestic utensils, crockery, the body's whole ambiance; Hellenism is the warmth of the hearth felt as something sacred; it is any
personal possession that joins part of the external world to a man,
any clothes placed on someone's shoulders by a random person, accompanied by that very same sacred shudder with which

> As the swift river froze
> And winter storms raged,
> With a downy hide they covered
> The holy old man.

Hellenism means consciously surrounding man with utensils
[*utvar'*] instead of indifferent objects; the metamorphosis of these
objects into the utensil, the humanization of the surrounding world;
the environment heated with the most delicate teleological warmth.
Hellenism is any stove near which a man sits, prizing its warmth as
something related to his own inner warmth. Finally, Hellenism is
the boat of the dead in which Egyptian corpses set sail, in which
everything is stored that is needed for continuation of a man's
earthly wanderings, including even an aromatic jar, a hand mirror,
and a comb. Hellenism is a system, in the Bergsonian sense of the
word, which man unfolds around himself, like a fan of phenomena
liberated from temporal dependence, commonly subordinated to an
inner bond through the human "I."
  In Hellenic terms, the symbol is a utensil, and therefore any object drawn into the sacred circle of man can become a utensil; and
therefore, a symbol, too. And so we may ask whether Russian poetry
needs a deliberately contrived Symbolism. Is this not a sin against
the Hellenic nature of our language that creates images as utensils
for the use of man?
  Essentially there is no difference between word and image. The
word is already a sealed image; one may not touch it. It is not suitable
for daily use; no one will light a cigarette from the icon-lamp. Such
sealed images are also very much needed. Man loves interdiction,
and even the savage puts a magical ban, a "taboo," on certain ob-

jects. And yet, the sealed image, removed from use, is hostile to man; in its own way, it is a scarecrow, a bugbear.

All that passes is merely a likeness. Let's take an example: a rose or the sun, a dove or a girl. For the Symbolist not one of these figures is interesting in itself; but rather the rose is an image of the sun, the sun is an image of the rose, the dove is an image of the girl, and the girl is an image of the dove. The figures are gutted like a stuffed owl and packed with a strange content. Instead of a symbolic forest, a taxidermist's shop.

That is where professional Symbolism is headed. The power of perception has been demoralized. Nothing is real or authentic. The terrible *contredanses* of "correspondences," all nodding to each other. Eternal winking. Not a single clear word; only hints and implications. The rose nods at the girl, the girl at the rose. Nobody wants to be himself. The epoch of Russian poetry dominated by the Symbolists surrounding the journal *The Scales* was quite remarkable indeed. Over two decades, it developed an enormous structure that stood on clay feet and might best be defined as the epoch of pseudo-symbolism. Let this definition not be understood as a reference to Classicism, denigrating the beautiful poetry and fruitful style of Racine. Pseudoclassicism is a nickname applied by academic ignorance that has since been fastened to a great style. Russian pseudo-symbolism is really pseudosymbolism. Jourdain discovered in the maturity of his years that all his life he had been speaking prose. The Russian Symbolists discovered that very same prose—the primal figurative nature of the word. They put a seal on all words, all images, designating them exclusively for liturgical use. This has very uncomfortable results—you can't get by or get up or sit down. Impossible to light a fire, because it might signify something that would make you unhappy.

Man was no longer master in his own house; it would turn out he was living in a church or in a sacred druidic grove. Man's domestic eye had no place to relax, nothing on which to rest. All utensils were in revolt. The broom asked holiday, the cooking pot no longer wanted to cook, but demanded for itself an absolute significance (as if cooking were not an absolute significance). They had driven the master from his home and he no longer dared to enter there. How is it to be then with the attachment of the word to its denotative significance? Isn't this a kind of bondage that resembles serfdom? But the word is not a thing. Its significance is not the equivalent of a translation of itself. In actual fact, there never was a time when anybody baptized a thing, called it by a thought-up name. It is most convenient and in the scientific sense most accurate to regard the word as an image; that is, a verbal representation. In this way the question of form and content is removed; assuming the phonetics are the form, everything else is the content. The problem of what is of primary significance, the word or its sonic properties, is also removed. Verbal representation is an intricate complex of phenomena, a connection, a "system." The signifying aspect of the word can be regarded as a candle burning from inside a paper lantern; the sonic representation, the so-called phonemes, can be placed inside the signifying aspect, like the very same candle in the same lantern.

The old psychology only knew how to objectivize representations and, while overcoming naïve solipsism, regarded representations as something external. In this case, the decisive instant was the instant of what was immediately given. The immediately given of the products of our consciousness approximates them to objects of the external world and permits us to regard representations as something objective. The extremely rapid humanization of science, including in this sense epistemology, too, directs us onto another path. Representations can be regarded not only as the objective-given of consciousness, but also as man's organs, quite like the liver or the heart.

Applied to the word, such a conception of verbal representations opens broad new perspectives and allows one to speculate on the creation of an organic poetics; not of a legislative, but of a biological character, destroying a canon in the name of a closer inner approximation to the organism, possessing all the features of biological science.

The organic school of the Russian lyric has taken upon itself the tasks of constructing such a poetics. I refer to the school that rose from the creative initiative of Gumilev and Gorodetsky in the beginning of 1912, to which Akhmatova, Narbut, Zenkevich, and the author of these lines were officially attached.[10] The very modest literature of Acmeism and the scarcity of theoretical work by its leaders render its study difficult. Acmeism arose out of repulsion: "Away with Symbolism, long live the living rose!"—that was its original slogan. It was Gorodetsky who in his time tried to graft onto Acmeism the literary world view called "Adamism," a sort of doctrine of a new earth and a new Adam. The attempt did not succeed. Acmeism did not adopt a world view; it brought in a series of new taste sensations, much more valuable than ideas; mostly, the taste for an integral literary representation, the image, in a new organic conception. Literary schools do not live by ideas, but by tastes; to bring along a whole heap of new ideas but not to bring new tastes means not to make a new school but merely to form a poetics. On the other hand, a school can be created by tastes alone, without any ideas. Not the ideas but the tastes of Acmeism were what turned out to be the death of Symbolism. The ideas seemed to have been partly taken over from the Symbolists, and Viacheslav Ivanov himself helped a good deal in constructing Acmeist theory. Yet behold the miracle: new blood flowed in the veins of Russian poetry. It is said that faith moves mountains, but with regard to poetry I would say: it is taste that moves mountains. Because a new taste developed in turn-of-the-century Russia, we saw such giants as Rabelais, Shakespeare, Racine pick up stakes and move our way to be our guests. Acmeism's upward thrust, its active love for literature with all its difficulties, is unusually great; and the lever of this active love is precisely a new taste, a masculine will to poetry and to a poetics, in the center of which stands man, not flattened to a pancake by pseudosymbolism, surrounded by symbols, that is by utensils, possessing literary representations, too, as a creature possesses its own organs.

More than once in Russian society we have had moments of inspired reading in the heart of Western literature. Thus, Pushkin, and with him his whole generation, read Chénier. Thus, the following generation, the generation of Odoevsky, read Schelling, Hoffmann,[11] and Novalis. Thus, the men of the sixties read their Buckle,[12] and, although neither party in this case possessed any dazzling genius, a more ideal reader could not be found. The Acmeist wind turned over the pages of Classics and Romantics, and these came open to the very place the age most needed. Racine opened to *Phaedra*, Hoffmann to *The Serapion Brothers*. We found Chénier's iambs and Homer's *Iliad*.

Acmeism was not merely a literary, but also a social phenomenon in Russian history. It brought a reinvigorated moral force back into Russian poetry. "I want to sail my free boat everywhere; and God and the Devil I'll glorify alike," said Briusov. This wretched affirmation of the void [*nichevochestvo*] will never repeat itself in Russian poetry. So far, the social pathos of Russian poetry has risen only to the conceptual level of "citizen"; but there is a higher principle than "citizen"—the concept "man" [*muzh*].

In distinction to the old civic poetry, the new Russian poetry has to educate not only the citizen but also the "man." The ideal of complete manliness is prepared by style and by the practical demands of our time. Everything has become heavier and bigger; so man, too, must stand more firmly, because man should be the firmest thing on the earth and should regard his relation to the earth as that of diamond to glass. The hieratic, that is to say, the sacred character of poetry, is dependent on the conviction that man is the firmest thing in the world.

The age quiets down, culture goes to sleep, a people is reborn, having given its best forces to a new social class; and this whole current bears the frail boat of the human word into that open sea of the immediate future, where there is no sympathetic understanding, where dreary commentary replaces the fresh wind of the hostility-and-sympathy of one's contemporaries. How then can one rig this boat for its distant trek, without having supplied it with everything necessary for so alien and so precious a reader. Once more I compare the poem to an Egyptian boat of the dead. In this boat, everything is equipped for life; nothing is forgotten.

Yet I see many objections beginning to arise and something of a reaction to Acmeism as it was originally formulated; a crisis similar to that of pseudosymbolism. For composing a poetics, pure biology won't do. However good and fruitful the biological analogy might be, with its systematic application a biological canon comes into being, no less oppressive and intolerable than the pseudosymbolical. From the physiological conception of art, "the superstitious abyss of the Gothic spirit" stares out. Salieri[18] is worthy of respect and burning love. It is not his fault that he heard the music of algebra as loudly as that of living harmony.

In the place of the Romantic, the idealist, the aristocratic dreamer of the pure symbol, of an abstract esthetic of the word, in place of Symbolism, Futurism, and Imaginism, we now have the living poetry of the word-object, and its creator is not the idealist-dreamer Mozart, but the stern and strict master craftsman Salieri, who now holds out his hand to that master of things and material values, the builder and producer of the material world.

Notes about Poetry

Contemporary Russian poetry didn't drop from heaven. It was anticipated by our country's entire poetic past—after all, didn't Iazykov's[1] clicking and clattering anticipate Pasternak, and doesn't this one example suffice to show how the poetic big-guns converse with one another in connecting salvos, not at all embarrassed by the indifference of the time that separates them? In poetry, it's always wartime. And it is only in epochs of social idiocy that there is peace or a truce. The root-conductors, like regimental commanders, take up arms against one another. The roots of words battle in the darkness, each "deriving" from the other sustenance and vital juices. The Russian conflict of unwritten secular speech, that is of the domestic root word, the language of peasant laymen, with the written speech of monks, with the hostile, Church-Slavic, Byzantine document, is felt to this day.

The first intelligentsia were the Byzantine monks, and they foisted an alien spirit and an alien form on the language. The black-cassocks, that is to say the intelligentsia, and the laity have always spoken different languages in Russia. The Slavicizing of Cyril and Methodius[2] was for its time the same as the Volapük[3] of our own day. Colloquial language loves accommodation. Out of hostile chunks it creates an alloy. Colloquial speech always finds the middle, convenient way. In its relationship to the whole history of language it is inclined to be conciliatory and is defined by its diffuse benevolence, that is to say, by its opportunism. Poetic speech on the other hand is never sufficiently "pacified," and in it, after many centuries, old discords are revealed. It is amber in which a fly buzzes, embedded ages ago in resin, the living alien body continuing to live even in its petrification. Everything that works in Russian poetry to the advantage of an alien monastic literature, any intelligentsia literature, that is, "Byzantium," is reactionary; and that means evil, bearing evil. Everything that inclines to the secularization of poetic speech, to driving out of it, that is, the monasticizing intelligentsia, Byzantium, brings good to the language, that is longevity, and helps it, as it might help a righteous man, to perform its ordeal of independent existence in the family of dialects. The opposite picture would be possible, let us say, if a people with a native theocracy, like the Tibetans, managed to liberate themselves from secular foreign conquerors like the Manchurians. In Russian poetry only those workers did a first-rate job who directly participated in the great process of making the language worldly, of secularizing it. These are Trediakovsky, Lomonosov, Batiushkov, Iazykov, and, most recently, Khlebnikov and Pasternak.

At the risk of seeming overly crude, of terribly oversimplifying my subject, I would depict the negative and positive poles in the field of poetic language as a widely luxuriant morphological flowering and a hardening of morphological lava under the semantic crust. A wandering root of multiple meanings animates poetic speech.

The root's multiplier, the index of its vitality, is the consonant. (The classical example is Khlebnikov's "Laughing" poem.) A word multiplies itself not through vowels but through consonants. Its consonants are the seed and the pledge of a posterity for a language.

A lowered linguistic consciousness amounts to the atrophy of the consonantal sense.

Russian verse is saturated with consonants and clatters and clicks and whistles with them. Real secular speech. Monkish speech is a litany of vowels.

Thanks to the fact that the conflict with monkishly intelligentsia-like Byzantium on the battleground of poetry abated after Iazykov, and it was a long time before a new hero appeared in this glorious arena, Russian poets one after the other began to deafen to the hum of the language, and grew deaf to the surf of sound waves, and only through an ear trumpet could they distinguish in the hum of the dictionary their own proper small vocabulary. An example: to the deaf old man in *W°oe from W'it*, the characters yell, "Prince, prince, back." A small vocabulary is no sin in itself, and it is not a vicious circle. It may even enclose the speaker in a circle of flame, and yet it is a sign that he does not trust his native soil and it isn't just anywhere that he dares place his foot. The Russian Symbolists were truly Stylites[4] of style: all of them together did not use more than five hundred words—the vocabulary of a Polynesian. But at least they were ascetics, performers of ordeals. They stood on logs. Akhmatova, now, stands on a parquet floor—this is already a parquet Stylitism. Kuzmin strews the parquet with grass so that it might resemble a meadow ("Evenings Some Other Where").

Pushkin has two expressions for innovators in poetry. One: "to fly away again, having stirred up in us, children of dust, a wingless desire." The other: "when the great Gluck[5] appeared and revealed new mysteries to us." Anyone who would lead his native poetry astray with the sound and form of alien speech would be an innovator of the first sort; that is, a seducer. It is untrue that Latin sleeps in Russian speech, untrue that Hellas sleeps in it. With as much justice one could conjure up Negro drums and the monosyllabic utterances of the Kaffirs in the music of Russian speech. Only Russian speech sleeps in Russian speech; only itself. It is a direct insult, and not praise, to say of a Russian poet that his verses sound like Latin. But what about Gluck?—Profound, captivating mysteries?—For Russian poetic fate the profound, captivating mysteries of Gluck are not to be found in Sanskrit or in Hellenism, but in the rigorous secularization of poetic speech. Give us the vulgate. We do not want a Latin Bible.

When I read Pasternak's *My Sister Life*, I experience that same pure joy of the quality of the vulgate, freed from the external influences of mundane speech, of Luther's dark quotidian speech, after the tense Latin, even if it had been understandable to all, certainly understandable to all, but unnecessary, once a kind of metalogic [*zaum*], but long having ceased to be metalogical, to the great chagrin of the monks. Thus the Germans rejoiced in their tile houses, when they opened for the first time their Gothic Bibles that still smelled of fresh printer's ink. And reading Khlebnikov can be compared with a still more magnificent and instructive spectacle, how our language could and should have grown, as one of the righteous, unburdened and undesecrated by historical adversities or by coercion. Khlebnikov's speech is so mundane, so vulgate, it is as though neither monks nor Byzantium nor intelligentsia-letters ever existed. His is an absolutely secular and mundane Russian speech, resounding for the first time in the history of Russian letters. If one takes such a view, the necessity of regarding Khlebnikov as some kind of sorcerer or shaman will vanish. He noted the language's paths of development, transitional, temporary, and this path of Russian oral destiny which never existed historically, which was realized only in Khlebnikov, was strengthened in his metalogic, which means nothing other than transitional forms that had managed not to be covered over by the semantic crust of the correctly and properly developing language.

When a ship after sailing near the shore moves out into the open sea, those who can't bear the rolling return to the shore. After

Khlebnikov and Pasternak, Russian poetry moves once more out into the open sea, and many of its customary passengers will have to take leave of the boat. I see them already standing with their suitcases near the gangway that has been dropped to the shore. But then, how welcome is each new passenger who climbs aboard at precisely this moment!

When Fet[6] made his appearance, the "silver and the tossing of a sleepy stream" agitated Russian poetry, and, as he was leaving, Fet said: "And with the burning salt of imperishable speech."

This burning salt of speech of some sort, this whistling, clicking, rustling, sparkling, splashing, this fullness of sound, this plenitude of life, this flood of images and feelings has rearisen with unheard-of force in the poetry of Pasternak. Before us is the significant patriarchal phenomenon of the Russian poetry of Fet.

Pasternak's magnificent domestic Russian poetry is already old-fashioned. It is tasteless because it is immortal; it is without style because it gasps on banalities with the classic delight of a trilling nightingale. Yes, Pasternak's poetry is a direct mating call (the partridge in his wood, the nightingale in spring), the direct consequence of a special physiological structure of the throat, just as much a mark of the species as plumage or a bird's crest.

> It is a suddenly suffused whistling,
> It is a crackling of compressed icicles,
> It is night frosting leaves,
> It is two nightingales in a duel.

To read Pasternak's verses is to clear one's throat, reinforce one's breathing, renovate the lungs; such verses must be a cure for tuberculosis. We do not have any healthier poetry now. It is kumiss after powdered milk.

Pasternak's book *My Sister Life* is for me a collection of excellent breathing exercises: each time the voice arranges itself anew, each time the powerful breathing apparatus adjusts itself differently.

Pasternak uses the syntax of a confirmed interlocutor, passionately and excitedly demonstrating something, but what is he demonstrating?

> Does the arum-lily ask
> Charity of the swamp?
> The nights breathe gratis
> Putrescent tropics.

So, swinging her arms, muttering, poetry plods along, staggering a bit, causing heads to spin, blessedly out of her mind, yet at the same time the only sober one, the only one awake in the whole wide world.

Certainly, Herzen and Ogarev,[7] when they stood on the Sparrow Hills as boys, experienced physiologically the sacred ecstasy of space and birdflight. Pasternak's poetry has told us about these moments: it is a shining Nike transported from the Acropolis to the Sparrow Hills.

The End of the Novel

What distinguishes the novel from the long story, the chronicle, the memoir, or any other prose form is that it is a composed, self-enclosed, extensive narrative, complete in itself, about the lot of a single person or a whole group of people. Saints' lives, for all their working out of the *fabula*,* were not novels, because they lacked worldly interest in the life story of their characters, illustrating instead some shared ideal. But the Greek story *Daphnis and Chloe* is considered the first European novel because this kind of interest appears there as a motive force, independently for the first time. Over a long period of time the novel form went on developing and gathered strength as it became the art of interesting the reader in the fate of individuals. As it does this, the art comes to fruition in two directions. Compositional technique turns biography into a *fabula*; that is, into a dialectically intelligible narrative, and, coinciding with the appearance of the *fabula*, another aspect of the novel develops—of an auxiliary nature, essentially—the art of psychological motivation. The *quattrocento* storytellers and the *Cent novelles nouvelles* confined themselves in their use of motivation to the juxtaposition of external situations, and this made their stories exceptionally dry and elegantly light and diverting. Novelist-psychologists like Flaubert and the Goncourts turned all their attention to psychological grounding at the expense of the *fabula* and handled this problem brilliantly, converting what had been an auxiliary device into a self-sustaining art.

Right up to our own days, the novel has been a central and urgent necessity, the form that summed up European art. *Manon Lescaut, Werther, Anna Karenina, David Copperfield, Le Rouge et le noir, La Peau de chagrin, Madame Bovary* were events in social life as much as they were artistic events. They produced in contemporaries who looked at themselves in the mirror of the novel a massive self-knowledge and resulted in imitation on a grand scale, as contempo-

* I have retained the Russian *fabula,* rather than translating it as "fable," to avoid confusion with the folkloric genre of the fable. It means "story" or "line of narrative."

raries adapted themselves to the typical images of the novel. The novel educated whole generations; it was an epidemic, a social mode, a school, and a religion. During the period of the Napoleonic wars, a vortex of imitative, lesser biographies formed around the central historical figure, around Napoleon's biography, without reproducing it in every detail of course, but playing variations on a theme. In *Le Rouge et le noir* Stendhal told one of these imitative biographies.

If originally the personae of the novel were unusual, gifted people, the opposite could be noted as the European novel began to decline: the ordinary man became the hero, and the center of gravity shifted to social motivation. That is, society made its appearance as a character participating in the action, as for example in Balzac or Zola.

All this prompts conjecture about an existing link between the fate of the novel and how at a given time the fate of personality in history is viewed. There is no need here to speak of the actual fluctuations that occur in the role of personality in history, but only about how this problem might be resolved at a given moment, insofar as such a resolution forms and nourishes the minds of contemporaries.

And so the nineteenth-century flowering of the novel is directly dependent on the Napoleonic epos, which greatly heightened the stock value of personality in history and, through Balzac and Stendhal, enriched the soil for the whole French and European novel. The typical biography of the usurper and man of destiny Bonaparte was scattered by Balzac through dozens of his so-called "novels of success" [*romans de réussite*], where the basic motive force is not love but career—that is, the striving to beat one's way from the lower and middle social layers into the upper.

Clearly, once we've entered the zone of powerful social movements, activities organized on a mass scale, the stock value of personality in history falls, and the power and influence of the novel fall with it. For the novel, the commonly acknowledged role of personality in history serves as a kind of pressure gauge, indicating the pressure of the social atmosphere. The measure of the novel is a human biography, or a system of biographies. From his very first steps, the new novelist felt that an individual fate did not exist, and he tried to transplant what he needed from the soil it grew in, with all its roots, all its accompaniments and attributes. Thus the novel always offers us a pattern of events, controlled by the biographical link, measured by a biographical measure, and sustaining itself com-

positionally only insofar as it responds to the centrifugal pull of our
planetary system; insofar as the centripetal pull, the pull of the center on the periphery, has not decisively asserted itself over the
centrifugal.

One may consider Romain Rolland's *Jean Christophe* the last example of the centrifugal, biographical European novel; that swan
song of European biography, with its majestic fluency and nobility
of synthetic devices which bring to mind Goethe's *Wilhelm Meister*.
Jean Christophe closes the circle of the novel; for all its contemporaneity, it is an old-fashioned work. In it is gathered the ancient
centrifugal honey of the German and Latin races. In order to create
the last novel, the two races that joined in the personality of Romain
Rolland were needed; and even this wasn't enough. *Jean Christophe*
is set in motion by that very same powerful jolt of the Napoleonic
revolutionary impetus, just as the whole European novel was, by way
of the Beethovenlike biography of Christophe, by way of its con-
tiguity with the powerful figure of the musical myth which came to
birth at the same Napoleonic floodtime in history.

What happens to the novel after this is simply a story of the dispersion of biography as a form of personal existence; more than
dispersion—the catastrophic collapse of biography.

The sense of allotted time a man has, in which he feels he may
act, conquer, love, go under—this sense of time composed the basic
tonality of the European novel, for, I repeat once more, the compositional measure of the novel is the human biography. A human life
by itself is not a biography and provides no backbone to the novel.
A man acting in the time of the old European novel appears as the
pivot of a whole system of phenomena that group themselves around
him.

Europeans are now cast out of their biographies, like balls from
the pocket of the billiard table, and in the determination of their
activity, as in the collision of balls on the billiard table, one principle
operates: the angle of fall is equal to the angle of deflection. A man
without a biography cannot be the thematic pivot of the novel, and
the novel on the other hand is unthinkable without an interest in
the fate of the separate individual, in the *fabula* and all that accompanies it. Besides, the interest in psychological motivation—the direction in which the declining novel so craftily escaped, already
sensing its coming ruin—is radically undermined and discredited by
the imminent impotence of psychological motives before those real

forces whose willful discarding of psychological motivation becomes more cruel from hour to hour.

The contemporary novel was at one and the same time deprived both of the *fabula*, that is, of the personality that acts in the time belonging to it, and of psychology, because psychology no longer substantiates action of any sort.

Badger's Burrow

(A. Blok: August 7, 1921–August 7, 1922)

I.

The first anniversary of Blok's[1] death should be a modest one:
August 7 is only just beginning to come alive in the Russian calendar. Blok's posthumous existence, his new fate, his *vita nuova*, is in
the time of its youth.

The swampish miasma of Russian criticism, the heavy poisoned
fog of Ivanov-Razumnik, Aikhenvald, Sorgenfrei,[2] and others,
which thickened in the past year, has still not dispersed.

Lyrical effusions about lyrics go on. The worst form of the lyrical
mating call. Conjectures. Arbitrary premises. Metaphysical guess-
work.

Everything is shaky, quirky: arbitrary, off-the-cuff pronounce-
ments.

One does not envy the reader who might wish to glean some
information about Blok from the literature of 1921–1922.

The works, the real "works" of Eikhenbaum and Zhirmunsky[3]
are lost in this litany, amid the swampy vapors of lyrical criticism.

From the very first steps of his posthumous life we have to learn
to grasp Blok, to fight the optical illusion of perception, with its
inevitable element of distortion. Gradually extending the realm of
unquestionable and universally compelling information about the
poet, we clear the road for his posthumous fate.

Establishing the poet's literary genesis, his literary sources, his
kinship and origins, takes us at once to solid ground. To the question
of what the poet wanted to say, the critic may answer or not; but
to the question of where he came from, he is obliged to provide an
answer . . .

Examining Blok's poetic course, one may distinguish two tendencies in it, two different principles; one, domestic, Russian, and
provincial; the other, European. The decade of the eighties cradled
Blok, and not for nothing did he return at the end of the road,
when he was already a mature poet, in the poem "Retribution," to
his life sources, to the eighties.

The domestic and the European are two poles, not only of Blok's

poetry but of all of Russian culture of the last decades. Beginning
with Apollon Grigoriev,[4] a deep spiritual rift began to show in
Russian society. There was a loss of contact with the major European
concerns, a deflection from the unity of European culture, a process
of separation from the great womb, a process some perceived as a
kind of heresy which they were afraid and ashamed to acknowledge
to themselves: all this had already come to pass. As if hurrying to
correct someone's mistake, to wipe out the guilt of a tongue-tied
generation whose memory was short and whose love was passionate
but limited, both for himself and for them, for the people of the
eighties, the sixties, and the forties, Blok solemnly swears:

> We love everything: the hell of Parisian streets
> And Venetian coolness,
> The distant fragrance of lemon groves
> And the smoky hulks of the Cologne Cathedral.

More than that, however, Blok had a love for history, an objective
historical attraction to that domestic period of Russian history which
passed under the sign of the intelligentsia and populism. The heavy
three-stress meter of Nekrasov was for him as magnificent as the
Works and Days of Hesiod. The seven-string guitar, Apollon
Grigoriev's friend, was for him no less sacred than the classical lyre.
He seized upon the gypsy ballad and made it the language of passion
on a national scale. In the brilliant light of Blok's knowledge of
Russian reality, Sophie Perovsky's[5] high mathematician's brow
already seems to waft gently with the marble chill of genuine immortality.

One does not cease to wonder at Blok's historical flair. A long
time before he begged the public to listen to the music of the
revolution, Blok was listening to the subterranean music of Russian
history—where even the most attuned ear caught only a syncopated
pause. From each line of Blok's poems about Russia, Kostomarov,
Soloviev, and Kliuchevsky[6] look out at you, especially Kliuchevsky,
the good genius, the house ghost, the guardian of Russian culture,
under whose protection no ordeal or calamity is to be feared.

Blok was a man of the nineteenth century and he knew that the
days of his century were numbered. He avidly extended and deepened his inner world in time, the way a badger digs in the earth,
arranging his dwelling, building it so it will have two exits. The
age is a badger's burrow, and the man who is a man of his own age
lives and moves about in a narrowly limited space, tries feverishly

to extend his dominions, and treasures most of all the exits from his underground burrow. Moved by this badger's instinct, Blok deepened his poetic knowledge of the nineteenth century. English and German Romanticism, the blue flower of Novalis, the irony of Heine, an almost Pushkinian yearning to touch his burning lips to the springs of European national folklore; those various springs, soothing in their purity and apartness, flowing separately, the English, the French, the German, had long tormented Blok. Among Blok's creations, there are those directly inspired by the Anglo-Saxon, the Romance, the German genius, and this immediacy of inspiration recalls to mind once more the "Feast in Time of Plague" and that place where the "night reeks of lemon and laurel" and the little song "I drink to the health of Mary." The whole poetics of the nineteenth century—*there* are the boundaries of Blok's power, that is where he is king, that is what his voice grows strong on, when his movements become authoritative and his intonations commanding. The freedom with which Blok handles the thematic material of this poetics suggests the notion that certain subjects, individual and incidental until recent times, have acquired before our very eyes the magnitude of myths. Such are the themes of Don Juan and Carmen. Mérimée's concise, exemplary story met with good fortune: Bizet's light and martial music, like a clarion call, spread through all the backwoods places the tidings of the Romance race's eternal youth and lust for life. Blok's poems offer the youngest member of the European family of legends and myths its most recent home. But the high point of Blok's historical poetics, the triumph of European myth, which moves freely with the traditional forms, without any fear of anachronism or modernity, is "The Steps of the Commendatore." Here the layers of time have been heaped one on the other in a freshly ploughed poetic consciousness, and the seeds of the old theme have yielded an abundant harvest. (*The automobile quiet, black as an owl . . . From a blessed, unknown distant land is heard the crowing of a cock.*)

II.

In literary matters, Blok was an enlightened conservative. In everything that concerned problems of style, rhythm, imagery, he was surprisingly cautious: there isn't a single break with the past. Imag-

ining Blok as an innovator in literature, one recalls an English lord
who with great tact introduces a new bill into the House. It was
more an English than a Russian kind of conservatism. A literary
revolution within the framework of tradition and irreproachable
loyalty. Beginning with a direct, almost a disciple's dependence
on Vladimir Soloviev[7] and Fet, Blok did not break with a single
commitment that he had undertaken, right up to the very end; he
did not cast away a single piety, did not trample on a single canon.
He merely complicated his poetic credo with newer and newer
pieties: thus, fairly late, he introduced the Nekrasov[8] canon into
his poetry, and much later experienced the direct canonical influence
of Pushkin, a very rare instance in Russian poetry. Blok's literary
susceptibility was not at all the result of characterlessness: he felt
style very strongly, as a *kind*, a species; therefore he sensed the life
of language and literary form not as break and destruction but as
interbreeding, the coupling of various species, strains, or as the
grafting of various fruits to one and the same tree.

The most unexpected and vivid of all Blok's works, *The Twelve*,
is nothing other than the use of a literary canon that had come into
being independently of him and had existed earlier, that of the
chastushka.[9] The poem *The Twelve* is a monumental dramatic
chastushka. The center of gravity is in the composition, in the
arrangement of parts, due to which the transitions from one
chastushka-like structure to another acquire a special expressiveness,
and each junction of the poem becomes the source for a discharge
of new dramatic energy; yet the power of *The Twelve* is not only in
its composition but in the material itself as well, drawn as it is
directly from folklore. Here the catchwords of the street are seized
upon and reinforced—often, single-day ephemerae like "She's got
*kerenki** in her stocking"—and with the greatest self-possession
they are woven into the general texture of the poem. The folkloristic
value of *The Twelve* recalls the conversations of the younger characters in *War and Peace*. Regardless of various idle interpretations,
the poem *The Twelve* is immortal, like folklore.

The poetry of the Russian Symbolists was extensive, predatory.
Balmont, Briusov, Andrei Biely opened up new regions, laid them
waste, and, like conquistadors, strove further. Blok's poetry, from
beginning to end, from the "Verses about the Beautiful Lady"

---

* Paper money, twenty- and forty-ruble notes, that came out in 1917 when
Kerensky was head of the provisional government.

to *The Twelve*, was intensive, culturally creative. The thematic development of Blok's poetry went from cult to cult. From "The Unknown Lady" and "The Beautiful Lady" through "The Puppet Show" and *The Snow Mask* to Russia and Russian culture, and beyond to the Revolution as the highest musical tension and the catastrophic essence of culture. The poet's spiritual frame inclined to catastrophe. And yet, cult and culture took on a concealed and protected source of energy, a steady and expedient movement, "the love which moves the sun and the other stars." Poetic culture arises from the effort to anticipate catastrophe, to make it dependent on the central sun of the whole system, whether it be that love of which Dante spoke, or the music at which in the long run Blok arrived.

One can say of Blok that he is the poet of the Unknown Lady and of Russian culture. Of course it would be obtuse to assume that the Unknown Lady and the Beautiful Lady are symbols of Russian culture. And yet, one and the same need for cult—that is, for an expedient discharge of poetic energy—guided his thematic creativity and found its highest fulfillment in service to Russian culture and Revolution.

The Nineteenth Century

Baudelaire's words about the albatross apply to the nineteenth century: "By the spread of his great wings, he is fastened to the earth."[1]

The beginning of the century still tried to struggle with the traction of earth, with convulsive hops, awkward and weighted half-flights; the end of the century already rests motionlessly, covered by the immense marquee of the outsize wings. The calm of despair. Its wings weigh it down, contrary to their natural function.

The great wings of the nineteenth century: its cognitive powers. The cognitive capacities of the nineteenth century had no correspondence with its will, its character, its moral growth. Like an immense cyclopean eye, the cognitive capacity of the nineteenth century turned to the past and the future. Nothing except sight, empty and rapacious, with a singular passion for devouring any object, any epoch.

Derzhavin on the threshold of the nineteenth century scratched on his slate board a few verses which could serve as the leitmotif of the whole oncoming century:

> The river of time in its flowing
> Bears off all works of men
> And drops into the abyss of oblivion
> Peoples, kingdoms, kings.
> And if something should yet remain
> Through sound of lyre and trumpet
> It will be devoured by Eternity's maw,
> And it won't escape the common fate.

Here, in the rusty language of the withered century, with all power and penetration, is expressed the hidden thought of the oncoming—the exalted lesson abstracted from it, its foundation given. The lesson—relativism, relativity: *and if something should yet remain . . .*

Note: This translation was originally published in *New Literary History* 1 (1974–1975):641–646.

The essence of the cognitive activity of the nineteenth century is projection. The century that has passed did not like to speak of itself in the first person but loved to project itself on the screen of strange epochs, and its life consisted of that, that was its movement. With its dreamless thought, as with an immense mad projector, it cast histories out over the dark sky; with gigantic illuminated tentacles it rummaged in the wastes of time; it plucked out of the darkness this or that chunk, burned it up with the blinding glitter of its historical laws, and indifferently allowed it once again to drop into nothingness as if nothing had happened.

It was not merely a single projector that fumbled along this terrible sky: all the sciences were turned into their own abstract and monstrous methodologies (with the exception of mathematics). The triumph of naked method over knowledge was essentially complete and exclusive—all the sciences spoke of their own method more openly, more eagerly, more animatedly than of their direct activity. Method determines science: as many methodologies as there are sciences. Most typical was philosophy: through the whole stretch of the century it preferred to limit itself to "Introductions to Philosophy," kept introducing without end, led you out somewhere or other, and then abandoned you. And all the sciences together fumbled along the starless sky (and this century's sky was amazingly starless) with their methodological tentacles, meeting no opposition in that soft, abstract emptiness.

I'm constantly drawn to citations from the naïve and clever eighteenth century, and now I am reminded of the lines from the famous Lomonosov missive:

> They think incorrectly about things, Shuvalov,
> Who consider glass lower than minerals.

From where does this enthusiasm come, this high-flown utilitarian enthusiasm, from where such an inner warmth that positively sets aglow this poeticizing about the fate of the industrial crafts? What a striking contrast to the brilliant, cold impersonality of the scientific thought of the nineteenth century!

The eighteenth century was an age of secularization, that is, of the rendering worldly of human thought and activity. Hatred for the priesthood, for hieratic cult, hatred for the liturgy, is deep in its blood. Not having been primarily an age of social struggle, it was nevertheless an interval of time when society was painfully aware of caste. The determinism inherited from the Middle Ages, weighed upon philosophy and enlightenment and upon its political experiments, all the way to the *tiers état*. The caste of priests, the caste of warriors, the caste of agriculturists—these were the concepts with which "enlightened minds" operated. These were not at all *classes*: all the enumerated elements were thought to be *necessary* in the sacred architectonics of *any* society. The immense, accumulated energy of social conflict sought to find a way out. The whole aggressive demand of the age, the whole force of its principled indignation, pounced upon the priestly caste. It seemed that the whole anvil of Great Principles served only to forge the hammer with which it would be possible to smash the hateful priests. There was not a century more sensitive to everything that smelled of priesthood—the smoke of incense scorched its nostrils and stiffened the backbone of a beast of prey.

> The bow rings, the arrow trembles,
> And, spiraling, Pithon died . . .

The liturgy was a thorn in the side of the eighteenth century. It saw nothing around itself that one way or another was not connected with the liturgy, that did not issue from it. Architecture, music, painting—all radiated from a single center, and this center was destined for destruction. In the composition of painting there is a certain question which conditions the movement and balance of colors: where is the source of light? Thus, the eighteenth century, which had rejected the source of light it had historically inherited, was obliged to resolve this problem all over again for itself. And it resolved it in an original way, having broken a window through to a paganism invented by itself, to a sham antiquity, inauthentic and by no means based on philology, but helpful, utilitarian, composed to satisfy a ripened historical need.

The rationalistic moments of mythology met this need of the time as well as anything could, permitting it to settle the waste sky with human images, pliant and obedient to the capricious vanity of the age. As for Deism, it tolerated anything; Deism was ready to tolerate everything as long as the modest significance of the underpainting was retained, as long as what was painted was not an empty canvas.

As the great French Revolution approached, the pseudoantique theatricalization of life and politics made greater and greater headway, and by the time of the Revolution itself, the practical participants were already moving and struggling in a thick crowd of personifications and allegories, in the narrow space of actual theatrical wings, on the boards of a staged antique drama. When real furies of ancient rage gathered within this pathetic cardboard theater, when they walked into the pompous gabble of civic holidays and municipal choruses, it was hard to believe at first; and only Chénier's poetry, a poetry of authentic antique rage, clearly showed that a union of intellect and the furies does indeed exist, that the ancient iambic spirit which had once inspired Archilochus to produce the first iambs still lived in the rebellious European soul.

The spirit of antique rage, with its festive luxury and dark majesty, made its appearance in the French Revolution. Isn't this what flung the Gironde at the Mountain and the Mountain at the Gironde? Wasn't this what broke out in the tongues of fire of the Phrygian cap and in the unprecedented thirst for mutual extermination that ripped open the womb of the Convention? Freedom, equality, and brotherhood—this triad left no place for the furies of authentic raging antiquity. They had not invited her to the feast, she came herself; they had not called her, she appeared unasked; they spoke with her in the language of intellect, but little by little she converted her most outspoken opponents into her followers.

The French Revolution ended when the spirit of antique rage departed; it had burned the priesthood, killed social determinism, completed the secularization of Europe. And then, there splashed out onto the shore of the nineteenth century, already misunderstood—not the head of the Gorgon, but a fascicle of seaweed. Out of the union of mind and the furies there was born a mongrel cur, equally strange to the high rationalism of the *Encyclopedia* and the antique madness of the revolutionary storm—Romanticism.

But, as it unfolded, the nineteenth century left the past a lot further behind than Romanticism had.

The nineteenth century was the carrier of Buddhist influence in European culture.[2] It was the bearer of an alien, hostile, and powerful principle with which all our history has struggled—an active, pragmatic, thoroughly dialectical and vital conflict of forces which had brought each other to fruition. The nineteenth century was the cradle of a Nirvana which did not allow a single ray of active knowledge to shine through.

> In an empty cave
> I am the rocking of a cradle
> Under somebody's hand,
> Silence, silence.

Latent Buddhism, an inclination inward, a wormhole. The age
did not preach Buddhism but bore it within, like an inner night,
like a blindness of the blood, like a secret terror and a head-spinning
weakness. Buddhism in science under the thin mask of a bustling
positivism; Buddhism in art in the analytical novel of the Goncourts
and Flaubert; Buddhism in religion peeking out from all the holes
in the theory of progress, preparing the triumph of the newest
theosophy, which is nothing other than the bourgeois religion of
progress, the religion of the apothecary Monsieur Homais, in preparation for further sailing rigged with metaphysical gear.

It seems to me not accidental, the inclination of the Goncourts and
those who thought like them, the first French Impressionists, to
Japanese art, to the print of Hokusai, to the form of the tanka[3] in
all its aspects; to a composition, that is, entirely immobile and self-
enclosed. All of *Madame Bovary* is written according to the system
of the tanka. The reason Flaubert wrote it so slowly and so painfully
is that after every five words he had to begin all over again.

The tanka is the favored form of molecular art. It is not a miniature, and it would be a gross mistake to confuse it with a miniature
because of its brevity. It has no scale because there is no action in it.
It doesn't relate to the world in any way, because it is itself a world.
It is the constant vortical movement inward of molecules.

The cherry branch and the snowy peak of a favorite mountain,
the patronesses of Japanese engravers, are reflected in the shining
lacquer of each phrase of the polished Flaubertian novel. Here
everything is covered with the lacquer of pure contemplation, and,
like the surface of the rosewood tree, the style of the novel is capable
of reflecting any object. If such works did not frighten contemporaries, this would be attributed to their striking insensitivity and lack
of artistic perceptiveness. Of all Flaubert's critics perhaps the most
penetrating was the royal prosecuting attorney, who sensed a certain
danger in the novel. Unfortunately, however, he did not seek it
where it was hidden.

The nineteenth century at its extreme simply had to arrive at the
form of the tanka—a poetry of nonbeing and Buddhism in art.

Essentially Japan and China are not at all the East, but rather the
extreme West: they are more Western than London or Paris. Our
past century really kept moving deeper into the West, and not the
East, but it merged with the Far East in its striving for the outer
limit.

Looking at the analytical French novel as the peak of nineteenth-century Western Buddhism, we become convinced of its total literary sterility. It has had no heirs, nor could it really have any—only naïve epigones, of which a large number still remain. Tolstoy's novels are pure epic and an entirely healthy European form of art. The synthetic novel of Romain Rolland broke sharply with the tradition of the French analytical novel and was related to the synthetic novel of the eighteenth century, mainly to Goethe's *Wilhelm Meister*, with which its basic artistic technique links it.

There exists a special kind of synthetic blindness to manifestations of the individual. Goethe and Romain Rolland depict psychological landscapes, landscapes of characters and spiritual conditions; but the form of the Japano-Flaubertian analytical tanka is alien to them. In the veins of every century there flows a foreign blood, not its own, and the stronger, the more intensive historically the age, the more heavily this foreign blood weighs.

After the eighteenth century, which understood nothing, possessed not the least feeling for the comparative-historical method, like a blind kitten in a basket, left abandoned amidst worlds incomprehensible to it, there arrived the century of omnicomprehension—the century of relativism with its monstrous capacity for reincarnating past ages—the nineteenth. Yet this taste for historical reincarnations and omnicomprehension proved to be not steady but transient, and our own century has begun under the sign of a sublime intolerance, exclusively, and the conscious noncomprehension of other worlds. In the veins of our century there flows the heavy blood of extremely distant monumental cultures, perhaps the Egyptian and Assyrian.

> The wind brought us comfort,
> And in the azure we sensed
> The Assyrian wings of the dragonflies,
> Partitions of elbow-jointed darkness.[4]

In relation to this new age, turned cruel and immense, we appear as colonizers. To Europeanize and humanize the twentieth century, to make it glow with a theological warmth—that is the task facing the survivors of the collapse of the nineteenth century, those who have been cast ashore by the will of the fates on a new historical continent.

And in this work it is easier to find support in the more remote rather than in the more immediate past. The elementary formulas, the general conceptions of the eighteenth century may once again come in handy. "The skeptical assessment of the *Encyclopedia*," the legal spirit of the social contract, naïve materialism once so arrogantly mocked, schematic intellect, the spirit of expediency may yet serve mankind. Now is not the time to fear rationalism. The irrational root of the oncoming epoch, the gigantic inextirpable double-stranded root, like the stone temple of an alien god, casts its shadow upon us. In days like these, the intellect of the Encyclopedists is the sacred fire of Prometheus.

Peter Chaadaev

I.

The trace Chaadaev left on Russian consciousness was so deep and unerasable as to suggest it had been made by diamond on glass. It is all the more remarkable in that Chaadaev was not what you might call a "public figure," neither a professional writer nor a tribune. By his whole turn of mind, he was a "private" man; what is called a *privatier*. Yet, as though aware that his personality belonged not to him but to posterity, he regarded it with a certain humility. Whatever he did, it turned out that he "served," that he performed a sacred task.

All those qualities that Russian life lacked, the existence of which it did not even suspect, joined together as if on purpose in the person of Chaadaev: an enormous inner discipline, a high-minded intellectualism, moral architectonics, and the cold of a mask, of a metal casing with which he encircled himself, aware that by the measure of the ages he was merely a shape, and so he went about preparing ahead of time the specific mold of his immortality.

Still more unusual for Russia was Chaadaev's dualism, the clear distinction he made between matter and spirit. In an unformed country, a country of half-animated matter and half-dead spirit, that ancient antinomy of the inert clod and the organizing idea was almost unknown. In Chaadaev's eyes, all of Russia still belonged to the world of the unformed and unorganized. He himself was flesh of the flesh of this Russia, and he regarded himself as raw material. The results achieved were amazing. The Idea organized his personality, not merely his mind, and gave this personality a structure, an architecture, subordinated it entirely to itself, overlooking nothing, and as a reward for this absolute subordination endowed it with absolute freedom.

A deep harmony, the virtual fusion of the moral and intellectual element, gives Chaadaev's personality its special firmness. It is hard to say where Chaadaev's intellectual personality leaves off and where his moral personality begins, so close are they to complete fusion. The strongest requirement of intellect was for him at the same time the greatest moral necessity.

I speak of the requirement of unity, which determines the structure of chosen intellects.

"What could we talk about, then?" he asked Pushkin in one of his letters. "I have, you know, just one idea, and if some other ideas should inadvertently pop into my brain, they would certainly get stuck on to that very idea immediately: and would that suit you?"

What then was the nature of this renowned "intellect" of Chaadaev's, this "proud" intellect, sung deferentially by Pushkin, hissed by the provocative Iazykov, if not a fusion of the moral with the intellectual principle, a fusion so characteristic of Chaadaev, in pursuit of which his personality came to its maturity.

With this deep, ineradicable demand for unity, for a higher historical synthesis, Chaadaev was born in Russia. The native of the plains wanted to breathe the air of Alpine heights, and, as we see, he found them within himself.

II.

In the West there is unity! From the time these words flared up in Chaadaev's consciousness, he no longer belonged to himself and tore himself away forever from "domesticity." He had enough manliness to tell Russia to her face the frightening truth—that she was cut off from global unity, severed from history, from "God's teachers of peoples."

The thing is that Chaadaev's understanding of history excludes the possibility of any *setting forth* on the historical path. According to his understanding, one could be on the historical path only prior to any beginning. History was a Jacob's ladder by which angels descended to earth. It must be called sacred, because of the continuity of the spirit of grace which lives in it. And so Chaadaev does not even mention "Moscow, the Third Rome." In this idea he could have seen only the stunted contrivance of the Kievan monks. Neither readiness alone nor good intentions are sufficient to "begin" history. It is unthinkable to *begin* it at all. Continuity is lacking, and unity. Unity cannot be created or invented or learned. Where there is no unity, at best there is "progress," but not history; the mechani-

cal movement of a clockhand, but not the sacred linkage and suc-
cession of events.

Like a man enchanted, Chaadaev kept staring at the one place
where this unity had become flesh, cautiously preserved, inherited
from generation to generation. "But the Pope! the Pope! Well, what
of it? Isn't he, too, simply an idea, a pure abstraction? Take a look
at this old man, being carried in his palanquin under a canopy, in
his triple crown, now just as a thousand years ago, as if nothing in
the world had changed: really, where in all this is the man? Isn't
this an all-powerful symbol of time—not of that time which passes,
but of that which remains motionless, through which everything
else passes, but which itself stands imperturbable and in which and
by means of which everything is brought to completion."

Such was the Catholicism of the snob of Zamoskvorech'e.

III.

And so, in August, 1825, a foreigner made his appearance in a sea-
coast village near Brighton, who united in his bearing the solemnity
of a bishop with the correctness of a worldly mannequin.

This was Chaadaev, who had fled Russia on the first boat that
came along, with such haste, as if some danger threatened him,
without any external need, but with the firm intent never to return.

The sickly, hypochondriacal, odd patient of foreign doctors, who
had never known any other contact with people except a purely intellectual one, concealing even from those close to him his terrible
spiritual upheaval, came to see *his* West, the realm of history and
majesty, native land of the spirit embodied in the church and in
architecture.

This strange journey which occupied two years of Chaadaev's life,
about which we know very little, is more like a languishing in the
desert than a pilgrimage. And then Moscow, the wooden separate-
wing residence, the "Apology of a Madman," and the long, measured years of preaching in the "Anglish" Club.

Is it that Chaadaev wearied? Is it that his Gothic thought submitted and ceased to raise up to the sky its lancet turrets? No, Chaadaev
did not submit, although time's blunt file scraped his thoughts as
well as others.

O precious scraps of the thinker's heritage! Fragments that break off just where one wishes elaborations above all, grandiose introductions about which one doesn't know whether they indicate a projected plan or its actual fulfillment. In vain the conscientious researcher sighs over what has been lost, the missing links. They never existed, and they were never lost: the fragmentary form of the *Philosophical Letters* is inherent in them, as is their essential nature of an extended introduction.

To understand the form and spirit of the *Philosophical Letters*, one needs to imagine that Russia serves them as an immense and awesome foundation. The yawning emptiness among the well-known written fragments is the thought of Russia that absents itself from them.

It is best not to touch on the "Apology." Certainly, it is not here that Chaadaev said what he thought about Russia.

And, like a hopeless flat plain, the last unfinished period of the "Apology" stretches on, this dreary, broadly prophetic beginning which at the same time promises nothing, after so much has already been said: "There is a certain fact which rules authoritatively over our historical movement, which passes like a red thread through our entire history, which contains within itself, so to speak, all its philosophy, which manifests itself in all the epochs of our social life and determines their character . . . And this is the fact of geography . . ."

From the *Philosophical Letters* one can learn only that Russia was the mainspring of Chaadaev's thought. *What* he thought about Russia remains a mystery. Having inscribed the excellent words, "Truth is more precious than country," Chaadaev did not reveal their prophetic meaning. Yet is it not an amazing sight, this "truth," surrounded on all sides as by some sort of chaos, by this alien and strange "native land"?

Let us try to develop the *Philosophical Letters* as if they were a photographic negative. Perhaps those places that become light will turn out to be precisely about Russia.

IV.

There is a great Slavic dream of the end of history in the Western sense of the word, as Chaadaev understood it. It is a dream of universal spiritual disarmament, after which a certain condition will

arrive, called "peace." The dream of spiritual disarmament has taken
such a hold on our domestic horizon that the rank-and-file member
of the Russian intelligentsia cannot imagine the final goal of progress
other than in terms of this unhistorical "peace." Not very long ago
Tolstoy himself addressed mankind with the summons to bring to
an end the false and unnecessary comedy of history and to begin
"simply" to live. It is this simplicity that makes the idea of "peace"
so irresistible:

> Pathetic man . . .
> What does he want? . . . The sky is clear,
> Beneath the sky, much room for all.

Earthly and heavenly hierarchies are forever being abolished for
their uselessness. Church, state, law disappear from consciousness
like stupid chimeras, with which man, to while away the time,
through stupidity, populated the "simple," "God-made" world, and
finally there remain, tête-à-tête, without tiresome intermediaries, a
pair—man and the universe:

> With the sky opposite, on the earth,
> An old man lived in a certain village.[1]

Chaadaev's thought is constructed as a strict perpendicular to traditional Russian thinking. He fled this formless paradise as from the
plague.

Certain historians have seen in colonization, in striving to settle
as freely as possible in expanses as vast as possible, the dominant tendency in Russian history.

In the powerful striving to populate the external world with ideas,
with values, and with images, in the striving which has already for
so many centuries formed the agony and the ecstasy of the West and
hurled its peoples into the labyrinth of history where they wander
to this day—one can perceive a parallel to this external colonization.

There, in the forest of the social church where the Gothic pine
needle admits no other light than the light of the idea, Chaadaev's
main thought took shelter and ripened, his mute thought about
Russia.

Chaadaev's West did not at all resemble the cleared paths of civilization. In the full meaning of the word, he discovered his own
West. Verily, into these thickets of culture the foot of man had not
yet entered.

V.

Chaadaev's thought, national in its sources, is national even where it joins with Rome. Only a Russian man could have discovered this West, which is denser, more concrete, than the historical West itself. Chaadaev, precisely by this right of being a Russian, entered upon the sacred soil of a tradition to which he was not bound by inheritance. There, where all is necessity, where each stone, covered by the cobweb of time, dreams, immured in its arch, Chaadaev carried moral freedom, the gift of the Russian land, its best flower. This freedom is worthy of the majesty congealed in architectural forms, it is as valuable as everything the West created in the realm of material culture, and I see how the Pope, "this old man, being carried in his palanquin under a canopy, in his triple crown," raised himself up that he might greet it.

It would be best to characterize Chaadaev's thought as national-synthetic. A synthetic nationality does not bow its head before the fact of national self-consciousness but rises above it in sovereign personality, characterized by its own way of life and therefore national.

Contemporaries were astonished at Chaadaev's pride; and he believed himself in his chosenness. In him there slumbered a hieratic solemnity, and even children felt the significance of his presence, although he did not in any way depart from common good manners. He felt himself chosen, the vessel of true nationality; yet the nation was no longer a fitting judge!

What a striking contrast to nationalism, to that beggary of the spirit which appeals incessantly to the monstrous tribunal of the crowd!

For Chaadaev, there was only one gift that Russia had: moral freedom, the freedom of choice. Never in the West had it been realized in such majesty, in such purity and fullness. Chaadaev took it up like a sacred staff and went to Rome.

I think that a country and a people have already justified themselves, if they have created even one completely free man who wanted and knew how to use his freedom.

When Boris Godunov, anticipating Peter's idea, sent young Russians abroad, not one of them returned. They did not return for the simple reason that there was no way back from being to nonbeing, that in stuffy Moscow they would have been stifled, who had partaken of the immortal spring of undying Rome.

But then, neither did the first doves return to the dovecote.

Chaadaev was the first Russian who, in actual fact, ideologically, had lived in the West and found the road back. His contemporaries felt this instinctively and valued terribly Chaadaev's presence among them.

They could point to him with superstitious awe, as once to Dante: "He was there, he saw—and came back."

And how many of us have spiritually emigrated to the West! And how many among us who live in unconscious duplicity, whose bodies are here, but whose spirits have remained there!

Chaadaev signifies a new deepened understanding of nationality as the highest flowering of personality and of Russia as the source of absolute moral freedom.

Having allotted us inner freedom, Russia presents us with a choice, and those who have made this choice are genuine Russian people, wherever they may attach themselves. But woe unto those who, after having circled about close to their home-nest, faintheartedly return!

Notes about Chénier

The eighteenth century is like a dried-up lake: with neither depth nor moisture, every underwater thing found itself on the surface. To people themselves, it was frightening, due to the transparency and emptiness of the concepts. *La Vérité, la Liberté, la Nature, la Déité*, especially *la Vertu*; they call forth an almost dizzying head-whirl of thought, like transparent, evaporated ponds. This century, which had been forced to walk along the ocean bottom as on a parquet floor, turned out to be preeminently a century of moralizing. People were astonished by the most trivial moral truths as if by rare sea shells. Human thought was suffocating from a cornucopia of false truths and yet could find no rest. Because, obviously, these all turned out to be insufficiently effective, it followed that they had to be endlessly repeated.

The Great Principles of the eighteenth century were always in motion, in a kind of mechanical flurry, like a Buddhist prayer wheel. Here is an example: the thought of antiquity had understood the Good as bounty or well-being; nothing here, as yet, of that inner emptiness of hedonism. The Good, well-being, health merged in a single representation, as a fully weighted, single-natured golden globe. Inside this concept there was no vacuum. And so this seamless nature of antique moralizing, by no means imperative, and by no means hedonistic, permits one even to doubt the *moral* nature of this consciousness: isn't it rather just a kind of hygiene; that is, a prophylaxis of spiritual health?

The eighteenth century lost a direct link with the moral consciousness of the ancient world. The seamless golden globe no longer made any music of its own. Cunning devices were used to draw sounds from it, considerations of the usefulness of the pleasant and the pleasure of the useful. This divested consciousness simply could not bear the idea of duty, and it made its appearance in the image "Roman Virtue," more suitable for supporting the equilibrium of bad tragedies than for administering the spiritual life of man. Yes, the link with authentic antiquity was lost for the eighteenth century; much more powerful was the link with the rigidified forms of scholastic casuistry, so that the Age of Reason appears as the direct heir

of scholasticism, with its rationalism, allegorical thinking, personifications of ideas, quite in the manner of the Old French poetics. The
Middle Ages had its own soul and an authentic knowledge of antiquity; and, not only in the matter of writing, but also in the loving
reproduction of the Classical world, it left the Age of Enlightenment
far behind. The muses had no fun around Intellect, and they were
bored with it, though they only reluctantly acknowledged this. Everything living and healthy went into knickknacks and trivia, because
there was less surveillance over these, while a child with seven nurses
(Tragedy) degenerated into a luxuriant sterile flower, precisely because the Great Principles had spent so much time bending over her
cradle and nursing her along. Younger forms of poetry that fortunately escaped this deadly tutelage would outlive the old that had
withered under its hand.

Chénier's[1] poetic path was a departure, almost a flight, from the
Great Principles to the living water of poetry, by no means to antiquity, but to a completely contemporary understanding of the
world.

In Chénier's poetry one seems to see a religious and perhaps a
childishly naïve presentiment of the nineteenth century.

The Alexandrine verse goes back to antiphony; that is, to a roll-
call exchange of the chorus, divided into two halves, which have the
same amount of time at their disposal for the expression of their
will. However, this equality of right is violated when one voice re-
linquishes part of the time belonging to it to the other. Time is the
pure and unvarnished substance of the Alexandrine. The distribution of time along the runnels of verb, subject, and predicate composes the autonomous inner life of the Alexandrine verse, regulates
its breathing, its tension, and its degree of saturation. Amidst all this
there takes place as it were a "struggle for time" among the elements
of the verse, during which each of them, like a sponge, tries to ab-
sorb into itself as large a quantity of time as possible, while encount-
ering in this effort the claims of the others. The triad of subject, verb,
and predicate, is not, in an Alexandrine verse, something invariable,
because these keep absorbing an alien content, and often the verb
appears with the significance and weight of the subject, the predicate
with the significance of action, that is, of the verb, and so forth.

Thus we have a fluidity of the relationships of the separate parts
of speech, their fusibility, their capacity for chemical transmutation
while retaining the absolute clarity and transparency of syntax that

is extremely characteristic of Chénier's style. The strictest hierarchy of predicate, verb, and subject on the monotonous canvas of the Alexandrine verse pattern traces the line of the image, communicates a prominence to the alternation of the paired lines.

Chénier belongs to a generation of French poets for whom syntax was a golden cage, from which they never dreamed of springing out. This golden cage was definitively constructed by Racine and furnished as a magnificent palace. The syntactical freedom of the medieval poets—Villon, Rabelais, the whole Old French syntax—remained behind, while the romantic uproar of Chateaubriand and Lamartine had not yet begun. A mean parrot guarded the golden cage—Boileau. Chénier faced the problem of creating an absolute plenitude of poetic freedom within the limits of the narrowest canon, and he solved this problem. The sense of the separate line as a living, indivisible organism and the sense of verbal hierarchy within the confines of this integral line are unusually characteristic of French poetry.

Chénier loved and sensed the separate, wandering line: he took a liking to the "Verse from the Epithalamion of Bion," and he preserved it.

It is in the nature of the new French line, founded by Clément Marot, father of the Alexandrine,[2] to weigh a word before it is uttered. Romantic poetics, however, assumes an outburst, unexpectedness, seeks after effect, unanticipated acoustics, and never knows what the song itself is costing it. From the powerful harmonic wave of Lamartine's "Lake" to the ironical little songs of Verlaine, Romantic poetry affirms the poetics of the unexpected. The laws of poetry sleep in the larynx, and all of Romantic poetry, like a necklace of dead nightingales, will not transmit, will not relinquish its secrets, knows no testament. A dead nightingale teaches nobody how to sing. Chénier ingeniously found a middle way between the Classical and the Romantic manner.

Pushkin's generation had already surmounted Chénier, because there had been Byron. One and the same generation could not grasp simultaneously "the sound of the new, miraculous lyre, the sound of the lyre of Byron," and the abstract, externally cold and rational poetry of Chénier which was nevertheless full of the obsessed rage of antiquity.

That by which Chénier still spiritually burned—the *Encyclopedia,*
Deism, the rights of man—was already for Pushkin the past, pure
literature:

> ... Diderot sat down on his rickety three-legged stool,
> Threw off his wig, shut his eyes in rapture,
> And preached away ...

The Pushkinian formula—the union of mind and the furies—
contains the two elements of the poetry of Chénier. The age was
such that no one managed to escape obsession. Only its direction
changed and it went off, now into the pathos of restraint, now into
the power of the accusatory iamb.

The iambic spirit descends upon Chénier like a fury. The imperative. The Dionysian character. Obsession.

Chénier would never have said, "You live for life's sake." He
was completely removed from the Epicureanism of the age, from
the Olympianism of the bigwigs and aristocracy.

Pushkin is more objective and more dispassionate, than Chénier
in his appraisal of the French Revolution. Where Chénier feels only
hatred and a living anguish, Pushkin knows how to contemplate and
has historical perspective: "Do you remember as well, Trianon, the
whir of those times of fun?"

Allegorical poetics. Very broad allegories, by no means fleshless,
among them, Liberty, Equality, Fraternity—for the poet and his
time these are almost living persons and interlocutors. He tries to
capture their features, he senses their warm breathing.

In "Jeu de paume" one observes a struggle between a journalistic
theme and the iambic spirit. Almost the entire poem is in thrall to
the newspaper.

The commonplace of a journalistic style:

> Pères d'un peuple, architectes des lois!
> Vous qui savez fonder d'une main ferme et sûre
> Pour l'homme un code solonnel.[3]

The Classical idealization of contemporaneity: the crowd of the
estates' representatives, making their way to the riding hall, accom-

panied by the people, is compared with the pregnant Latona, almost a mother.

> Comme Latone enceinte, et déjà presque mère,
>   Victime d'un jaloux pouvoir,
> Sans asile flottait, courait la terre entière.[4]

The dissolution of the world into intelligently operating forces. The only one who turns out to be singularly unintelligent is man. The entire poetics of civil poetry is a search for curbs—*frein*: "*...l'oppresseur n'est jamais libre...*"[5]

What are Chénier's poetics? Maybe he has not one but several in different periods or, more precisely, moments of poetic consciousness?

These can be differentiated: the pastoral-shepherdly (*Bucoliques*, *Idylles*)[6] and the grandiose construction of an almost "Scientific Poetry."

Is the influence of Montesquieu and of English common law on Chénier not confirmed, in connection with his stay in England? Isn't there anything he wrote, like the Pushkinian line, "Here a flaming onslaught, there a stern rebuff..."? Or is his abstract mind alien to Pushkinian practicality?

Although the Old French literary tradition had been completely forgotten, some of its devices went on being automatically reproduced, because they had entered into the blood.

Strange, after the antique elegy with all its accessories, where there are the earthenware jug, the reed, the brook, the beehive, the rosebush, the swallow, and the friends and interlocutors and witnesses and spies of the lovers, to find in Chénier an inclination to a completely worldly elegy in the spirit of the Romantics; almost Musset-like, as, for example, the third elegy to "Camille," a worldly love letter delicately unforced and agitated, where the epistolary form is almost liberated from its mythological contingencies, and the animated conversational style of a man who thinks and feels in the Romantic manner flows freely forth:

> Et puis d'un ton charmant, la lettre me demande
> Ce que je veux de toi, ce que je te commande!

Ce que je veux! dis-tu. Je veux que ton retour
Te paraisse bien lent; je veux que nuit et jour
Tu m'aimes (nuit et jour hèlas! je me tourmente).
Présente au milieu d'eux, sois seule, sois absente;
Dors en pensant à moi! rêve-moi près de toi;
Ne vois que moi sans cesse, et sois toute avec moi.[7]

In these lines one hears Tatiana's letter to Onegin, the same domesticity of language, the same sweet heedlessness, better than any caution, and it is just as much at the heart of the French language, just as spontaneous in French as Tatiana's letter is in Russian. For us, through the crystal of the Pushkinian lines, these lines sound almost Russian:

The pink wafer goes dry
On the inflamed tongue.

Thus in poetry the boundaries of the national are destroyed, and the elements of one language exchange greetings with those of another over the heads of space and time, for all languages are linked by a fraternal bond, which strengthens itself on the freedom and domesticity of each, and within this freedom they are fraternally akin, and, each from its own home, they call out to each other.

François Villon

Astronomers accurately predict the return of a comet after a long
interval of time. For those who know Villon, the phenomenon of
Verlaine presents just such an astronomic wonder. The vibrations of
these two voices are strikingly similar. Yet, in addition to tone of
voice and biography, the two poets are linked by an almost identical
mission with regard to the literature contemporary to them. Both
were fated to emerge in epochs of artificial hothouse poetry, and,
just as Verlaine destroyed the *serres chaudes* of Symbolism, Villon
flung his challenge to the powerful Rhetorical school, which could
quite rightly be considered the Symbolism of the fifteenth century.
The well-known *Roman de la Rose* built for the first time the im-
permeable wall within which that tepid atmosphere went on thick-
ening, which the allegories created by this Romance needed in order
to breathe. Love, Danger, Hatred, Perfidy are not dead abstractions.
They are not fleshless. Medieval poetry lends these phantoms an
astral body as it were and fusses tenderly over the artificial atmosphere so vital to the support of their fragile existence. The garden
where these peculiar personages live is enclosed by a high wall. The
lover, as the beginning of the *Roman de la Rose* narrates, has been
wandering around this wall for a long time in a vain search for the
elusive entry.

Poetry and life in the fifteenth century were two independent,
hostile dimensions. It is difficult to believe that Maître Alain Char-
tier was subjected to real persecution and suffered mundane discom-
forts after having incensed the public opinion of his day by too stern
a judgment on the Cruel Lady, whom he drowned in the well of
tears, after a brilliant trial which observed all the niceties of medieval jurisprudence. Fifteenth-century poetry was autonomous: the
place it occupied in the culture of its time resembled that of a state
within the state. Let us recall the Court of Love of Charles VI:
there were over seven hundred varied official ranks, beginning with
the highest signory and ending with petty bourgeois and lower

Note: This translation was originally published in *New Literary History* 1
(1974–1975):633–639.

clercs. The exclusively *literary* nature of this institution explains its contempt for social partitioning. The hypnotic power of literature was so great that members of similar associations wandered about the streets adorned with green wreaths—the symbol of being in love—wishing to extend the literary dream into reality.

François de Montcorbier (de Loges) was born in Paris in 1431, during the time of English rule. The poverty that surrounded his cradle matched the misfortune of the people and, specifically, the misfortune of the capital. One might have expected that the literature of the time would be suffused with a patriotic pathos and a thirst for revenge for the offended dignity of the nation. However, neither in Villon nor in his contemporaries do we find such feelings. France, occupied by foreigners, showed herself a real woman. Like a woman in captivity, she devoted her main attention to the details of her customary and cultural toilette, sizing up the conquerors with curiosity. High society, right behind its poets, was carried away as before by fantasy into the fourth dimension of the Gardens of Love and the Gardens of Delight, and for the common people the lights of the taverns were lit in the evenings, and on holidays farces and mysteries were played.

The feminine-passive nature of the epoch left a profound imprint on the fate and on the character of Villon. Throughout his whole aimless life he carried the firm conviction that someone had to look after him, to manage his affairs and extract him from difficult situations. Even as a mature man, thrown into the basement-dungeon of Meung sur Loire by the Bishop of Orléans, he called plaintively to his friends: "Le laisserez-vous là, le pauvre Villon?"[1] The social career of François de Montcorbier began from the time that Guillaume de Villon, the worthy canon of the monastery church of Saint Benoît le Bétourné, took him under his tutelage. By Villon's own acknowledgement, the old canon was "more than a mother" to him. In 1449 he received the baccalaureate degree; in 1452, the licenciate and master's degree. "O Lord, if I had studied in the days of my heedless youth and dedicated myself to good morals, I would have received a house and a soft bed. But what's the use of talking! I escaped from school like a cunning urchin: as I write these words, my heart bleeds." Strange as it may seem, Maître François Villon had several students, at one time, and instructed them, as best he could, in scholastic wisdom. But, with his characteristic self-honesty, he acknowledged he had no right to be called Maître and in his ballads preferred to call himself a "poor little scholar." And it really was especially difficult for Villon to keep working because, as luck would have it, the years of his study coincided with the student agitations of 1451–1453.

Medieval people loved to consider themselves children of the city, of the church, of the university. But the "children of the university" were exceptionally inclined to mischief. A heroic hunt was organized for the most popular signboards of the Paris market. The Stag was to marry off the She-Goat to the Bear, and the Parrot was meant to be a gift. The students stole a boundary stone from the estate of Mademoiselle de Bruyères, erected it on top of Mount St. Genevieve, calling it *la vesse*, and, having won it from the authorities by force, fastened it to the spot with iron bands. On this round stone they placed another one, oblong in shape—"Pet au Diable"[2]— and they worshipped there nights, strewing the stones with flowers, dancing around them to the sounds of flute and tambourine. The furious butchers and the offended lady brought suit. The provost of Paris declared war on the students. Two jurisdictions clashed, and the audacious ringleaders had to go on their knees with lit candles in their hands to beg mercy of the rector. Villon, who undoubtedly stood at the center of these events, engraved them in his romance "Le Pet au Diable," which has not come down to us.

Villon was a Parisian. He loved the city and idleness. Toward nature he nourished no tenderness of any sort, and even mocked at her. Even in the fifteenth century, Paris was the kind of sea in which one could swim without being bored, forgetting about the rest of the universe. Yet how easy to run aground on one of the numberless reefs of an idle existence! Villon becomes a murderer. The passivity of his fate is remarkable. Almost as though it awaits the occasion of its realization, all the same whether that be good or bad. In a foolish street brawl of the fifth of June, Villon kills the priest Sermoise with a heavy stone. Sentenced to hanging, he appeals; pardoned, he makes his way into exile. Vagabondage decisively shattered his morality, bringing him in touch with the Coquille criminal band, a member of which he then became. On returning to Paris, he takes part in the great burglary in the Collège de Navarre and immediately flees to Angers—because of a broken heart, as he would assert; in actual fact, to make preparations for robbing his rich uncle. Disappearing from the Parisian horizon, Villon publishes his *Petit Testament*. Years of aimless wandering follow, with pauses at feudal courts and in prisons. Amnestied by Louis XI on October 2, 1461, Villon experiences a deep creative unrest, his thoughts and feeling become exceptionally sharp, and he composes the *Grand Testament*, his memorial for the ages. In November, 1463, François Villon was the eyewitness of a quarrel and a murder on the Rue St. Jacques. Here our information about his life comes to an end and his dark biography breaks off.

The fifteenth century was cruel to personal destinies. It turned many of its respectable and sober people into Jobs, murmuring in the depths of their gloomy dungeons and accusing God of injustice. A special kind of prison poetry was created, suffused with biblical bitterness and severity, insofar as these modes were accessible to the courtly Romance soul. From this chorus of convicts, however, Villon's voice may be sharply distinguished. His revolt is more like a legal action than like a mutiny. He knew how to combine in one and the same person the plaintiff and the defendant. In his attitude to himself, Villon never exceeds certain limits of intimacy. He is tender, attentive, concerned with himself no more than a good lawyer would be with his client. Self-pity is a parasitic emotion, corruptive of the spirit and the organism. But the dry juridical pity which Villon affords himself is for him a source of boldness and firm conviction in the justice of his "case." A most unscrupulous, "amoral" man, like a proper heir of the Romans, he lives entirely in a legal world and cannot conceive of any relationships outside of feudal jurisdiction and the norm. A lyric poet is by his nature a bisexual being capable of endless fission in the name of interior dialogue. In none was this "lyrical hermaphroditism" more pronounced than in Villon. What a varied selection of enchanting duets: the offended and the comforter, mother and child, judge and accused, property-owner and beggar.

All his life, property beckoned to Villon like a musical siren and made a thief out of him . . . and a poet. A pathetic vagabond, he appropriated for himself goods that were inaccessible to him, with the aid of his witty irony.

Our contemporary French Symbolists are in love with things, like property-owners. Perhaps the very "soul of things" is nothing other than the feeling of the property-owner, spiritualized and ennobled in the laboratory of subsequent generations. Villon was highly conscious of the abyss between subject and object, but understood it as the impossibility of possession. The moon and other neutral "objects" are irrevocably excluded from his poetic usage. But then he comes instantly to life when the talk turns to roast duck in sauce, or to eternal bliss, which he never loses final hope of acquiring.

Villon depicts a bewitching *intérieur*, in Dutch taste, while peeking through the keyhole.

Villon's sympathies for the dregs of society, for everything suspect and criminal, are by no means an expression of his demonism. The shady company which he so quickly and intimately joined captivated his feminine nature with its abundance of passion, its powerful rhythm of life, which he could not find in other spheres of society. One ought to listen with what taste Villon tells in the "Ballade de la grosse Margot" about the profession of *souteneur* (pimp), to which he obviously was no stranger: "When clients come I grab the jug and run for wine." Neither waning feudalism nor the newly emergent bourgeoisie, with its tendency to Flemish headiness and importance, could provide an outlet for the immense dynamic ability stored and concentrated by some kind of miracle in this Parisian *clerc*. Dry and dark, eyebrowless, thin as a chimera, with a head that suggested according to his own testimony a husked and roasted nut, hiding his sword in the half-feminine dress of the student, Villon lived in Paris like a squirrel in a wheel, without knowing a moment's rest. He loved in himself the predatory lean little beast and cherished his own shabby little hide: "Is it not true, Granier, I did well that I appealed," he writes to his own prosecutor after having been spared the gallows; "it isn't every beast would know how to extricate himself that way." If Villon had been able to give his poetic credo, he undoubtedly would have exclaimed like Verlaine: "Du mouvement avant toute chose!"[3]

A powerful visionary, he dreams his own hanging on the eve of probable execution. But, strangely enough, with incomprehensible acrimony and rhythmic animation, he depicts in his ballad how the wind rocks the bodies of the unfortunate, to and fro, capriciously ... Even death he endows with dynamic qualities and even here he contrives to manifest his love for rhythm and movement ... I think it was not demonism that captivated Villon, but the dynamism of crime. For all I know there is an inverse relationship between the moral and the dynamic development of the soul. In any case, both the *Testaments* of Villon, the big and the little (that feast of magnificent rhythms the like of which French poetry had not previously known) are incurably amoral. Twice the pathetic vagabond writes his will, disposing of his imaginary property to the right and to the left, as a poet, ironically asserting his mastery over all the things that he wished to possess: if Villon's spiritual experiences, for all their originality, were not distinguished by any special depth, his human relationships, the tangled web of his acquaintances, links, calculations, formed a pattern of genial complexity. This man contrived to place himself in a vital, urgent relationship to an immense number of people of the most varied callings, from all levels of the social hierarchy, from thief to bishop, from bar girl to prince. With what pleasure he tells their little secrets! How precise and keen he is! Villon's *Testaments* are captivating if for no other reason than that such a mass of accurate information is communicated in them. It strikes the reader that he can use them, and he feels himself the poet's contemporary. The present moment can bear the weight of centuries, preserve its wholeness, and retain it "now." One only needs to know how to dig it out of the soil of time without damaging its roots—otherwise it will wither. Villon knew how to do this. The bell of the Sorbonne that interrupted his work on the *Petit Testament* sounds to this day.

Like the princes of the troubadours, Villon "sang in his own Latin." Once, as a scholar, he heard about Alcibiades—and, as a result, the unknown lady *Archipiade* joins the graceful procession of ladies of former times.

The Middle Ages hung on tight to its children and did not voluntarily relinquish them to the Renaissance. Authentic medieval blood flowed in the veins of Villon. To this he owed his integrity, his temperament, his spiritual originality. The physiology of the Gothic—there was such a thing, after all, and the Middle Ages were precisely a physiologically gifted epoch—substituted for a world view for Villon and rewarded him, and then some, for the absence of a traditional link with the past. Moreover it secured him a worthy place in the future, because nineteenth-century French poetry drew its strength from the very same national treasure house of Gothic. It will be said. what does the splendid rhythm of the *Testaments*, now tricky, like bilboquets, now slow, like a church cantilena, have in common with the craftsmanship of the Gothic builders? Yet isn't Gothic the triumph of dynamics? One more question: what is more mobile, more fluent, the Gothic cathedral or the oceanic surge? How if not by a sense of architectonics is that magical balance of stanzas to be explained in which Villon dedicates his soul to the Trinity by way of the Virgin in "Chambre de la divinité"— nine heavenly legions. This is no anemic flight on the little wax wings of immortality, but an architecturally based ascension, corresponding to the tiers of the Gothic cathedral. He who first proclaimed in architecture the mobile equilibrium of masses and built the crossed vault genially expressed the psychological essence of feudalism. The medieval man considered himself part of the world-building, as necessary and as constrained as any stone in the Gothic structure, bearing with dignity the pressure of his neighbors and entering as an inevitable stake into the general play of forces. To serve meant not only to be active for the common good. Unconsciously, the medieval man considered the bare fact of his existence as a service, as a kind of heroic deed. Villon, the last-born, epigone of the feudal world-sense, turned out to be unreceptive to its ethical side, to the sense of mutual commitment and guarantee! The steadfast, the moral in Gothic was quite foreign to him. On the other hand, to make up for that, by no means indifferent to its dynamics, he lifted it to the level of amoralism. Villon twice received pardons —*lettres de rémission*—from kings: Charles VII and Louis XI. He was firmly convinced that he would receive just such a letter from God, forgiving him all his sins. Perhaps in the spirit of his dry and rational mysticism he projected the ladder of feudal jurisdictions into infinity, and in his soul there dimly wandered a wild, but profoundly feudal insight, that there is a God beyond a God . . .

"I know well that I am not the son of an angel crowned by the diadem of a star or of another planet," said of himself that poor Parisian scholar, capable of much for the sake of a good supper.

Such negations are worth as much as positive certitude.

Uncollected Essays and Fragments

Pushkin & Scriabin (Fragments)

Pushkin and Scriabin[1] are two transmutations of a single sun, two transmutations of a single heart. Twice the death of an artist gathered the Russian people and kindled the sun over them. They served as an example of a collective Russian demise, they died a *full* death, as people are said to live a full life; their personality, while dying, extended itself to a symbol of the whole people, and the sun-heart of the dying remained forever at the zenith of suffering and glory.

I wish to speak of Scriabin's death as of the highest act of his creativity. It seems to me the artist's death ought not to be excluded from the chain of his creative achievements, but rather examined as the last conclusive link. From this wholly Christian point of view, Scriabin's death is amazing. It not only is remarkable as the fabulous posthumous growth of the artist in the eyes of the masses, but also serves as it were as the source of this creativity, as its teleological cause. If one were to tear the veil of death from this creative life, it would flow freely from its cause—that is, death—which disposes itself around it as if around its own proper sun, and absorbs its light.

Pushkin was buried at night. Was buried secretly.[2] The marble of St. Isaac's—that magnificent sarcophagus—never did receive as expected the solar body of the poet. At night they placed the sun in its coffin, and the runners of the sled that carried the poet's dust off to the funeral service squeaked in the January frost.

I recall the picture of the Pushkin funeral to evoke in your memory the image of a nighttime sun,[3] the image of the last Greek tragedy created by Euripides—a vision of the unfortunate Phaedra.

In the fateful hours of purification and storm, we have raised Scriabin aloft, whose sun-heart burns above us; yet alas! this is not the sun of redemption but the sun of guilt. Affirming Scriabin as her symbol at the time of the World War, Phaedra-Russia . . .

. . . Time can go backward: the whole course of our most recent history, which with terrific force has turned away from Christianity to Buddhism and theosophy, testifies to this . . .

There is no unity! "Worlds are many, all dispose themselves in their orbits, god reigns over god." What is this: hallucination or the end of Christianity?

There is no personality! "I"—it's a transient condition; you have many souls and many lives! What is this: hallucination or the end of Christianity?

There is no time! The Christian chronology is in danger, the frail ledger of the years of our era is lost—time tears backward with a roaring hum and a swoosh, like a blocked torrent—and the new Orpheus flings his lyre in the seething spume: there is no more art . . .

Scriabin is the next stage after Pushkin of Russian Hellenism, one more consistent disclosure of the Hellenistic nature of the Russian spirit. Scriabin's immense value for Russia and for Christianity was determined by the fact that he was a *raving Hellene.* Through him, Hellas entered into a blood relationship with the Russian sectarians who burned themselves in their coffins. In any case, he is much closer to them than to the Western theosophists. His chiliasm was a purely Russian passion for salvation; what there is of antiquity in him is the madness with which he expressed this passion.

. . . Christian art is always an action based on the great idea of redemption. It is an "imitation of Christ" infinitely various in its manifestations, an eternal return to the single creative act that began our historical era. Christian art is free. It is, in the full meaning of the phrase, "art for art's sake." No necessity of any kind, even the highest, clouds its bright inner freedom, for its prototype, that which it imitates, is the very redemption of the world by Christ. And so, not sacrifice, not redemption in art, but the free and joyful imitation of Christ—that is the keystone of Christian esthetics. Art cannot be a sacrifice, for a sacrifice has already been made; cannot be redemption, for the world along with the artist has already been redeemed. What then is left? A joyful commerce with the divine, like a game played by the Father with his children, a hide-and-seek of the spirit! The divine illusion of redemption, which is Christian art, is explained precisely by this game Divinity plays with us, permitting us to stray along the byways of mystery so that we would, as it were of ourselves, come upon salvation, having experienced catharsis, redemption in art. Christian artists are as it were the freedmen of the idea of redemption, rather than slaves, and they are not preachers. Our whole two-thousand-year-old culture, thanks to the miraculous mercy of Christianity, is the *world's release into free-dom* for the sake of play, for spiritual joy, for the free "imitation of Christ."

Christianity took its place and stood there in an absolutely free relationship to art, and this no human religion of any kind has been able to do either before or after it.

Nourishing art, giving art of its flesh, offering it in the way of a sturdy metaphysical foundation the most real fact of redemption, Christianity demanded nothing in return. Christian culture is there-fore not threatened by the danger of inner impoverishment. It is in-exhaustible, infinite, because, triumphing over time, again and again it condenses grace into magnificent clouds and lets it pour out in life-giving rain. One cannot be sufficiently emphatic in pointing out the fact that, for its character of eternal freshness and unfadingness, European culture is indebted to the mercy of Christianity in its rela-tionship to art.

Still unstudied is the realm of Christian dynamics—the spirit's activity in art as a free self-affirmation in the basic fact of redemp-tion—in particular, music.

In the ancient world music was considered a destructive element. The Hellenes feared flutes, considering Phrygian harmony danger-ous and seductive, and Terpander had to fight for each new string of the lyre with great effort. The untrusting attitude toward music as a dark and suspicious element was so strong that the state took music under its tutelage, declaring it a state monopoly, civic har-mony, eunomia. But even in this form, the Hellenes could not bring themselves to grant music its independence: the word seemed to them a necessary antidote, a loyal guard, a constant companion of music. The Hellenes did not know *pure* music, properly speaking— it belongs entirely to Christianity. The mountain lake of Christian music managed to hold out against enemy attacks only after that profound transformation that turned Hellas into Europe.

Christianity did not fear music. With a smile, the Christian world said to Dionysus: "Well, go ahead, give it a try; order your maenads to tear me apart: I am all wholeness, all personality, all welded unity!" This confidence that the new music has in the decisive triumph of personality, integral and unharmed, is as strong as that. This confidence in personal salvation—I would say—enters Christian music as an overtone, while working the coloration of Beethoven's sonority into the white marble of Sinai's glory.

Voice is personality. The piano is a siren. Scriabin's break with the voice, his great bewitchment with the siren of pianism, signals the loss of the Christian sense of personality, of the musical "I am." The wordless, strangely mute chorus of Prometheus goes on being the same seductive siren.

Beethoven's catholic joy, the synthesis of the Ninth Symphony, that "triumph of white glory," is inaccessible to Scriabin. In this sense he broke away from Christian music and went his own way . . .

The spirit of Greek tragedy has awakened in music. Music has completed its cycle and returned from whence it came: once again, Phaedra calls out to the nurse, once again Antigone demands libation and burial for the beloved body of her brother.

Something has happened to music, some sort of wind has swooped down and broken the dry and sonorous rushes. We demand a choir; the murmur of the thinking reed has begun to bore us. . . . For a long, long time we played with music, without suspecting the danger that lurks in it, and while (perhaps from boredom) we were inventing a myth not invented but born, foam-born, purple-born, of imperial origin, the legitimate heir of the myths of antiquity— the myth of forgotten Christianity.

. . . of the vineyards of the old Dionysus: I seem to see the closed eyes and the light, triumphant, small head, tilted slightly upward. This is the muse of remembering—the lightfoot Mnemosyne, senior in the circle of the dance. From her light, fragile face, the mask of oblivion falls, her features smooth out; memory triumphs, though it be at the cost of death: to die means to remember, to remember means to die. . . . To remember no matter what it might entail! To fight oblivion, even to the death: that is Scriabin's motto, that is the heroic tendency of his art! In this sense I said Scriabin's death was the highest act of his creativity, that it showers him with a blinding and unexpected light.

. . . finished—was in full swing. Anyone who feels himself a Hellene must be on his guard now as two thousand years ago. You can't Hellenize the world once and for all the way you can repaint a house. The Christian world is an organism, a living body. The tissues of our world are renewed by death. We have to struggle with the barbarism of a new life, because there, in the new life which

is in full bloom, death is unvanquished! While death exists in the
world Hellenism *will be*, because Christianity *Hellenizes death*. . . .
The Hellenic, fructified by death, is just what Christianity is. The
seed of death, having fallen on the soil of Hellas, burst miraculously
into bloom: our whole culture has grown from this very seed; we
keep the ledger of the years from that moment when the land of
Hellas accepted it. Everything Roman is sterile, because the soil
of Rome is stony, because Rome is Hellas deprived of grace.

Scriabin's art has a direct relationship to that historical task of
Christianity that I call the Hellenization of death, and through this
receives its profound meaning.

. . . there is music—it contains in itself the atoms of our being. To
the degree that melody in its pure form corresponds to the unique
feeling of personality as Hellas knew it, so harmony is characteristic of the complex post-Christian sense of "I." Harmony was a
sort of forbidden fruit for the world as yet not implicated in the
Fall. The metaphysical essence of harmony is in the narrowest sense
connected with the Christian concept of time. Harmony is crystallized eternity, it is all in a cross section of time, in that section of
time that knows only Christianity. . . . the mystics energetically
reject eternity in time, while accepting this cross section available
only to the righteous, while affirming eternity—a Kantian category
cloven by the sword of the seraph. The center of gravity of Scriabin's music lies in harmony: harmonic architectonics.

The Morning of Acmeism

I.

Amidst the immense emotional excitement surrounding works of art, it is desirable that talk about art be marked by the greatest restraint. For the immense majority, a work of art is enticing only insofar as it illuminates the artist's perception of the world. For the artist, however, his perception of the world is a tool and an instrument, like a hammer in the hands of a stonemason, and the only thing that is real is the work itself.

To live is the artist's highest self-esteem. He wants no other paradise than being, and when he's told about reality, he only smiles bitterly, because he knows the infinitely more convincing reality of art. The spectacle of a mathematician proclaiming the square of a ten-digit number without stopping to think about it fills us with a certain astonishment. Too often, however, we overlook the fact that the poet raises a phenomenon to its tenth power, and the modest exterior of a work of art often deceives us concerning the prodigiously condensed reality that it possesses. In poetry this reality is the word as such. Just now, for example, while expressing my thought as accurately as possible, yet not at all in poetic form, I am speaking essentially with the consciousness, not with the word. Deaf-mutes understand one another very well, and railroad signals perform their quite complicated assignments without recourse to help from the word. Thus, if one is to regard the sense as the content, one must regard everything else in the word as mechanical ballast that only impedes the swift transmission of the thought. The "word as such" was slow to be born. Gradually, one after the other, all the elements of the word were drawn into the concept of form; only the conscious sense, the Logos, is regarded even to this day erroneously and arbitrarily as the content. From this needless honor, Logos only loses; Logos requires only an equal footing with the other elements of the word. Our Futurist, who could not cope with the conscious sense as creative material, frivolously threw it overboard and in essence repeated the same crude error as his predecessors.

For the Acmeists the conscious sense of the word, the Logos, is just as splendid a form as music for the Symbolists.

And if, among the Futurists, the word as such still crawls on all fours, in Acmeism it has for the first time assumed the more dignified upright position and entered upon the Stone Age of its existence.

II.

The cutting edge of Acmeism is not the stiletto and not the pinprick of Decadence. Acmeism is for those who, seized by the spirit of building, do not meekly renounce their gravity, but joyfully accept it in order to arouse and make use of the forces architecturally dormant in it. The architect says: I build. That means, I am right. The consciousness of our own rightness is what we value most in poetry, and scornfully discarding the pick-up-sticks of the Futurists, for whom there is no higher pleasure than to hook a tough word with a crochet hook, we are introducing the Gothic into the relationships of words, just as Sebastian Bach established it in music.

What kind of idiot would agree to build if he did not believe in the reality of his material, the resistance of which he must overcome? A cobblestone in the hands of an architect is transformed into substance, and the man for whom the sound of a chisel splitting stone is not a metaphysical proof was not born to build. Vladimir Soloviev used to experience a special kind of prophetic horror before gray Finnish boulders. The mute eloquence of the granite block disturbed him like an evil enchantment. But Tiutchev's stone that "rolled down from the mountain to the valley floor, torn loose itself, or flung by a sentient hand," is the word. The voice of matter sounds in this unexpected fall like articulate speech. To this call one can answer only with architecture. Reverently the Acmeists pick up the mysterious Tiutchevan stone and lay it in the foundation of their building.

The stone thirsted as it were for another being. It was itself the discoverer of the dynamic potential concealed within it, as if it were asking to be let into the "groined arch" to participate in the joyous cooperative action of its fellows.

III.

The Symbolists were bad stay-at-homes. They loved voyages; yet they felt bad, ill at ease, in the cage of their own organisms and in that universal cage which Kant constructed with the help of his categories.

The first condition for building successfully is a genuine piety before the three dimensions of space—to look on the world not as a burden or as an unfortunate accident, but as a God-given palace. Really, what is one to say about an ungrateful guest who lives off his host, takes advantage of his hospitality, yet all the while despises him in his soul and thinks only of how to put something over on him. One can build only in the name of the "three dimensions," because they are the conditions for all architecture. That is why an architect has to be a good stay-at-home, and the Symbolists were bad architects. To build means to fight against emptiness, to hypnotize space. The fine arrow of the Gothic belltower is angry, because the whole idea of it is to stab the sky, to reproach it for being empty.

IV.

We tacitly understand a man's individuality, that which makes him a person, and that which forms part of the far more significant concept of the organism. Acmeists share a love for the organism and for organization with the Middle Ages, a period of physiological genius. In its pursuit of refinement the nineteenth century lost the secret of genuine complexity. That which in the thirteenth century seemed a logical development of the concept of the organism—the Gothic cathedral—now has the esthetic effect of something monstrous; Notre Dame is a celebration of physiology, its Dionysian orgy. We do not wish to divert ourselves with a stroll in a "forest of symbols," because we have a more virgin, a denser forest—divine physiology, the infinite complexity of our own dark organism.

The Middle Ages, while defining man's specific gravity in its own way, felt and acknowledged it for each individual quite independently of his merits. The title *maître* was used readily and without hesitation. The most humble artisan, the very least clerk, possessed the secret of down-to-earth respect, of the devout dignity so characteristic of that epoch. Yes, Europe passed through the labyrinth of a fine tracery-work culture, when abstract being, unadorned personal existence, was valued as a heroic feat. Hence the aristocratic intimacy that links all people, so alien in spirit to the "equality and fraternity" of the Great Revolution. There is no equality, no competition—there is the complicity of those united in a conspiracy against emptiness and nonbeing.

Love the existence of the thing more than the thing itself and your own being more than yourself—that is the highest commandment of Acmeism.

v.

A = A: what a splendid poetic theme. Symbolism languished and longed for the law of identity; Acmeism makes it its watchword and offers it instead of the dubious *a realibus ad realiora.**

The capacity for astonishment is the poet's greatest virtue. Still, how can one not be astonished by that most fruitful of all laws, the law of identity? Whoever has been seized with reverent astonishment before this law is undoubtedly a poet. Thus, once having acknowledged the sovereignty of the law of identity, poetry acquires in lifelong feudal possession all that exists, without condition or limitation. Logic is the kingdom of the unexpected. To think logically means to be perpetually astonished. We have fallen in love with the music of proof. For us logical connection is not some little ditty about a finch, but a symphony with organ and choir, so intricate and inspired that the conductor must exert all his powers to keep the performers under his control.

How persuasive is the music of Bach! What power of proof! One must demonstrate proof, one must go on demonstrating proof endlessly: to accept anything in art on faith alone is unworthy of an artist, easy and tiresome . . . We do not fly; we ascend only such towers as we ourselves are able to build.

---

* Symbolism's slogan, as provided by Viacheslav Ivanov in the collective work *Borozdy i mezhi* [Furrows and boundaries]. (Mandelstam's note.) Slogan means "from the real to the more real."

VI.

The Middle Ages are dear to us because they possessed to a high
degree the sense of boundary and partition. They never mixed different levels, and they treated the beyond with immense restraint. A
noble mixture of rationality and mysticism and the perception of the
world as a living equilibrium makes us kin to this epoch and impels
us to derive strength from works that arose on Romance soil around
the year 1200. And we shall demonstrate our rightness in such a
way that the whole chain of causes and consequences from alpha to
omega will shudder in response; we shall teach ourselves to carry
"more lightly and more freely the mobile chains of being."

Literary Moscow

Moscow-Peking: here it is continentality that triumphs, the spirit of a Middle Empire; here the heavy tracks of the railroads have been spliced together into a tight knot; here the Eurasian continent celebrates its eternal name day.

Whoever isn't bored by Middle Empire is a welcome guest in Moscow. There are some who prefer sea-smell and some who prefer world-smell.

Here the cabdrivers drink tea in the taverns as if they were Greek philosophers; here, on the flat roof of a modest skyscraper, they show nightly an American detective drama; here, without attracting anybody's attention, a decorous young man on the boulevard whistles a complex aria from *Tannhäuser* in order to earn his bread, and in half an hour an artist of the old school, sitting on a park bench, will do your portrait for you on a silver academic medal; here the boys selling cigarettes travel in packs, like the dogs of Constantinople, and do not fear competition; people from Iaroslav are selling pastries, and people from the Caucasus have sat down in the coolness of the delicatessen. There isn't a single man here, provided he's not a member of the all-Russian union of writers, who would go to a literary discussion in the summertime, and Dolidze,[1] at least for the summer, moves in spirit to Azurketa, where he's been planning to move these past twelve years.

When Mayakovsky went about scouring poets in alphabetical order at the Polytechnic Museum, there were some young people in the auditorium who actually volunteered to read their own poems when their turn came, to make Mayakovsky's job easier. This is possible only in Moscow and nowhere else in the world; only here are there people who, like Shiites, are ready to prostrate themselves so that the chariot of that stentorian voice might pass over them.

In Moscow, Khlebnikov could hide himself from human eyes, like a beast of the forest, and, without even being noticed, he exchanged the hard beds of the Moscow flophouses for a green Novgorodian grave. And yet it was in Moscow, too, that I. A. Aksenov, when that happened, in the most modest of modest literary gatherings, placed a beautiful wreath of analytical criticism on the grave of the departed great archaic poet, illuminating Khlebnikov's archaicism by means of Einstein's principle of relativity and revealing the link between his creative work and the old Russian moral ideal of the sixteenth and seventeenth centuries. And this was at the very time that the enlightened Petersburg *Literary Messenger* could respond at best with an insipid, arrogant remark about the "great loss." From out of town, with a different perspective, one can see more easily: all is not well with Petersburg; it has forgotten how to speak in the language of time and wild honey.

As far as Moscow is concerned, the saddest symptom is the pious needlework of Marina Tsvetaeva,[2] who seems to echo the dubious solemnity of the Petersburg poetess Anna Radlova.[3] The worst thing about Literary Moscow is women's poetry. The experience of the last years has shown that the only woman who has entered the circle of poetry with the rights of a new muse is the Russian study of poetry called to life by Potebnia[4] and Andrei Biely and nourished to maturity in the formalist school of Eikhenbaum, Zhirmunsky, and Shklovsky.[5] To the lot of women has fallen the enormous realm of parody, in the most serious and formal sense of this word. Feminine poetry is an unconscious parody of poetic inventiveness as well as of reminiscence. The majority of Muscovite poetesses are bruised by metaphor. These are poor Isises, doomed to an eternal seeking for the second part of the poetic comparison which has been lost somewhere, and which must return its primal unity to the poetic image, to Osiris.

Adalis[6] and Marina Tsvetaeva are prophetesses, and so is Sophie Parnok.[7] Prophecy, as domestic needlework. While the formerly elevated tone of masculine poetry, the intolerable bombastic rhetoric, has given way to a more normal conversational pitch, feminine poetry continues to vibrate on the highest notes, offending the ear, offending the historical, the poetic sense. The tastelessness and the historical insincerity of Marina Tsvetaeva's poems about Russia—pseudonational and pseudo-Muscovite—are immeasurably beneath the poems of Adalis, whose voice now and again acquires a masculine force and certainty.

Inventiveness and remembrance go hand in hand in poetry. To remember means also to invent. He who remembers is also an inventor. The radical illness of Moscow's literary taste lies in forgetting this double truth. Moscow has been specializing in inventiveness, no matter what.

Poetry breathes through both the mouth and the nose, through remembrance and inventiveness. One needs to be a fakir in order

to deny oneself one of these modes of breathing. The passion for
poetic breathing by way of remembrance was expressed in that
heightened interest with which Moscow greeted Khodasevich's[8]
arrival. He is a man who's been writing verses for about twenty-five
years now, thank God; yet he has suddenly found himself in the
position of a young poet just beginning.

As from the Taganka to the Pliushchikha, literary Moscow spread
out enormously from MAF to the Lyrical Circle.[9] At one end, something like inventiveness; at the other, remembrance. Mayakovsky,
Kruchenykh,[10] Aseev on the one side; on the other, given the complete absence of domestic resources, there was a need to resort to
visiting players from Petersburg in order to draw the line. And so
one needn't talk about the Lyrical Circle as though it were a Muscovite phenomenon.

What, then, goes on in the camp of pure inventiveness? Here, if
one leaves out the completely unsound and unintelligible Kruchenykh—and I say this, not because he's left-wing or extreme, but
because there is after all such a thing in the world as simple nonsense . . . (And yet, Kruchenykh's attitude to poetry is passionate and
very intense, and this makes him interesting as a personality.) Here
Mayakovsky goes on resolving the great, elementary problem of
"poetry for all, not just for the elite." An extensive broadening of
the space contiguous to poetry naturally takes place at the expense of
intensivity, pithiness, poetic culture. Splendidly informed about the
richness and complexity of world poetry, Mayakovsky, in founding
his "poetry for all," had to send everything obscure to the devil;
everything, that is, that assumed the least bit of poetic preparation in
his audience. And yet to address in verse an audience completely
unprepared poetically is as thankless a task as trying to sit on a pike.
The completely unprepared audience will grasp absolutely nothing,
or else poetry, emancipated from culture of any kind, will quite
cease to be poetry, and then, due to some strange quality in human
nature, will become accessible to an enormous audience indeed. Yet
Mayakovsky writes poetry, and quite cultivated poetry: that is, his
refined *raeshnik*, whose stanza is broken by a weighty antithesis,
saturated with hyperbolic metaphors and sustained in the monotonous brief *pauznik*.* It is therefore quite in vain that Mayakovsky

---

* The *raeshnik* is a verse form deriving from the country-fair side-show
barker, who used to call attention to his show by spouting rhymes. The
pauznik is a meter, usually of three feet, with an unequal number of un-
stressed syllables between the stressed syllables; i.e., with pauses.

impoverished himself. He is threatened with the danger of becoming a poetess, and it has already half come to pass.

If Mayakovsky's poems express the tendency toward universal accessibility, what speaks out in Aseev's[11] is our time's passion for organization. The brilliant rational imagery of his language produces the impression of something freshly mobilized. There is essentially no difference between the snuffbox poetry of the eighteenth century and Aseev's twentieth-century mechanical poetry. A sentimental rationalism on the one hand, an organizational rationalism on the other. A purely rationalistic, electro-mechanical, radioactive, and in general technological poetry is impossible, for a single reason that should be equally close to the poet and the mechanic: rationalistic mechanical poetry does not store up energy, gives it no increment, as natural irrational poetry does; but only spends, only disperses it. The discharge is equal to the windup. As much comes out as is wound up. A mainspring cannot give back more than has been put into it beforehand. This is why Aseev's rationalistic poetry is not rational, why it is sterile and sexless. A machine lives a deep and animated life, but it gives forth no seed.

By now the passion for inventiveness in poetic Moscow is already passing. All the patents have already been taken out, and there have been no new patents for some time. The double truth of inventiveness and remembrance is as much needed as bread. That is why in Moscow there is not a single real poetic school, not a single lively poetic circle, for all the factions somehow find themselves on one side or the other of a divided truth.

Inventiveness and remembrance are the two elements by which the poetry of B. Pasternak is moved. Let us hope that his poems will be studied in the immediate future, and that they will not suffer the mass of lyrical stupidities (inflicted by our critics) that has befallen all Russian poets, beginning with Blok.

World cities like Paris, Moscow, London are amazingly tactful in their relationship to literature, permitting it to hide in any trench, to disappear without trace, to live without a permit, or under another name, or not to have an address. It is as absurd to talk of Muscovite literature as it is of a world literature. The first exists only in the imagination of the reviewer, just as the second exists only in the name of a worthy Petersburg publishing house. To the man who has not been forewarned, it might seem that there is no literature at all in Moscow. If he should accidentally meet a poet, the latter would wave his hands and look as though he were in a terrible hurry to be off somewhere, and he would disappear through the green gates of the boulevard accompanied by the blessings of the cigarette boys, who know better than anyone else how to estimate the value of a man and how to bring out in him the most remote possibilities.

Literary Moscow: Birth of the *Fabula*

I.

Once upon a time the monks in their chill Gothic refectories ate more or less lenten fare, while listening to a reader, to the accompaniment of a prose that was quite good for its time, from the book of *Chet'i-Minei.** It was read aloud, not only for instruction; the reading was added to the refectory as table music, and, freshening the heads of those who dined, the seasoning provided by the reader supported the harmony and orderliness at the common table.

But imagine, if you will, almost any social group, the most enlightened, the most modern, wishing to renew the custom of reading aloud at table and inviting a reader; and this reader, wishing to please everybody, brings along Andrei Biely's *St. Petersburg* and he reads it to the group. Well, he begins. The results are incredible. Somebody has something stuck in his throat; somebody else is eating his fish with his knife; a third person burns himself swallowing the mustard.

It is impossible to imagine such an occasion, such an event, such a group occasion, to which Andrei Biely's prose might conceivably serve as an accompaniment. Its rhythmic periods are reckoned on the scale of a Methusalean age; incompatible with any kind of human activity. The tales of Scheherazade, on the other hand, were measured to 366 days, one for every night of a Leap Year, and the *Decameron* befriended the calendar, attentive to the shifting of day and night. Why mention the *Decameron*! Dostoevsky makes excellent table reading; well, if not just yet, then he will in the very near future, when, instead of weeping over him and being moved by him, as chambermaids are touched by Balzac and by good cheap novels, people will apprehend him in a purely literary way, and then for the first time they will have read and understood him.

Extracting pyramids from your own depths is an indigestible, unsociable activity; it is a stomach probe. It's not entertainment, but a surgical operation. From the time that the plague of psychological

Note: See footnote, p. 85.
* Book of saints' lives and similar edifying reading, divided according to the calendar. (Title Slavonicized from the Greek.)

experimentation penetrated literary consciousness, the prose writer has become a surgeon and prose a clinical catastrophe, to our taste quite unpleasant; and a thousand times I'll drop the belletristic psychologizing of Andreev, Gorky, Shmelev, Sergeev-Tsensky, Zamiatin,[1] for the sake of the magnificent Bret Harte in the translation of an unknown student of the nineties: "Without saying a word, with a single motion of hand and foot, he flung him from the staircase and turned very calmly to the unknown lady."

Where is that student now? I'm afraid he is unjustly ashamed of his literary past and in his leisure hours places himself at the disposal of the psychologist-authors to be vivisected, though now it's no longer the clumsy ones from the clinic of *The Miscellanies of Knowledge*,[2] where the least operation, the extraction of the tooth of a member of the intelligentsia, threatened blood poisoning, but rather the excellent surgeons of Andrei Biely's polyclinic, equipped with all the resources of antiseptic Impressionism.

II.

Merimée's *Carmen* ends with a philological discussion about where in the family of languages the gypsy dialect belongs. The highest tension of mood and plot is unexpectedly resolved by a philological tract; yet it sounds approximately like the epode of a tragic chorus: "And everywhere there are ill-fated passions, and against the fates is no defense." This happened before Pushkin.

Why should we then be especially surprised if Pilniak[3] or the Serapions[4] introduce notebooks into their narration, building estimates, Soviet circulars, newspaper advertisements, excerpts from chronicles, and God knows what else. Prose belongs to nobody. It is essentially anonymous. It is the organized motion of a verbal mass cemented together by whatever comes to hand. The basic element of prose is accumulation. It is all fabrication, morphology.

Our current prose writers are often called eclectics; that is, collectors. I think this is not meant as an insult; it's a good thing. Every real prose writer is precisely an eclectic, a collector. Personality to the side, make way for anonymous prose. This is why the names of the great prose writers, those contractors of grandiose literary plans, anonymous in essence, collective in execution, like Rabelais' *Gargantua* and *Pantagruel* or *War and Peace*, are transformed into legend and myth.

In Russia, this passion for anonymous, collective prose coincided with the Revolution. Poetry itself demanded prose. It had lost all sense of scale—because there was no prose. It achieved an unhealthy flowering and could not satisfy the demands of the reader to be given access to the pure and direct activity of verbal masses, bypassing the author's personality, bypassing everything that is incidental, personal, and causes suffering (the lyric).

Just why is it that the Revolution turned out to be propitious for the renaissance of Russian prose? Precisely for the reason that it advanced the type of anonymous prose writer, the eclectic, the collector, who does not create verbal pyramids from the depths of his own spirit, the modest Pharaonic overseer who supervises the slow but true construction of real pyramids.

III.

Russian prose will begin its advance when the first prosewriter appears who is independent of Andrei Biely. Andrei Biely is the peak of Russian psychological prose. He soared to the top with astonishing energy; yet with his high-flown and varied devices he merely completed the spadework of his predecessors, the so-called belletrists.

Can it be that his pupils, the Serapion Brothers and Pilniak, are returning to the bosom of belles-lettres, closing in this way a cycle of rotations, and that all that remains for us now is to wait for the reappearance of the *Miscellanies of Knowledge*, where psychology and *byt** will re-engender the old novel, the novel of the convict with the wheelbarrow?

As soon as the *fabula* disappeared, *byt* appeared in exchange. Earlier, Jourdain had not surmised that he was speaking prose; earlier, people did not know there was *byt*.

Byt is dead *fabula*; it is a decomposing plot, a convict's wheelbarrow which psychology drags after itself, because after all it needs to lean on something, on a dead *fabula* if there isn't a living one. *Byt* is a foreignism, the always falsely exotic; to the eyes of those

* A word that has no precise equivalent in English. "Way of life," "mores," but assuming that these form a discernible pattern. A literary genre that emphasizes the way of life of a society or a segment of society as expressed in daily life, the ordinary, the quotidian, the daily round.

who live in the same house it does not exist: the native knows how to notice only what is needed, what is to the point, but to the tourist, the foreigner (the belletrist) it's another matter. He stares at everything and keeps talking about everything, inopportunely.

Our present Russian prose writers, like the Serapions and Pilniak, are just as much psychologists as their predecessors were before the Revolution, before Andrei Biely. They have no *fabula*. They do not lend themselves to being read aloud at table. Only their psychology is chained to another convict's wheelbarrow—not to *byt*, but to folklore. I'd like to speak in more detail about just what difference this makes, because the watershed between *byt* and folklore is a serious matter. They are not at all one and the same thing. Folklore is a better brand. Higher quality.

Byt is a kind of night-blindness to things. Folklore is a conscious strengthening, an accumulation of linguistic and ethnographic material. *Byt* is the deadening of plot; folklore is the birth of plot. Listen intently to folklore and you will hear how thematic life stirs there, how the *fabula* breathes, and, in any folkloric entry, the *fabula* is present in embryo; here interest begins, here everything is fraught with the *fabula*, flirts, intrigues, and threatens with it. The brood hen sits on a heap of straw and clucks and cackles; the folkloric prose writer clucks and cackles about something, too, and whoever has a taste for it listens to him. In actual fact, he's doing something worth doing—he's hatching the *fabula*.

The Serapions and Pilniak (their older brother, and he needn't be set apart from them) cannot please the serious reader; they are suspect because of their use of the anecdote; that is to say, they threaten with the *fabula*. Of the real *fabula*—that is, of deep narrative breathing—there is not a trace; but the anecdote tickles with its whiskers through every crack, quite as in Khlebnikov.

> Winging with the goldletter of most delicate veins
> The grasshopper stowed into the belly of the basket
> A multitude of varied grasses and faiths.

"A multitude of varied grasses and faiths," is what Pilniak, Nikitin, Fedin, Kozyrev and others, and Lidin (another Serapion not initiated into the brotherhood for some reason) and Zamiatin and Prishvin have.[5] The beloved anecdote, the first free and joyful fluttering of the *fabula*, emancipation of the spirit from the melancholy monk's cowl of psychology.

IV.

Meanwhile, let us dig in. Folklore is coming at us like a voracious caterpillar. In teeming locust swarms, jottings, notes, remarks, sayings, quotation marks, small talk, observations come crawling. A great gypsy-moth invasion, threat to cropped field. Thus, in literature, the turn of the *fabula* and folklore is legitimized, and folklore gives birth to *fabula*, as the voracious caterpillar gives birth to the delicate moth. If we did not notice this change earlier, it was because folklore was not trying to consolidate itself and tended to disappear without a trace. But as a period of accumulation, a period of voracious invasion, the folklore period preceded the flowering of any kind of *fabula*. And since it did not aspire to literature, not having been labeled as such, it remained within the contents of private letters, within the tradition of home-grown storytellers, in only partly published journals and memoirs, in petitions and chancery messages, in juridical protocols and in placards.

There may be some people (who knows?) who actually *like* those discourses of Pilniak, which are like the ones Leskov[6] placed on the lips of his first railroad conversationalists, who were whiling away the boredom of the not-too-rapid transport. In all of Pilniak, however, I much prefer the epic conversation in the bathhouse, of the deacon with a certain Draube, on the theme of what sense the universe makes: there, you won't find a single strophe beginning with "something," nor a single lyrical simile, intolerable in prose, but the elementary play of the *fabula* being born, as, you will recall, in Gogol, approaching Pliushkin's, you can't at first distinguish "whether it's a man or a woman; no, it's a woman; no, a man."

At the same time as the folklore line in prose, the purely *byt* line goes on to this day. One should overlook all the differences that characterize the Serapions, Pilniak, Zamiatin, Prishvin, Kozyrev, and Nikitin, because of the common badge of folklore by which they are united, their pledge of vitality. As the legitimate children of folklore they all slip into using anecdote. The only one who absolutely does not slip into anecdote is Vsevolod Ivanov,[7] and what I said above about *byt* relates to him.

If you listen attentively to prose at a time when folklore flourishes, you will hear something that resembles the rich ringing of grasshoppers coupling in the air. This is the universal sound of contemporary Russian prose, and I don't wish to take this ringing sound apart, since it was not invented by the clockmaker, since it is com-

posed of an incalculable multitude of winging grasses and faiths. In
the period inevitably ensuing, in the period of the flourishing *fabula*,
with these multitudes thick upon each other, the voices of the grasshoppers will be transformed into the sonorous singing of the skylark—of the *fabula*, and then the skylark's high notes will ring out,
of which the poet said:

> Fluent, frisky, sonorous, clear—
> He has shaken me to the depth of my soul.

Storm & Stress

From this time on, readers will no longer perceive the body of Russian poetry of the first quarter of the twentieth century as "Modernism," with all the ambiguity and semicontempt inherent in the conception, but simply as Russian poetry. What has taken place is what one might call the welding together of the backbone of two poetic systems, two poetic epochs.

The Russian reader, who has lived through not one but several poetic revolutions during this quarter of a century, has learned to seize, more or less immediately, on what is objectively valuable in the multiformity of the poetic creation surrounding him. Every new literary school—be it Romanticism, Symbolism, or Futurism—comes to us artificially inflated as it were, exaggerating its own exclusive significance, while failing to be aware of its external historical limitations. It passes inevitably through a period of "Storm and Stress." Only subsequently, usually when the main proponents of the school have already lost their freshness and their capacity for work, does it become clear what its real place in literature is, and what objective value it created. And after the high-water mark of Storm and Stress, the literary flood tide willy-nilly subsides to its natural channel, and it is precisely these incomparably more modest boundaries and outlines that are remembered ever after. Russian poetry of the first quarter of the century twice lived through a harshly expressed period of Storm and Stress. One was Symbolism, the other Futurism. Both major currents wanted to freeze at the crest of their wave, and failed to do so; because history, preparing the crests of new waves, authoritatively ordered them, at the designated time, to recede, to return to the lap of the common maternal element of language and poetry. However, in their poetic development, Symbolism and Futurism, which complemented each other historically, were essentially of quite different types. Symbolism's "Storm and Stress" should be seen as a stormy and fiery process of making European and world poetry accessible to Russian literature. And so this stormy phenomenon had essentially an outward cultural meaning. Early Russian Symbolism was a very powerful blast of air from the West. Russian Futurism is much closer to Romanticism. It contains all the traits of a national

poetic revival, in the course of which its reworking of the national
treasury of language and of a deep native poetic tradition once more
brings it closer to Romanticism, unlike the alien nature of Russian
Symbolism, which had been a *Kulturträger*, a hauler of poetic culture from one base to another. Following this essential distinction
between Symbolism and Futurism, the former may be cited as an
example of outward, the latter of inward striving. Symbolism hinged
on a passion for great themes of a cosmic and metaphysical nature.
Early Russian Symbolism is the realm of Great Themes and Big
Ideas, with a capital letter, borrowed directly from Baudelaire, Edgar
Poe, Mallarmé, Swinburne, Shelley, and others. Futurism for the
most part lived by the poetic device, and developed not the theme
but the device; that is, something internal, innate in language.
Among the Symbolists, the theme was brandished like a shield pro-
tecting the device. The themes of the early Briusov, Balmont, and
others were extremely distinct. Among the Futurists it is difficult to
separate the theme from the device, and the inexperienced eye will
see in, say, the works of Khlebnikov, nothing more than pure device
or naked metalogic.

It is easier to sum up the Symbolist period than the Futurist, because the latter has not come to so distinct an end and was not so
abruptly broken off as Symbolism, which was extinguished by hostile
influences. Almost imperceptibly Futurism has renounced the ex-
cesses of its Storm and Stress period. It has continued to elaborate,
in the spirit of the common history of the language and our poetry,
those of its elements that have turned out to be of objective value.
To sum up Symbolism is relatively easy. Of the early stage of Symbolism, swollen and afflicted with the dropsy of great themes, almost
nothing remains. Balmont's grandiose cosmic hymns have turned out
childishly weak and inept in poetic practice. The renowned urbanism
of Briusov, who entered poetry as the singer of the universal city,
has dimmed with time, since Briusov's phonic and imagistic material
seemed to be anything but inherent in his favorite theme. Andrei
Biely's transcendental poetry turned out not to be up to preventing
its metaphysical meaning from losing the sheen of its fashionable-
ness and becoming a bit of a ruin. The complex Byzantine-Hellenic
world of Viacheslav Ivanov presents a somewhat better case. While
he was essentially as much the pioneer and colonizer as the other
Symbolists, he did not treat Byzantium and Hellas as foreign countries marked for conquest, but rightly saw in them the cultural
sources of Russian poetry. Due, however, to the lack of a sense of

measure, characteristic of all the Symbolists, he overfreighted his
poetry with Byzantine-Hellenic images and myths, which signifi-
cantly cheapened it. About Sologub and Annensky one ought to
speak separately, since they never participated in the Storm and
Stress of Symbolism. Blok's poetic fate is most tightly bound to
Russian poetry of the nineteenth century, and so one must speak
separately about him, too. And here one has to mention the work of
the younger Symbolists, or Acmeists, who wished not to repeat the
mistakes of early Symbolism, swollen with its dropsy of great themes.
Estimating their powers much more soberly, they renounced the illu-
sions of grandeur of early Symbolism and replaced them, some with
monumentality of device, others with clarity of exposition, with far
from equal success.

No single poetic heritage has ever aged and deteriorated in such
a short time as Symbolism. It would even be more correct to call
Russian Symbolism a pseudosymbolism, to call attention to its misuse
of great themes and abstract conceptions, inadequately embodied in
its language. The pseudosymbolic, that is, a large part of what the
Symbolists wrote, preserves for the history of literature only a relative interest. That which has some objective value lies hidden under
heaps of stage props and pseudosymbolist rubbish. What was the
hardest-working and noblest generation of Russian poets paid a
heavy tribute to the age in which they lived and their cultural task.
Let us begin with the father of Russian Symbolism, Balmont. Strikingly little of Balmont has survived; a dozen poems perhaps.
That which has survived, however, is truly superb: both in its
phonetic brilliance and its deep sense of roots and sounds, it bears
comparison with the best examples of metalogical poetry. It isn't
Balmont's fault that his undemanding readers turned the development of his poetry in the worst possible direction. In his best poems
—"O night, stay with me" [O noch', pobud' so mnoi"] and "The
Old House" ["Staryi dom"]—he extracted from the medium of
Russian verse new and never-to-be-repeated sounds of a foreign,
almost a kind of seraphic, phonetics. For us, this is explained by the
special phonetic quality of Balmont, by his exotic perception of consonant sounds. It is here rather than in his vulgar musicality that the
source of his poetic power is to be found. In Briusov's best (non-
urban) poems, one feature, making him the most consistent and able
of Russian Symbolists, will never fade with age. This is his capacity
to approach his theme, his total authority over it, his capacity to draw
from it all it can and must give, to exhaust it completely, to find for
it a correct and capacious stanzaic vessel. His best poems are models

of absolute mastery over the theme: "Orpheus and Eurydice," "Theseus and Ariadne," "The Demon of Suicide" ["Demon samoubistva"]. Briusov taught Russian poets to respect the theme as such. There is also something to be learned from his latest books: *Distances* [*Dali*] and *Last Dreams* [*Poslednye mechty*]. Here he provides examples of the breadth of his verse and of his astonishing capacity to deploy thought-filled words of varied imagery in a space of frugal dimension. In *The Urn* [*Urna*] Andrei Biely enriched the Russian lyric with sharp prosaisms from the German metaphysical vocabulary, displaying the ironical sound of philosophic terms. In his book *Ashes* [*Pepel*] he skillfully introduces polyphony, that is, many voices, into Nekrasov's poetry, the themes of which are subjected to an original orchestration. Biely's musical populism is reduced to a gesture of beggarlike plasticity that accompanies the immense musical theme. Viacheslav Ivanov is more genuinely native and in the future will be more accessible than all the other Russian Symbolists. A large part of the fascination for his majestic manner stems from our philological ignorance. In no other Symbolist poet does one hear so distinctly the hum of his lexicon, the powerful clamor of popular speech surging forward and waiting its turn like a bell: "Mute night, deaf night" ["Noch' nemaia, noch' glukhaia"], "The Maenad" ["Menada"], etc. His apprehension of the past as the future relates him to Khlebnikov. Viacheslav Ivanov's archaism stems not from his choice of themes, but from his incapacity to think in relative terms, that is, to compare different periods. Viacheslav Ivanov's Hellenic poetry was not written after or at the same time as Greek poetry, but before it, because not for one moment does he forget that he is speaking in his own barbarous native tongue.

These were the founders of Russian Symbolism. None of them worked in vain. In each of them there is something to be learnt at the present moment, or at any moment you like. Let us turn to those contemporaries of theirs on whom fell the bitter lot of avoiding the historical mistakes of their kindred but at the price of exclusion from the invigorating riot of the first Symbolist feasts. Let us turn to Sologub and Annensky.

Sologub and Annensky began their work as early as the nineties, completely unnoticed. Annensky's influence left its mark with unusual force on the Russian poetry that came after him. Our first teacher of psychological acuity in the new Russian lyric, he transmitted the art of psychological composition to Futurism. Sologub's influence, with almost equal force, manifested itself in a purely negative way: having brought to an extreme simplicity and perfection, by way of a lofty rationalism, the devices of the old Russian literature of the period of decline—including Nadson, Apukhtin and Golenishchev-Kutuzov[1]—having cleansed these devices of their trashy emotional admixture and having painted them the color of original erotic myth, he rendered impossible all attempts to return to the past, and he had, it would seem, practically no imitators. Organically compassionate on behalf of banality, keening tenderly over some dead word, Sologub created a cult of ghastly and outlived poetic formulas, inspiriting them with a miraculous and terminal life. Sologub's early poetry and his collection *Ring of Fire* [*Plamennyi krug*] are a cruel and cynical disposal of the poetic stereotype, not an enticing example, but rather a terrible warning to the brave idiot who might in the future try to write such verse.

Annensky, with the same resoluteness as Briusov, introduced the historically objective theme into poetry, and he introduced psychological constructivism into the lyric. Burning with a thirst to learn from the West, he had no teachers worthy of his vocation and was forced to pretend to be an imitator. Annensky's psychologism is not a caprice and not the ephemeral flash of an exquisite sensibility; it is genuine, firm construction. A straight path connects Annensky's "Steel Cicada" ["Stal'naia tsikada"] with Aseev's "Steel Nightingale" ["Stal'noi solovei"]. Annensky taught us how to use psychological analysis as a working tool in the lyric. He was the real forerunner of psychological construction in Russian Futurism, so brilliantly represented by Pasternak. To this day, Annensky has not found his Russian reader and is known only by Akhmatova's vulgarization of his methods. He is one of the most authentic originals in Russian poetry. One would like to transfer every poem in his books, *Quiet Songs* [*Tikhie pesni*] and *The Cypress Chest* [*Kiparisovyi larets*], into an anthology.

If Russian Symbolism had its Vergils and Ovids, it also had its Catulluses, not so much with regard to their relative stature as to the nature of their work. Here one must mention Kuzmin[2] and Khodasevich. These are typical minor poets, with all the purity and charm of sound characteristic of minor poets. For Kuzmin the major line in world literature would seem in general never to have existed. He's all bound up in a prejudice against it and in a canonization of the minor line, no higher than the level of Goldoni's comedy and Sumarokov's love songs. He cultivated rather successfully in his poems a conscious carelessness and baggy awkwardness of speech,

sprinkled with Gallicisms and Polonisms. Enkindled by the minor
poetry of the West—Musset, let us say—he writes a *New Rolla* and
creates for the reader the illusion of the completely artificial and
premature decrepitude of Russian poetic language. Kuzmin's poetry
is the prematurely senile smile of the Russian lyric. Khodasevich
cultivated Baratynsky's theme: "My gift is meager and my voice is
soft" ["Moi dar ubog i golos moi negromok"] and worked every
possible variation on the theme of the prematurely born child. His
minor line stems from the poems of the secondary poets of the Pushkin and post-Pushkin periods, the domestic amateur poets like
Countess Rostopchina, Viazemsky, and others.[3] Coming from the
best period of Russian poetic dilettantism, the period of the domestic album, the friendly epistle in verse, the casual epigram, Khodasevich carried the intricacy and the tender coarseness of idiomatic
popular Moscow speech as it had been used in the noble literary
circles of the last century right into our own. His poetry is very national, very literary, and very elegant.

An intense interest in the whole range of Russian poetry, from
the powerfully clumsy Derzhavin to that Aeschylus of the Russian
iambic line, Tiutchev, preceded the advent of Futurism. All the old
poets at that time—roughly before the beginning of the World
War—suddenly seemed new. A fever of reappraisal and the hasty
correction of historical injustice and short memory seized everyone.
Essentially, *all* Russian poetry at that time struck the new inquisi-
tiveness and the renovated hearing capacity of the reader as metalogical. A revolutionary reappraisal of the past preceded the revolution in creativity. Affirmation and legitimation of the real values of
the past is just as much a revolutionary act as the creation of new
values. Most unfortunately, however, memory and deed soon parted
company; they did not proceed hand in hand. Futurizers and his
torizers very quickly found themselves in two hostile camps. The
futurizers indiscriminately rejected the past, though their rejection
was no more than dietetic. For hygienic reasons they denied themselves a reading of the old poets, or they read them surreptitiously,
without letting on in public. And the historists prescribed themselves exactly the same kind of diet. I would even go so far as to say
that many respectable literary men, right up to recent times when
they were forced to do it, did not read their contemporaries. It would
seem that the history of literature had never before known such an
irreconcilable hostility and lack of understanding. The hostility between the Romantics and the Classicists, let us say, was child's play

compared to the abyss that opened up in Russia. But quite soon a criterion came to hand that facilitated a meeting of minds in this impassioned literary litigation between two generations: whoever does not understand the new has no comprehension of the old, and whoever comprehends the old is bound to understand the new as well. Only misfortune results when, instead of the real past with its deep roots, we get "former times." "Former times" means easily assimilated poetry, a henhouse with a fence around it, a cosy little corner where the domestic fowl cluck and scratch about. This is not work done upon the word, but rather a rest from the word. The boundaries of such a world of comfortable repose from active poetry are now defined approximately by Akhmatova and Blok, and not because Akhmatova or Blok, after the necessary winnowing of their works, are bad in themselves—for Akhmatova and Blok were never meant for people with a moribund sense of language. And if the linguistic consciousness of the age approached its death in them, it was dying gloriously. It was "that which in a rational being we call the heightened diffidence of suffering," and certainly not the inveterate stupidity bordering on malicious ignorance of their dedicated opponents and adherents. Akhmatova, using the purest literary language of her time, adapted with extraordinary steadfastness the traditional devices of the Russian folksong, and not only Russian, but the folksong in general. What we find in her poems is by no means a psychological affectation, but the typical parallelism of the folksong, with its acute asymmetry of two adjacent theses, on the pattern of: "My elderbush is in the yard; my uncle is in Kiev." This is where her twofold stanza with the unexpected thrust at the end comes from. Her poems are close to the folksong not only in structure but in essence, asserting themselves always and invariably as laments. Keeping in mind the poet's purely literary lexicon, filtered through her clenched teeth, these qualities make her especially interesting, allowing one to discern a peasant woman in this twentieth-century Russian literary lady.

Blok is the most complex phenomenon of literary eclecticism, a gatherer of the Russian poetry strewn and scattered by the historically shattered nineteenth century. The great work of collecting Russian poetry accomplished by Blok is still not clear to his contemporaries and is felt by them only instinctively as melodic power. Blok's acquisitive nature, his effort to centralize poetry and language, recalls the state-building instinct of the historic figures of Muscovy. His is a firm, stern hand as far as any provincialism is concerned: everything for Moscow, which in the given case is to say, for the historically formed poetry of the traditional language used by this proponent of a centralized poetic state. Futurism is all in its provincialisms, in its tumult reminiscent of the medieval appanages, in its folkloric and ethnographic cacophony. Try looking for that in Blok! Poetically, his work went at right angles to history and serves to prove that the government of language lives its own special life.

Fundamentally, Futurism ought not to have directed its barbs against the paper fortress of Symbolism, but rather against the living and genuinely dangerous figure of Blok. And if it failed to do this, it was only because of its characteristic inner piety and its literary propriety.

Futurism confronted Blok with Khlebnikov. What could they say to each other? Their battle continues, even in our own time when neither the one nor the other is any longer among the living. Like Blok, Khlebnikov thought of language as if it were a state, only not spatial, not territorial, but temporal. Blok is contemporary to the marrow of his bones; his time will go to rack-ruin and be forgotten; yet he will remain in the consciousness of generations to come as a contemporary of his own time. Khlebnikov does not know what a contemporary is. He is a citizen of all history, of the whole system of language and poetry. He is like some sort of idiotic Einstein who doesn't know how to tell which is closer, a railroad bridge or the *Igor Tale*. Khlebnikov's poetry is idiotic in the authentic, innocent, Greek sense of the word. His contemporaries could not and cannot forgive him the absence in his work of any reference to the madness of his own time. How terrifying it must have seemed when this man, oblivious of his interlocutor, without distinguishing his own time from all the ages, yet appeared in a persona that seemed unusually sociable, and gifted to a high degree with the purely Pushkinian gift of poetic small talk. Khlebnikov jokes, and nobody laughs. Khlebnikov makes light, elegant allusions, and nobody understands them. A very large part of what Khlebnikov has written is not more than light poetic small talk as he understood it, corresponding to the digressions from *Evgeny Onegin*, or to Pushkin's "Order yourself some macaroni with Parmesan in Tver, and make an omelette" ["Zakazhi sebe v Tveri/ S parmezanom makaroni,/ I iaichnitsu svari"]. He wrote comic dramas—*The World from its End-side* [*Mir s kontsa*]—and tragic buffonades—*Miss Death* [*Baryshnia smert'*]. He provided models of a marvelous prose, virginal and, like the story of a child, incomprehensible, because of the onrush of images and ideas pushing and crowding one another right out of consciousness. Each line he wrote is the beginning of a new long poem. Every tenth line is an aphorism, seeking a stone or bronze plaque on which to come to rest. It wasn't even poems or epics that Khlebnikov wrote, but a huge all-Russian prayer-and-icon book, from which for centuries upon centuries everyone who has the requisite energy will be able to draw.

Alongside Khlebnikov, as if for contrast, the mocking genius of fate placed Mayakovsky, with his poetry of common sense. There is common sense in any poetry. But specific common sense is nothing other than a pedagogical device. Schoolteaching that instills previously well-established truths into childish heads makes use of visual aids—that is, of a poetic tool. The pathos of common sense is part of schoolteaching. Mayakovsky's merit is in his poetic perfection of schoolteaching, in applying the powerful methods of visual education to the enlightenment of the masses. Like a schoolteacher, Mayakovsky walks about with a globe of the world or some other emblem of the visual method. He has replaced the repulsive newspaper of recent times, in which no one could understand anything, with a simple, wholesome schoolroom. A great reformer of the newspaper, he has left a profound imprint in our poetic language, simplifying its syntax to the limit of the possible and directing the noun to the place of honor and primacy in the sentence. The force and precision of his language make Mayakovsky akin to the traditional carnival side-show barker.[4] Both Khlebnikov and Mayakovsky are national to such a degree that populism—that is, folklore with a crude sugar-coating—would seem to have no place beside them. It continues to exist, however, in the poetry of Esenin, and to some degree in that of Kliuev, too.[5] The significance of these poets is in their rich provincialisms, which link them to one of the basic tendencies of our age.

Aseev stands completely to Mayakovsky's side. He has created the lexicon of a well-qualified technician. He is a poet-engineer, an organizer of work. In the West such people—that is, engineers, radiotechnicians, inventors of machines—tend to be poetically mute, or they read François Coppée.[6] It is characteristic of Aseev that he places the machine, as an expedient contraption, at the foundation of his poetry, without really talking about the machine at all. The plugging in and plugging out of the lyrical current provides an impression of swift fusing and powerful emotional discharge. Aseev is exceptionally lyrical and sober with regard to the word. He never poeticizes, but simply plugs in the lyrical current, like a good electrician, using the materials he needs.

Now the dikes that artificially held back the development of our poetic language have already given way, and any glossy, dress-uniform innovativeness strikes one as unnecessary and even reactionary.

The truly creative epoch in poetry is not that of invention, but that of imitation. When the prayer books have been written, then it is time to begin the service. The last poetic prayer book to be issued for common use throughout all the Russias was Pasternak's. *My Sister Life* [*Sestra moia zhizn'*]. Not since Batiushkov's time has such a new and mature harmony resounded in Russian poetry. Pasternak is not a fabricator or a parlor magician, but the founder of a new harmonic mode, a new structure of Russian versification that corresponds to the maturity and toughness achieved by the language. By means of this new harmony one can say whatever one likes. Everybody will use it, whether he wants to or not, since it has become henceforth the common property of all Russian poets. Up to now the logical structure of a sentence has become archaic along with the poem in which it appears; that is, it was only the briefest means for expressing the poetic meaning. Owing to frequent use in poetry, customary logical progression had become effaced and imperceptible as such. Syntax, which is the circulatory system of poetry, was stricken with sclerosis. Then comes a poet who reanimates the virginal strength of the logical structure of the sentence. It was just this in Batiushkov that astonished Pushkin, and Pasternak awaits his Pushkin.

Humanism & Modern Life

There are certain periods that say they have nothing to do with man: that say he should be used, like brick, like cement; that say he should be built from, not for. Social architecture takes its measure from the scale of man. Sometimes it becomes hostile to man and nourishes its own majesty by belittling and deprecating him.

Assyrian captives swarm like chickens under the feet of the immense king; warriors, who personify the state-power hostile to man, kill bound pygmies with their long spears; and the Egyptians and the Egyptian builders dispose of the human mass as if it were inert matter, of which there is always bound to be a sufficient supply, which has to be provided in any quantity that may happen to be required.

But there is another social architecture; and of this, too, man is the scale and the measure. It does not, however, use man as material from which to build, but builds for the sake of man; it does not build its majesty on the insignificance of personality, but on a higher expediency that corresponds to the needs of the individual.

Everybody senses the monumentality of form of the oncoming social architecture. The mountain is still not visible, but already it casts its shadow over us, and we who have grown unaccustomed to monumental forms of social life, having become accustomed to the politico-legal flatness of the nineteenth century, move about in this shadow with fear and perplexity, not knowing whether it is the wing of oncoming night, or the shadow of our native city that we are about to enter.

Simple mechanical immensity and bare quantity are hostile to man, and it is not some new social pyramid we find enticing, but social Gothic: the free play of weights and forces, a human society, conceived as a dense and complex architectural forest, where everything is expedient and individual, and where every part echoes in exchange with the immense whole.

The instinct for social architecture—that is, the structuring of life in majestic monumental forms that would seem to far exceed the direct needs of man—is deeply inherent in human societies, and no mere whim dictates it.

Reject social structure, and even the simplest dwelling, the one most indubitably necessary for all, man's home, will collapse.

In countries threatened by earthquake, people build close to the ground, and this tendency to flatness, this rejection of architecture, beginning with the French Revolution, runs through the whole legal life of the nineteenth century, all of which passed in the tense expectation of a subterranean shock, a social blow.

But the earthquake did not spare the flat dwellings either. The chaotic world smashed its way into both the English "home" and German *Gemüt*; chaos sings in our Russian stoves, chaos knocks in our chimney dampers and grates.

How to preserve the human dwelling from these awesome quakes? Where to bolster its walls against the subterranean shocks of history? And who will dare to say that the human dwelling, the free house of man, ought not to stand on the earth as its best ornament and the most solid thing that exists?

The legal thought of the last generations turned out to be powerless to protect the very thing for the sake of which it had come into being, over which it had struggled and on which fruitlessly reflected.

No statutes on the rights of man, no principles of property and inalienability insure the human dwelling any longer; they do not save homes from catastrophe; they provide neither certitude nor security.

The Englishman more than others concerns himself (hypocritically) with legal guarantees of the person, but he has forgotten that the concept "home" came into being many centuries ago in his own country as a revolutionary concept, as a natural justification for the first social revolution in Europe, deeper and more akin to our own time, as a type, than the French Revolution.

The monumentality of the oncoming social architecture is implicit in its vocation to organize world economy according to the principle of a worldwide domesticity to serve the needs of man, extending the circle of his domestic freedom to boundaries that are worldwide, blowing the flame of his individual hearth to the dimensions of a universal flame.

The days to come seem cold and frightening to those who do not understand this, but the inner warmth of the days to come, the warmth of expediency, economy, and teleology, is as clear to the contemporary humanist as the heat of the kindled stove of our own day.

If an authentically humanistic justification is not at the base of the coming social architecture, then it will crush man as Assyria and Babylonia did.

The fact that the values of humanism have become rare now, as though removed from circulation and hidden, isn't at all a bad sign. Humanistic values have merely gone underground and hoarded themselves away, like gold currency, but, like the gold supply, they secure the whole ideational commerce of contemporary Europe and from their underground administer it all the more authoritatively.

Switching to gold currency is a matter for the future, and in the realm of culture it will mean the exchange of current ideas—paper issue—for the gold coinage of the European humanistic heritage; and it is not under the spade of the archeologist that the excellent florins of humanism will ring; but they will see their day, and as sound current coin they will start circulating from hand to hand, when the time comes.

Fourth Prose

I.

Benjamin Fedorovich Kagan[1] approached this matter with the spare, sage prudence of a wizard or that of an Odessite Newton. All of Benjamin Fedorovich's conspiratorial activity rested on infinitesimals. Benjamin Fedorovich saw the law of salvation as a matter of maintaining a tortoiselike pace. He allowed himself to be shaken out of his professorial cubicle, answered the telephone at all hours, neither renounced nor refused anything or anyone, but for the most part what he tried to do was hold back the dangerous course of the disease.

The availability of a professor, what's more a mathematician, in this improbable affair of saving five lives by way of those cognizable, yet utterly imponderable integral progressions that are called "pulling strings," evoked expressions of satisfaction everywhere.

Isaiah Benediktovich[2] behaved himself from the very first as if the disease might be contagious, something catching, like scarlet fever, so that he, too, Isaiah Benediktovich, might, for all he knew, be shot. Isaiah Benediktovich went bustling about without rhyme or reason. He seemed to be racing from doctor to doctor, imploring them to disinfect him immediately.

If Isaiah Benediktovich had had his way, he would have taken a taxi and driven all over Moscow at random, without any plan, imagining that that was how one performed the ritual.

Isaiah Benediktovich would keep asserting and constantly recalling that he had left a wife behind him in Petersburg. He even managed to acquire a secretary of sorts, a small, stern, very sensible companion, a woman who was a relative of his and who had already begun to baby him. To put it briefly, by appealing to different people at different times, Isaiah Benediktovich seemed, as it were, to be inoculating himself against the firing squad.

All Isaiah Benediktovich's relatives had died in their Jewish beds of carved walnut. As a Turk will travel to the black stone of Kaaba,[3] so these Petersburg bourgeois descended from rabbis of patrician blood, brought into touch with Anatole France by way of the translator Isaiah, made pilgrimages to the very most Turgenevian and Lermontovian spas, preparing themselves by taking the cure for their transition to the hereafter.

In Petersburg Isaiah Benediktovich had been living the life of a good Frenchman, eating his *potage*, choosing acquaintances as innocuous as the croutons in his bouillon, and making visits, according to his profession, to two stock jobbers in junk translation.

Isaiah Benediktovich was good only at the very beginning of the "string pulling," during the mobilization and, as it were, the alarm. After that he faded, drooped, stuck out his tongue, and those very relatives of his pooled their money and sent him back to Petersburg.

I have always wondered where the bourgeois gets his fastidiousness and his so-called probity. Probity is the quality that relates the bourgeois to the animal. Many Party members relax in the company of a bourgeois for the same reason that grown-ups need the society of rosy-cheeked children.

The bourgeois is of course more innocent than the proletarian, closer to the uterine world, to the baby, the kitten, the angel, the cherubim. In Russia there are very few of these innocent bourgeois, and the scarcity has a bad effect on the digestion of authentic revolutionaries. The bourgeoisie in its innocent aspect must be preserved, entertained with amateur sports, lulled on the springs of Pullman cars, tucked into envelopes of snow-white railway sleep.

II.

A boy in goatskin booties, in a tight-fitting velveteen Russian coat, with his locks combed carefully back, stands there surrounded by mammas, grandmammas, and nursemaids, and beside him stands a cook's brat or a coachman's waif—some kid from the servants' quarters. And this whole howling pack of sniveling, pulling, hissing archangels is urging Little Lord Fauntleroy on:

"Go on, Vasenka, let him have it!"

Now Vasenka lets him have it, and the old maids, the vile toads, nudge each other and hold back the mangy little coachman's kid.

"Go on, Vasenka, you let him have it, and we'll grab him by the curly-locks and we'll waltz 'im around . . ."

What's this? A genre painting in the manner of Venetsianov? A scene by some serf-artist?

No, this is a training exercise for a Komsomol baby under the guidance of his agit-mammas, grandmammas, and nursemaids, so Vasenka can stomp him. Vasenka can let him have it, while we hold the scum down, while we waltz around . . .

"Go on, Vasenka, let him have it . . ."

III.

A crippled girl approached us from a street as long as a streetcarless night. She puts her crutch to one side and sits down as quickly as she can, so she can look like everybody else. Who is this husbandless girl? She is the light cavalry . . .[4]

We shoot cigarettes at one another and adjust our Chinese dialect, encoding into brute-cowardly formulae the great, powerful, forbidden concept of class. Brute terror pounds on the typewriters, brute terror proofreads a Chinese dialect on sheets of toilet paper, scribbles denunciations, hits those that are down, demands the death penalty for prisoners. Like little kids drowning a kitten in the Moscow River while a crowd watches, our grown-up kids playfully put on the pressure; at noon recess they give it the big squeeze: "Hey, come on and push it under. So you can't see it any more." That's the sacred rule of lynch law.

—A shopkeeper on the Ordynka short-weighted a working-woman: kill him!

—A cashier shortchanged somebody a nickel—kill her!

—A manager signed some nonsense by mistake—kill him!

—A peasant stashed away some rye in his barn—kill him!

A girl approaches us, limping on her crutch. One of her legs is foreshortened, and her crude prosthetic shoe reminds one of a wooden hoof.

And who are we? We are school children who don't study. We are a Komsomol volunteer. We are rowdies by permission of all the saints.

Filipp Filippych had a toothache. Filipp Filippych had not and would not come to class. Our notion of study has as much to do with science as a hoof with a foot, but this doesn't bother us.

I have come to you, my artiodactylous friends, to stomp with my peg leg in the yellow socialist arcade-complex created by the unbridled fantasy of that reckless entrepreneur Giber out of elements of a chic hotel on Tver Boulevard, out of the night telegraph and telephone exchange, out of a dream of universal incarnate bliss disguised as a permanent foyer with a buffet, out of a permanently open office with saluting clerks, out of a postal-telegraph, throat-tickling dryness of the air.

Here we have a permanent bookkeepers' night under the yellow flame of second-class railroad lamps. Here, as in Pushkin's tale, a Jew and a frog get married, that is, we have a wedding ceremony permanently going on between a goat-hoofed fop spawning theatrical fish eggs and his unclean mate from the same bathhouse, the Moscow editor-coffinmaker, who turns out brocade coffins on Monday, Tuesday, Wednesday, and Thursday. He rustles his paper shroud. He opens the veins of the months of the Christian calendar that still preserve their pastoral-Greek names: January, February, March . . . He is the terrifying and illiterate horse doctor of proceedings, deaths, and happenings, and he is pleased as can be when, like a fountain, the black horse blood of our epoch spurts forth.

IV.

I went to work for the newspaper *Moscow Komsomol* straight from the caravanserai of TSEKUBU.[5] There were twelve pairs of earphones there, almost all broken, and a reading room without books, remodeled from what had been a chapel, where people slept like snails on small round sofas.

The service staff at TSEKUBU hates me because of my straw baskets and because I'm not a professor.

In the afternoon I would go to observe the high water and I firmly believed that the obscene waters of our Moscow River would flow over the scholarly Kropotkin Embankment and TSEKUBU would telephone for a boat.

Mornings I would drink pasteurized cream right on the street, straight from the bottle.

I would take somebody else's soap from the professors' shelves and wash myself in the evenings, and I was not caught once.

People would come there from Kharkov and Voronezh and would be on their way to Alma-Ata. They accepted me as one of their own and took counsel with me as to which republic might work out best for them.

At night TSEKUBU was locked up like a fortress and I would bang my stick against the window.

Every decent man received telephone calls at TSEKUBU, and in the evening a servant would hand him his messages as if he were giving a priest a funerary list of souls to be prayed for. The writer Alexander Grin[6] lived there, and the servants cleaned his clothes with a brush. I lived at TSEKUBU like everybody, and no one bothered me until I myself moved out in the middle of summer.

When I moved to another apartment, my fur coat[7] lay draped across the cab, as it does when a patient has been dismissed from hospital after a long illness, or a convict released from prison.

v.

Things have reached the point where in the literary trade I value only raw meat, only the crazy excrescence:

> And by the falcon's cry, the entire
> Gorge was wounded to the bone.

That's the sort of thing I need.

All the works of world literature I divide into those that have been authorized and those that have been written without authorization. The former are all trash; the latter, stolen air. As to writers who receive authorization first, and then write, I would like to spit in their face; I would like to beat them on the head with a stick and sit them all down around a table in Herzen House,[8] and put a glass of police-tea in front of each one of them and hand each one of them personally a steaming sample of Gornfeld's[9] urinalysis.

I'd forbid such writers to marry and have children. How can they have children? Our children, after all, must carry on for us, must finish saying what was most important for us to say. And how can they, when their fathers have sold out, to a pock-marked devil, for three generations to come?

Now that's a tidy little literary page.

vi.

I have no manuscripts, no notebooks, no archives. I have no handwriting, because I never write. I alone in Russia work from the voice, while all around me the pack of accomplished pig-dogs writes. What the hell kind of writer am I? Get out of here, you fools!

On the other hand, I have a lot of pencils and they are all stolen and of different colors. One can sharpen them with a Gillette blade.

The blade of the Gillette razor with its slightly notched beveled edge has always seemed to me one of the noblest products of the steel industry. The good Gillette blade cuts like sedgegrass, bends but doesn't break in the hand, something like a Martian's calling card, or a note from some punctilious devil, with a hole drilled in the middle.

The Gillette razor blade is the product of a dead trust, whose shareholders include packs of American and Swedish wolves.

VII.

I am a Chinaman; nobody understands me. Hack-shmack![10] Let's go to Alma-Ata, where the people have raisin-eyes, where the Persian has eyes like fried eggs, where the Sart has sheep's eyes.

Hack-shmack! Let's go to Azerbaijan!

I had a patron once—People's Commissar Mravian-Muravian,[11] antic People's Commissar of the Armenian land, that younger sister of the Land of Judea. He sent me a telegram.

Dead is my patron, the People's Commissar Mravian-Muravian. Gone from the Erevan anthill is the black ant-commissar. No longer will he come to Moscow, in the international car of the train, as naïve and curious as a priest from a Turkish village.

Hack-shmack! Let's go to Azerbaijan!

I had a letter for People's Commissar Mravian. I took it to the secretaries in the Armenian residence in the cleanest, most ambassadorial street in Moscow. I was just about to depart for Erevan on an assignment from the ancient People's Commissariat of Education to conduct a terrifying seminar for those roundheaded youths in their poor monastery of a university.

If I had gone to Erevan, for three days and three nights I would have been hopping off the train to eat buttered bread with black caviar at the station buffets.

Hack-shmack!

On the way I would have read Zoshchenko's very best book and

I would have been happy as a Tatar who had just stolen a hundred rubles.

Hack-shmack! Let's go to Azerbaijan!

I would have taken fortitude with me in my yellow straw basket with its great heap of clean-smelling linen, and my fur coat would have hung on a golden nail. And I would have gotten out at the station in Erevan with my winter coat in one hand and my elder's walking stick—my Jewish staff[12]—in the other.

VIII.

There is a splendid line of Russian poetry which I will never tire of declaiming in the dog-smelling Moscow nights, a line from which, when uttered, as from a spell, the unclean spirits disperse. Guess what line, friends. It inscribes itself on the snow like sleigh runners, it clicks in the lock like a key, it darts into a room like frost: ". . . I didn't shoot the poor bastards in the dungeons . . ."[13] There you have a symbol of faith, there you have the genuine canon of a real writer, a true mortal enemy of Literature.

In Herzen House there is a certain lactile vegetarian, a philologist with a Chinaman's noggin, of that breed that tiptoes about our blood-soaked Soviet land intoning *hao-hao, shango-shango*, while heads are being lopped off, a certain Mitka Blagoi,[14] a piece of high-school rubbish, authorized by the Bolsheviks, in the name of the advancement of science, to stand guard in a special museum over the length of cord with which Seriozha Esenin hanged himself.

And I say: Blagoi to the Chinese! To Shanghai with him! To the Chinks—that's where he belongs! Ah, to think, what Mother Philology once was, and what she has now become . . . Pure-blooded and uncompromising she was; cur-blooded and all-compromising she has become.

IX.

To the number of murderers and apprentice-murderers of Russian poets, the murky name of Gornfeld has been added. This paralytic d'Anthès,[15] this Uncle Monia from Basseiny Street, who preaches morality and statesmanship, carried out the orders of a regime completely alien to him, orders which he accepted about as he would a touch of indigestion.

Dying of Gornfeld is as foolish as dying because of a bicycle or a parrot's beak. But a literary murderer can also be a parrot. I, for instance, was almost killed by a polly named after His Majesty King Albert and Vladimir Galaktionovich Korolenko.[16] I am quite pleased that my murderer is alive and has in a sense survived me. I feed him sugar and listen with pleasure as he recites aloud from *Eulenspiegel*, "The ashes are knocking at my heart," alternating this phrase with another not less beautiful: "There is no torment in the world greater than the word . . ." A man who can title his book *Torments of the Word* is born with the Cain's mark of the literary murderer on his brow.

I only met Gornfeld once, in the dirty editorial office of some unprincipled rag where, as in the buffet at Kvisisan, some spectral figures hovered. There was still no ideology then and nobody to whom to complain if somebody insulted you. When I recall that orphaned state—how did we manage to live then!—huge tears roll down my face . . . Somebody introduced me to this two-legged critic, and I shook his hand.

Dear Uncle Gornfeld, why did you go complain to the *Stock Exchange News*, I mean to the *Evening Red Gazette*,[17] in the Year of Our Soviet 1929? You would better have gone weeping to Mr. Propper, into his pure literary Jewish waistcoat. You would better have told your woes to your banker, with his sciatica, kugel, and tallith . . .

X.

Nikolai Ivanovich[18] has a secretary. And, in truth, to tell you the truth, she is quite a squirrel, a tiny little rodent. She nibbles a nut with every visitor and goes running to the telephone like an inexperienced young mother to her sick baby.

A certain scoundrel told me that truth was *mria* in Greek.

And so our little squirrel is genuine truth with a capital letter in Greek; and at the same time she is that other truth, that stern card-carrying Virgin—Party Truth . . .

The secretary, frightened and attentive, like a hospital nurse, doesn't so much work there as live in the office's anteroom, in the telephone-dressing-room. Poor Mria from the anteroom with her telephone and her classical newspaper!

This secretary differs from others in that she sits like a nightnurse on the threshold of power, defending the wielder of power as if he were gravely ill.

XI.

No, really, bring me to court by all means! Allow me to be submitted as evidence! . . . Permit me, so to speak, to put myself on file. Do not deprive me, I implore you, of my own trial . . . The legal proceedings aren't over yet and, I make so bold as to assure you, they never will be. What happened before was only the overture. Bosio[19] herself will sing at my trial. Bearded students in checked plaids, mingling with policemen in capes, under the baton of their goat of a choir director, ecstatically chanting a syncopated version of the Eternal Memory,[20] will carry a police coffin with the remains of my case out of the smoke-dimmed halls of the district court.

> Papa, papa, papochka,
> Where, oh where is Mamochka?
> From the Writers' Union, down two blocks,
> She came home with the black pox.
> Mama's eye has lost its sight
> And the case is sewn up tight.

Alexander Ivanovich Herzen! . . . Allow me to introduce myself . . . It seems that in your house . . . As host, you are in some sense responsible . . .

You deigned to go abroad, did you . . . Something disagreeable has happened here in the meantime . . . Alexander Ivanovich! Sir! How can it be! There is absolutely no one to turn to!

XII.

In a certain year of my life, grown men from a tribe I despise with all the strength of my soul, and to which I neither wish to nor ever will belong, conceived the intention of collectively committing against me an ugly and repellent ritual. The name of this ritual is literary pruning, or dishonoring, and it is performed according to the custom and the calendrical needs of the writers' tribe, and in it a sacrificial victim is designated by vote of the elders.

I insist that writerdom, as it has taken shape in Europe and especially in Russia, is incompatible with the honorable title of Jew, of which I am proud. By blood, burdened with its inheritance from shepherds, patriarchs, and kings, rebels against the shifty gypsydom of the writers' tribe. A creaking camp of unwashed Romanies kidnapped me when I was still a child and for a certain number of years dawdled along its obscene routes, vainly trying to teach me its only craft, its only art—stealing.

Writerdom is a race with a revolting smell to its hide and the very filthiest means of preparing its food. It is a race that camps and sleeps in its own vomit, expelled from cities and hounded in villages; yet anywhere and everywhere it is close to the authorities, who always grant it special accommodations in red-light districts as they do to prostitutes. For, anywhere and everywhere, literature carries out one assignment: it helps superiors keep their soldiers in line, and it helps judges dispose arbitrarily of the condemned.

A writer is a mixture of parrot and priest. He is a polly in the very loftiest sense of that word. He speaks French if his master is French, but, sold to Persia, he'll say "Pol's a fool" or "Polly wants a cracker" in Persian. A parrot has no age and knows not day from night. If he bores his master, he's covered with a dark cloth, and, for literature, that becomes a surrogate for night.

XIII.

There were two Chénier brothers.[21] The despicable junior belongs entirely to literature; the executed senior himself excluded literature.

Jailers love to read novels, and more than anyone else have a need for literature.

In a certain year of my life, bearded adult men in peaked fur caps brandished a flint knife over me, with the aim of deballing me. Judging by the evidence, these were the priests of the tribe: they smelled of onion, novels, and goatmeat.

And it was all as frightening as in a child's dream. *Nel mezzo del' cammin di nostra vita*[22]—midway on the journey of our life, I was stopped in the dense Soviet forest by bandits who called themselves my judges. They were elders with veins protruding from their necks and little goose-heads unfit to bear the burden of their years.

For the first and only time in my life, literature had need of me, and it crumpled me, pawed me, and pressed me flat, and it was all frightening, as in a child's dream.

XIV.

I bear moral responsibility for the fact that the ZIF publishing house did not write out a contract with the translators Gornfeld and Karia-kin. I—dealer in precious furs, practically suffocating under a load of literary pelts—bear moral responsibility for the fact that I inspired a Petersburg lout with the desire to allude in a libelous anecdote to that warm Gogolian fur coat, torn by night in the open square from the shoulders of that most ancient Komsomol member, Akaky Aka-kievich.[23] I tear off my literary fur coat and trample it underfoot. In nothing but my jacket, and in thirty-degree frost, I will run three times around the concentric boulevard rings of Moscow. I shall flee from the red-light district hospital of the Komsomol arcade into a mortal chill, if only not to see those twelve lit Judas-windows of that obscene house on Tver Boulevard, if only not to hear the clink of silver and the counting of printer's sheets.

XV.

Honored Romanies of Tver Boulevard, we have written a novel to-gether, you and I, of which you have not even dreamed. I am very fond of coming across my name in official papers, in court-ordered subpoenas and other stern documents. Here the name has a com-pletely objective ring to it: a sound new to the ear and, I must say, quite interesting. From time to time, I, too, am a bit curious to know what it is I am forever doing wrong. What kind of apple is this Mandelstam anyway, who's supposed to have been doing such-and-such for so long, and who—the scoundrel—keeps on evading the issue? . . . How much longer is he going to keep on evading the issue? That's why I profit nothing with the passage of the years; others gather dignity and respect with every passing day, while for me, quite the contrary, time flows backward.

I am guilty. Here there can be no two opinions. I shall not wriggle out of this guilt. I live in insolvency. I save myself by evasion. How much longer am I to go on evading?

When a tin subpoena arrives, or a reminder, Greek in its austere simplicity, from a social organization—when they demand that I name my accomplices, stop my thieving, tell where I get my counterfeit money, and sign a warrant not to travel beyond certain designated limits—I agree immediately, but then I start evading again right away, as if nothing had happened. And so it goes.

In the first place: I ran away from somewhere, and I must be sent back, settled, investigated, and corrected. In the second place, they assume I am somebody else. No way of proving my identity. In my pockets, trash: cryptic notes from the previous year, telephone numbers of dead relatives and addresses of God knows whom. In the third place, I signed a pact, either with Beelzebub or the State Publishing House, grandiose and unfulfilled, on Whatman paper, smeared with mustard and emery-powder pepper, in which I bound myself to return twice over everything acquired, to regurgitate fourfold everything I misappropriated, and to perform sixteen times running that impossible, that unthinkable, that unique thing that might, in part, acquit me.

I became more stiff-necked every year. As though by a streetcar conductor's steel punch, I am riddled with holes and stamped with my own surname. Whenever anyone calls me by my first name and patronymic, I tremble. I simply cannot accustom myself to such honor! To be called Ivan Moiseich, even if just once in my life! Hey, Ivan,[24] go scratch the dogs! Mandelstam, go scratch the dogs! Some little Frenchman might be called "*cher maître*," dear teacher—but me? "Mandelstam, go scratch the dogs!" To each his own.

I grow old, and with the stump of my heart I scratch the master's dogs, and they never get enough, they never get enough . . . With canine tenderness, the eyes of Russian writers look at me and they implore: drop dead! Where does it come from, this lackey's malice, this sniveling contempt for my name? Even the gypsy had a horse, but I am horse and gypsy in one person . . .

Tin subpoenas under my little pillow . . . The forty-sixth little old contract instead of a halo and a hundred thousand lighted cigarettes instead of candles . . .

XVI.

No matter how much I work, no matter if I carry horses on my back
or if I turn millstones, I shall never become a worker. My work, no
matter what form it might take, is seen as mischief, as lawlessness,
as incidental. But that's the way I want it, and so I agree. I subscribe
with both hands.

Here's a different approach: for me, it is the hole in the doughnut[25] that has value. What of the dough of the doughnut? You can
devour the doughnut, but the hole will remain.

That's what real work is: Brussels lace. The main thing is what
supports the pattern: air, punctures, truancy.

In my case, brethren, work does me no good; it doesn't go on my
record.

We have a Bible of work, but we do not appreciate it. I mean
Zoshchenko's stories. He's the only man who has shown us a worker,
and we've trampled him in the dirt. But I demand monuments for
Zoshchenko in every city and boondock of the Soviet Union, or at
the very least, as for Grandpa Krylov, in the Summer Garden.[26]

Now there's a man whose work reeks with truancy, in whose work
Brussels lace lives!

At night on the Ilinka when the department stores and the trusts
are asleep and conversing in their native Chinese, at night anecdotes
go walking along the Ilinka. Lenin and Trotsky walk arm in arm as
though nothing has happened. One has a little pail and a fishing rod
from Constantinople in his hand. Two Jews go walking, an inseparable pair. One asks questions, the other answers; and the one keeps
asking, always asking, while the other keeps evading, always evading, and in no way can they be parted.

A German organ-grinder walks by with his Schubertian barrel
organ—such a failure, such a parasite . . . *Ich bin arm*. I am poor.

Sleep, my dear . . . M.S.P.O.[27] . . .

Viy[28] is reading the telephone book on Red Square. Lift up my
eyelids . . . Give me the Central Committee . . .

Armenians from Erevan walk by with green-painted herrings.
Ich bin arm. I am poor.

And in Armavir on the town coat of arms there is written: A dog
barks and the wind carries it.[29]

Journey to Armenia

Journey to Armenia

On the island of Sevan, which is conspicuous for two most dignified architectural monuments that date back to the seventh century, as well as for the mud huts of flea-bitten hermits only recently passed away, thickly overgrown with nettles and thistles, but not scarier than the neglected cellars of summer houses, I spent a month enjoying the lake water that stood at a height of four thousand feet above sea level and training myself to the contemplation of the two or three dozen tombs scattered as if they were a flowerbed amidst the monastery's recently renovated dormitories.

Daily at five o'clock on the dot, the lake, which teems with trout, would boil up as though a huge pinch of soda had been thrown into it. It was what you might fully call a mesmeric seance for a change in the weather, as if a medium had cast a spell on the previously tranquil limewater, producing first a playful little ripple, then a bird flock twittering, and finally a stormy Ladogan frenzy.

It was at such a time impossible to deny oneself the pleasure of measuring off three hundred paces along the narrow beachpath that lay opposite the somber Gunei shore.

Here the Gökcha forms a strait five times broader than the Neva. The superb fresh wind would tear into one's lungs with a whistle. The velocity of the clouds kept increasing by the minute, and the incunabular surf would hasten to issue a fat, hand-printed Gutenberg Bible in half an hour under the gravely scowling sky.

Not less than 70 percent of the island's population consisted of children. They would clamber about like wild little beasties over the monks' graves, bombard some peaceful snag on the lake bottom, whose icy spasms they took for the writhing of a sea serpent, or bring out of their murky tenements the bourgeois toads and the grass snakes with their jewellike feminine heads, or chase back and forth an infuriated ram who could in no way figure out how his poor body stood in anybody's way and who would keep shaking his tail, grown fat in freedom.

The tall steppe grasses on the lee hump of Sevan Island were so strong, juicy, and self-confident that one felt like carding them out with an iron comb.

The entire island is Homerically strewn with yellowed bones—remnants of the local people's pious picnics.

Moreover, it is literally paved with the fiery red slabs of nameless graves, some sticking up, others knocked over and crumbling away.

At the very beginning of my stay the news came that some stone-masons digging a pit for the foundation of a lighthouse on the long and melancholy spit of land called Tsamakaberda had come across a cemetery containing burial urns of the ancient Urartian people. I had previously seen a skeleton in the Erevan Museum, crammed into a sitting position in a large clay amphora, with a little hole drilled in its skull for the evil spirit.

Early in the morning I was awakened by the chirring of a motor. The sound kept marking time. A pair of mechanics were warming the tiny heart of an epileptic engine, pouring black oil into it. But the moment it got going, its tongue twister—something that sounded like "Not-to-eat, not-to-drink, not-to-eat, not-to-drink"—would fizzle out and extinguish itself in the water.

Professor Khachaturian, over whose face an eagleskin was stretched, beneath which all the muscles and ligaments stood out, numbered and with their Latin names, was already strolling along the wharf in his long black frock coat, cut in the Ottoman style. Not only an archeologist, but also a teacher by calling, he had spent a great part of his career as director of a secondary school, the Armenian gymnasium in Kars. Invited to the chair of archeology in Soviet Erevan, he carried with him both his devotion to the Indo-European theory and a smoldering hostility to Marr's Japhetic fabrications, as well as his astonishing ignorance of the Russian language and of Russia, where he had never before been.

Having somehow struck up a conversation in German, we sat down in the launch with Comrade Karinian, former chairman of the Armenian Central Executive Committee.

This proud and full-blooded man, doomed to inactivity, to smoking long cardboard-tipped Russian cigarettes, to such a gloomy waste of time as reading Onguardist[1] literature, evidently found it difficult to give up the habit of his official duties, and Lady Boredom had planted her fat kisses on his ruddy cheeks.

The motor went on muttering, "Not-to-eat, not-to-drink," as if it were reporting to Comrade Karinian. The little island rapidly dropped away behind us, as its bearlike back with the octagons of the monasteries straightened. A swarm of midges kept pace with the launch, and we sailed along in it as in a veil of muslin across the milky morning lake.

In the excavation, we really did unearth both clay crocks and human bones, but in addition we also found the haft of a knife stamped with the ancient trademark of the Russian N. N. factory.

Nevertheless, I respectfully wrapped up in my handkerchief the porous, calcified little crust of somebody's skull.

Life on any island—be it Malta, St. Helena, or Madeira—flows past in precious expectation. This has its charm and its inconvenience. In any case, everyone is constantly busy; people drop their voices a bit and are slightly more attentive to each other than on the mainland with its thick-fingered roads and its negative freedom.

The ear lobe is more delicately molded and takes on a new twist.

It was my good fortune that a whole gallery of clever, thoroughbred old men had collected on Sevan: there was the respected regionalist Ivan Iakovlevich Sagatelian, the archeologist Khachaturian whom I have already mentioned, and finally a vivacious chemist named Gambarian.

I preferred their quiet company and the thick black coffee of their talk to the flat conversations of the young people, which revolved, as they do everywhere, around examinations and sports.

The chemist Gambarian speaks Armenian with a Moscow accent. He has voluntarily and merrily Russified himself. He is young in heart and has a dry, sun-baked body. He's the pleasantest man, physically, and a wonderful partner at games.

He was annointed with a kind of military oil, as though he'd just come back from a military chapel, which proves nothing, however, since this is an air that sometimes clings to quite excellent Soviet people.

With women he is a chivalrous Mazeppa,[2] flattering Maria with his lips alone; in the company of men, he is the sworn enemy of caustic remarks and vanity; yet, if he is insulted in a quarrel, he will flare up like a Frankish fencer.

The mountain air made him younger; he would roll up his sleeves and fling himself at the little fishnet that served the volleyball court, drily working his small palm.

What is there to say about Sevan's climate?

"Gold currency of cognac in the secret cupboard of the mountain sun."

The dacha's little glass-stick oral thermometer was carefully passed around from hand to hand. Dr. Gertsberg was frankly bored on this island of Armenian mothers. He seemed to me the pale shadow of an Ibsen problem, or some actor from the Moscow Art Theater at his dacha.

The children would show him their narrow little tongues, sticking them out for an instant like chunks of bearmeat . . .

But, toward the end of our stay, we did have a bout of foot-and-mouth disease, brought in via milk cans from the far shore of Zeinal, where some ex-Khlysty,[3] who had long since ceased to rejoice, had lapsed into silence in their somber Russian huts.

For the sins of the grown-ups, however, the foot-and-mouth disease struck only the godless children of Sevan.

One after another, the wiry-haired, pugnacious children would droop with a ripe fever onto the arms of the women, onto pillows.

Once, competing with Kh., a youngster from the Komsomol, Gambarian ventured to swim around the whole island of Sevan. His sixty-year-old heart couldn't make it, and even Kh. was exhausted and had to leave his friend and return to the starting point, where he flung himself half-alive onto the pebble beach. Witnesses to the accident were the volcanic walls of the island fortress, which at the same time precluded any thought of mooring there . . .

What an alarm went up then! There turned out not to be any lifeboat on Sevan, although one had been requisitioned.

People rushed about the island, proud in their awareness of an accident that was irreparable. The unread newspaper rattled like tin in the hands. The island felt nauseated, like a pregnant woman.

We had neither telephone nor pigeon-post to communicate with the shore. The launch had left for Elenovka about two hours before, and, no matter how you strained your ear, not even a chirring could be heard on the water.

When the expedition led by Comrade Karinian, equipped with blanket, cognac bottle, and so on, returned with Gambarian, all stiff with cold but smiling, whom they had managed to pick up on a rock, he was met with applause. That was the most splendid hand-clapping I ever heard in my life: a man was being congratulated on the fact that he was not yet a corpse.

At the fishing wharf in Naraduz, where we were taken for an excursion that fortunately managed to cast off without any choral singing, I was impressed by the hull of a completely finished barge that had been pulled up in its raw state onto the trestle of the wharf. It was a good Trojan horse in size, and its fresh musical proportions resembled the box of a bandore.

There were curly shavings around. The salt was eating into the earth, and the fish scales glimmered like little discs of quartz.

In the cooperative dining room which was just as log-cabin and Mynheer-Peter-the-Great as everything else in Naraduz, we sat side by side to eat the thick artel soup of cabbage and mutton.

The workers noticed that we had no wine with us and, as befits proper hosts, filled our glasses.

I drank a toast in spirit to the health of young Armenia, with its houses of orange stone, to its white-toothed commissars, to its horse sweat and its restless stomp of waiting-lines: and to its mighty language which we are unworthy to speak and of which, in our incompetence, we can only steer clear. "Water" in Armenian is *dzhur*. "Village" is *g'iur*.

I shall never forget Arnoldi.

He walked on an orthopedic limb, but in such a manly way that everyone envied him his walk.

The scholarly high command of the island lived along the highway in Molokan⁴ Elenovka, where, in the half-shadow of the scientific Executive Committee, the gendarmelike mugs of formaldehyde-preserved giant trout turned blue.

Ah, these visitors!

An American yacht, swift as a telegram, that cut the water like a lancet, had brought them to Sevan—and Arnoldi would step out onto the shore, that terror of science, that Tamerlane of good spirits.

I had the impression that a blacksmith lived on Sevan who used to make his shoes, and he used to visit the island in order to consult with him.

There is nothing more pleasant and instructive than to immerse yourself in the society of people of an entirely different race, whom you respect, with whom you sympathize, of whom you are, though a stranger, proud. The Armenians' fullness of life, their rough tenderness, their noble inclination for hard work, their inexplicable aversion to any kind of metaphysics, and their splendid intimacy with the world of real things—all this said to me: you're awake, don't be afraid of your own time, don't be sly.

Wasn't this because I found myself among people, renowned for their teeming activity, who nevertheless told time not by the railroad station or the office clock, but by the sundial, such as the one I saw among the ruins of Zvartnots in the form of the zodiac or of a rose inscribed in stone?

ASHOT OVANESIAN

The Institute of Peoples of the East is located on the Bersenev Embankment next door to the pyramidal Government House. A little further along, a ferryman used to ply his trade, charging three pennies for a crossing and loading his boat to the gunwales.

The air on the Moscow River Embankment is viscid and mealy.

A bored young Armenian came out to greet me. In addition, one could also see, among the Japhetic books with their spiky script, like a Russian cabbage butterfly in a library of cactuses, a blond young lady.

My amateurish arrival caused no one to rejoice. A request for help to study Old Armenian touched no heart among these people, of whom, moreover, the woman herself lacked this key of knowledge.

As a result of my incorrect subjective orientation,[5] I have fallen into the habit of regarding every Armenian as a philologist . . . Which is, however, not all wrong. These are people who jangle the keys of their language even when they are unlocking nothing particularly valuable.

My conversation with the young graduate student from Tiflis flagged and ended on a note of diplomatic reserve.

The names were names of highly esteemed Armenian writers, Academician Marr[6] was mentioned, who had just dashed through Moscow on his way from the Udmurt or Vogul' District to Leningrad, and the spirit of Japhetic learning was praised, which penetrates to the deep structure of all speech . . .

I was already getting bored and glancing more and more often out the window at a bit of overgrown garden, when into the library strode an old man with despotic manners and a lordly bearing.

His Promethean head radiated a smoky ash-blue light like the most powerful carbide lamp . . . The blue-black locks of his wiry hair, fluffed out with a certain disdain, had something of the reinforced strength of an ensorcelled bird feather.

There was no smile on the broad mouth of this black-magician, who never forgot that speech is work. Comrade Ovanesian's head had the capacity of distancing itself from his interlocutor, like the top of a mountain that only chanced to resemble a head. But the dark-blue-quartz-frowning of his eyes was worth anyone else's smile.

"Head" in Armenian is *glukh'e*—with a short breath after the *kh* and a soft *l* . . . It's the same root as in Russian [*glava*, or *golova*] . . . And would you like a Japhetic novella? If you please:

"To see," "to hear," and "to understand"—all these meanings coalesced at one time into a single semantic bundle. At the very deepest stages of language, there were no concepts, only directions, fears and longings, needs and apprehensions. The concept "head" was shaped over a dozen millennia out of just such a vague bundle of mists, and its symbol became . . . deafness [*glukhota*].

You'll get it all mixed up anyway, dear reader, and it is not for me to teach you.

ZAMOSKVORECH'E[7]

Not long before that, as I had been rooting about under the staircase in the musty-pink house on the Iakimanka, I found a tattered book by Signac defending Impressionism.[8] The author explained "the law of optical blending," glorified the method of working with little dabs of the brush, and instilled in the reader a sense of the importance of using only the pure colors of the spectrum.

He based his arguments on citations from Eugène Delacroix, whom he idolized. Now and then he would refer to Delacroix's *Journey to Morocco* as if he were leafing through a codex of visual training that every thinking European was obliged to know.

Signac was trumpeting on his chivalric horn the last, ripe gathering of the Impressionists. Into their bright camps he summoned the Zouaves, the burnooses, and the red skirts of the Algerian women.

At the very first sounds of this emboldening theory that braces the nerves, I felt the shiver of novelty; it was as if someone had called me by name . . .

It seemed to me as if I had changed my clodhopper city shoes for a pair of light Moslem slippers.

I'd been blind as a silkworm all my long life.

Moreover, a lightness invaded my life, my always arid and disorderly life, which I imagine to myself as a kind of ticklish waiting for a lottery in which everyone wins a prize, from which I might extract whatever I wanted: a piece of strawberry soap, a spell of sitting in the archive of the Archprinter's chambers, or my longed-for journey to Armenia, of which I never ceased to dream.

It must be terribly impertinent, talking to the reader about the present in that tone of absolute courtesy we, for some reason, have yielded to the memoirists.

I think it comes from the impatience with which I live and change my skin.

The salamander suspects nothing of the black-and-yellow mottling on its back. The thought has never occurred to it, that these spots are arranged in two chains, or else fused together into a solid path, depending on the dampness of the sand, or on whether the papering of the terrarium is cheerful or gloomy.

As for that thinking salamander, man, who puzzles out the next-day's weather—if only he could choose his own coloration!

Next door to me there lived some stern families of philistines [*obyvateli*].⁹ God had denied these people affability, which does, after all, make life pleasanter. They had morosely linked themselves together into a passionately consuming consumers' association, and they kept tearing off the days due them in the ration-coupon booklet, and they would smile and smile as if they were pronouncing the word "cheese."

Their rooms were stocked inside like handicraft shops, with various symbols of kinship, longevity, and domestic fidelity. White elephants prevailed, big ones and small ones, artistic renditions of dogs, and sea shells. The cult of the dead was not alien to them, nor a certain respect for those who were absent. It seemed these people with their Slavic faces, fresh and cruel, slept in a photographer's prayer-room.

And I thanked my lucky stars that I was only an accidental guest of Zamoskvorech'e and would not spend my best years there. Nowhere, never, have I felt with such force Russia's watermelon-emptiness; the brick-colored sunsets over the Moscow River, the color of the brick-tea brought to mind the red dust of the Ararat blast furnace.

I felt like getting back as soon as I could to the place where people's skulls are equally beautiful, whether at work or in the grave.

All around there were, God help us, such cheery little houses with such nasty little souls and timidly oriented windows. Seventy years ago or less they used to sell serf girls here, who had been taught to sew and stitch hems, quiet little things, quick to catch on.

The stale old lindens, deaf with age, lifted their brown forked trunks in the courtyard. Frightening in their somehow bureaucratic thickness, they heard and understood nothing. Time fed them with lightning flashes and watered them with downpours; thunder or bromide, it was all the same to them.

Once a meeting of the adult males who lived in the house resolved to chop down the oldest linden and cut it up for firewood.

They dug a deep trench around the tree. The ax began to hack at the indifferent roots. Doing a woodcutter's work requires certain skills. There were too many volunteers. They fussed about, like the incompetent executors of some foul verdict.

I called to my wife: "Look, it's about to fall!"

Meanwhile, however, the tree was resisting with a kind of sentient force. It seemed to have become fully conscious again. It despised those who were harrassing it and the pike's teeth of the saw.

Finally, they threw a noose of thin laundry twine around the dry
place where the trunk forked—the very place that marked the tree's
great age, its lethargy, and its verdant outburst—and began to rock
it gently back and forth. It shook like a tooth in a gum, but remained
king of the hill. A moment later, the children ran up to the toppled
idol.

That year the directors of Tsentrosoiuz [the Central Union of
Consumer Cooperatives of the USSR] approached Moscow University with the request that they recommend a man who could be sent
to Erevan. They had in mind someone to supervise the production
of cochineal, a kind of insect few people knew about. An excellent
carmine dye is made from the cochineal when it is dried and ground
to powder.

The university selected B. S. K., a well-educated young zoologist.
B. S. lived with his old mother on Bolshaia Iakimanka, belonged to
the trade union, would snap to attention, out of pride, before anyone
and everyone, and, out of the entire academic milieu, singled out
for admiration old Sergeev, who had made and installed with his
own hands all the tall red cabinets in the zoology library and who
could unerringly name the wood of already finished lumber with his
eyes closed, just by running his palm along it, whether it was oak,
ash, or pine.

B. S. was not in any way a bookworm. He studied science as he
went; had once had something to do with the salamanders of the
famous Viennese professor Kammerer, who had committed suicide;
and more than anything else on earth loved the music of Bach, especially one invention for wind instruments that went flying upward
like some Gothic firework.

B. S. was a fairly experienced traveler within the USSR. In both
Bukhara and Tashkent his field shirt had been sighted and his infectious military laugh had resounded. Everywhere he went, he
planted friends. Not so long ago, a certain mullah, a holy man, since
buried on a mountain, had sent him a formal announcement of his
death in pure Farsi. In the mullah's opinion, the fine, erudite young
man—when he had used up his supply of health and engendered
enough children, but not before—should come join him.

Hooray for the living! Every labor is worthy!

Reluctantly, B. S. got ready to go to Armenia. He kept running
after buckets and bags to collect the cochineal and complaining about
the slyness of bureaucrats who wouldn't issue him packing materials.

Parting is the younger sister of death. For those who respect fate's reasonings, the ritual of farewell contains an ominous nuptial animation.

Now and then the front door would slam and up the mousy stairs from the Iakimanka guests of both sexes would arrive: students from Soviet aviation schools, those carefree skaters on air; staff members of distant botanical stations; some who specialized in mountain lakes; people who had been in the Pamirs and in western China; and, simply, young people.

Then began the filling of goblets with Muscovite wines, and the sweet demurrals of the ladies and girls; tomato juice spurted, and so did a general, unsequential chatter: about flying, about looping the loop, when you don't notice that you've been turned upside down, and the earth, like some huge brown ceiling, comes rushing at your head; about the high cost of living in Tashkent, about Uncle Sasha and how he had the grippe, about everything . . .

Someone told the story about the man with Addison's disease who sprawled himself out on the Iakimanka and lived there: drank vodka, read the newspapers, vehemently played dice, and at night removed his wooden leg and used it for a pillow.

Someone else compared this Iakimanka Diogenes with a medieval Japanese woman, and a third person shouted that Japan was a country of spies and bicyclists.

The subject of the conversation kept merrily slithering away, like a ring passed behind the back, and dominant over the table talk was the knight's move, which always swerves to one side . . .

I don't know how it is for others, but for me a woman's charm is augmented if she happens to be a young traveler, who has spent five days of a scientific trip lying on a hard bench of the Tashkent train, who knows her way around in Linnaean Latin, who knows where she stands in the dispute between the Lamarckians and the epigeneticists, and who is not indifferent to the soybean, the cotton plant, or the chicory.

And on the table there is an elegant syntax of confused, heteroalphabetical, grammatically incorrect wildflowers, as if all the preschool forms of vegetative being were coalescing into a pleophonic anthology-poem.

As a child, a stupid vanity, a false pride, had kept me from ever going out to look for berries or stooping down over mushrooms. Gothic pine cones and hypocritical acorns in their monks' hoods pleased me more than mushrooms. I would stroke the pine cones.

They bristled. They were good. They were persuading me. In their shell-like tenderness, in their geometrical harum-scarum, I sensed the rudiments of architecture, the demon of which has accompanied me all my life.

I almost never spent any time in summer houses on the outskirts of Moscow. Of course, automobile trips to Uzkoe on the Smolensk road don't count, past those fat-bellied log huts where the truck farmers had piled up heaps of cabbages like cannonballs with green fuses. Those pale green cabbage-bombs, heaped up in shameless abundance, reminded me vaguely of the pyramid of skulls in Vereshchagin's dull painting.

It's not like that now, but I suppose the break came too late.

Only last year on the island of Sevan in Armenia, as I went strolling in the waist-high grass, I was captivated by the shameless burning of the poppies. Bright to the point of surgical pain, looking like counterfeit badges from some cotillion, big, too big for our planet, fireproof, dream-faced moths, they grew on repulsive hairy stalks.

I envied the children . . . They hunted enthusiastically for poppywings in the grass. I would stoop down, then again . . . Fire in my hands, as if a blacksmith had lent me some coals.

Once in Abkhazia I came upon whole streaks of northern wild strawberries.

At a height of several hundred feet above sea level, young forests clothed that whole hilly region. The peasants hoed the sweet reddish earth, preparing little holes for botanical transplants.

How happy this coral coinage of the northern summer made me! The ripe glandular berries hung in triads and pentads, and they sang in batches, and in tune.

So, B. S., you'll be leaving first. Circumstances do not yet permit me to follow you. I hope they'll change.

You'll be staying at 92 Spandarian Street, with those very nice people, the Ter-Oganians. Do you remember how it was? I'd come running to see you down Spandarian Street, swallowing the acrid construction dust for which young Erevan is famous. I still found pleasure and novelty in the ruggedness, the roughnesses and solemnities of the valley of Ararat, which had been repaired right up to its wrinkles; in the city, which seemed to have been upended by divinely inspired plumbers; and in the broad-mouthed people with eyes that had been drilled straight into their skulls—the Armenians.

Past the dry pump houses, past the conservatory, where a quartet was being rehearsed in the basement and one could hear the angry voice of the professor shouting "Lower! lower!"—that is, give a diminishing movement to the adagio—to your gateway.

Not a gate, but a long cool tunnel cut into your grandfather's house, and at the end of it, as through a spyglass, there flickered a little door covered with greenery, so unseasonably tarnished that one might have thought it had been burnt with sulphuric acid.

When you look around, your eyes need more salt. You catch forms and colors—and it is all unleavened bread. Such is Armenia.

On the little balcony you showed me a Persian pen case covered with a lacquer painting the color of blood baked with gold. It was offensively empty. I wanted to sniff its venerable musty little panels which had served sirdar justice and those instantaneous verdicts ordering men to have their eyes put out.

Then you withdrew into the walnut twilight of the Ter-Oganians' apartment and returned with a test tube and showed me the cochineal. Reddish-brown peas lay on a little wad of cotton.

You had taken that sample from the Tatar village of Sarvanlar, about twenty versts from Erevan. From there, you can see Father Ararat quite clearly, and in that dry borderland atmosphere you can't help feeling like a smuggler. Laughing, you told me a story about a certain splendid glutton of a girl, member of a friendly Tatar family in Sarvanlar . . . Her sly little face was always smeared with sour milk and her fingers were greasy with mutton fat . . . At dinnertime, you, who do not suffer in any way from undue fastidiousness, nevertheless quietly put aside a sheet of the lavash for yourself, because the little glutton was in the habit of resting her feet on the bread as on a stool.

I would watch as the accordion of infidel wrinkles would come together and draw apart on your forehead; I should think it the most inspired part of your physical appearance. These wrinkles—seemingly rubbed by your lambskin cap—reacted to every significant phrase, and they rambled all over your forehead, staggering and swaggering and stumbling about. There was something Godunov-Tatar[10] about you, my friend.

I used to compose similes for your character and grew more and more accustomed to your anti-Darwinian essence; I studied the liv-

ing language of your long, ungainly arms, created for the sake of
a handshake in a moment of peril and for passionate protestations,
while walking, against natural selection.

In Goethe's *Wilhelm Meister* there is a little man named Jarno,
a scoffer and a naturalist. He disappears for weeks at a time into the
latifundias of his model world, spends his nights in tower rooms or
chilly sheets, and emerges for dinner from the depth of his steadfast
castle.

This Jarno belonged to a peculiar order, founded by a large landowner named Lothario for the purpose of educating his contemporaries in the spirit of *Faust*, Part II. The society had a broad network
of secret agents extending all the way to America, a network organized along Jesuit lines. Secret conduct lists were kept, tentacles
would stretch out, people would get caught.

It was this Jarno who had the job of keeping Meister under surveillance.

Wilhelm was traveling with his little boy Felix, the son of the unfortunate Marianna. A paragraph of his instructions forbade him to
spend more than three days in any one place. The rosy-cheeked
Felix—a frisky, didactic child—would herbalize and exclaim, "*Sag
mir, Vater,*" would keep shooting distant questions at his father,
breaking off bits of mineral rock, and striking up one-day acquaintances.

Goethe's well-behaved children are generally a tiresome lot. As
Goethe depicts them, children are little Cupids of curiosity, each
with a quiver of pointed questions slung over his shoulder . . .

So Meister meets Jarno in the mountains.

Jarno literally tears Meister's three-day pass out of his hands. Behind them and before them lie years of separation. So much the
better! All the more resonant the echo for the geologist's lecture in
that sylvan university!

And that's why the warm light shed by oral instruction, the clear
didacticism of a friendly conversation, greatly surpasses the illuminating and instructive action of books.

I gratefully recall one of those Erevan conversations of ours,
which now, after a year or so has passed, have already been aged by
the confidence of personal experience and which possess an authenticity that helps us get a sense of ourselves in our commitment.

The talk turned around the "theory of the embryonic field," proposed by Professor Gurvich.

The rudimentary leaf of the nasturtium has the form of a halberd or of an elongated, twofold purse that begins to resemble a little tongue. Or it looks like a flint arrowhead from the Paleolithic. But the tension in the field of force that rages around the leaf first transforms it into a figure of five segments. The lines of the cave arrowhead get stretched into the shape of an arc.

Take any point and join it by a bunch of coordinates to a straight line. Then extend these coordinates, intersecting the line at various angles, to a section of identical length, then join them together again, and you get convexity!

But later the force field sharply changes its game and drives the form to its geometrical limit, the polygon. A plant is a sound evoked by the wand of a termenvox,[11] pulsating in a sphere oversaturated with wave processes. It is the envoy of a living storm that rages permanently in the universe—akin in equal measure to stone and lightning! A plant in the world—that is an event, a happening, an arrow; and not boring, bearded "development"!

Not long ago, B. S., a certain writer repented in public for having been an ornamentalist, or for having been one to the extent of his poor, sinful powers.

I think a place is prepared for him in the seventh circle of Dante's hell, where the bleeding thornbush grew. And when some tourist or other out of curiosity breaks a twig off that suicide, he will beg in a human voice, like Pier della Vigna: "Don't touch! You're hurting me! Or have you not pity in your heart? We were men, who now are trees . . ."

And a drop of black blood will fall . . . [Dante, *Inferno*, XIII, 32–37]

What Bach, what Mozart, composes variations on the theme of the nasturtium leaf? Finally, a phrase flared up: "the world-record speed of the pod of a bursting nasturtium."

Who has not felt envious of chess players? You sense in the room a peculiar field of estrangement, from which a chill hostile to non-participants flows.

But these little Persian horses made of ivory are immersed in a power-solvent. The same thing happens to them as happens to the nasturtium of the Moscow biologist E. S. Smirnov and the embryonic field of Professor Gurvich.

The threat of removal hangs over each figure throughout the game, during the whole stormy phenomenon of the tournament. The chessboard swells up from the attention concentrated on it. The chess figures grow, when they fall into the radial focus of a maneuver, like milky-cap mushrooms in Indian summer.

The problem is solved not on paper, and not in the camera obscura of causality, but in a live Impressionist milieu, in Edouard Manet's and Claude Monet's temple of air, light, and glory.

Is it true that our blood radiates mitogenetic rays that the Germans have captured on a phonograph disc, rays which, I was told, help to intensify the cell division of tissue?

All of us, without suspecting it, are the carriers of an immense embryological experiment: for even the process of remembering, crowned with the victory of memory's effort, is amazingly like the phenomenon of growth. In one as well as the other, there is a sprout, an embryo, the rudiment of a face, half a character, half a sound, the ending of a name, something labial or palatal, sweet legume on the tongue, that doesn't develop out of itself but only responds to an invitation, only stretches out *toward*, justifying one's expectation.

With these belated musings, B. S., I hope to repay you, if only in part, for having disturbed your chess game in Erevan.

SUKHUM

At the beginning of April I arrived in Sukhum—a city of mourning, tobacco, and fragrant vegetable oils. Here is where one should
begin studying the alphabets of the Caucasus; here every word starts
with *a*. The language of the Abkhazians is powerful and sonorous,
but abounds in the upper and lower guttural compound sounds,
which make pronunciation difficult; one might say it was torn out of
a larynx overgrown with hair . . .

I'm afraid the kindly bear Baloo has not yet been born to teach
me, as he did the boy Mowgli of Kipling's jungle, the excellent language of "Achoo!"—although in the distant future I foresee acade-
mies for the study of the groups of Caucasian languages, scattered
over the whole world. The phonetic ore of Europe and America
will run out. Its deposits have their limits. Even now young people
are reading Pushkin in Esperanto. To each his own.

But what an awesome warning!

One can easily get a panoramic view of Sukhum from Mount
Cherniavsky, as it is called, from Ordzhonikidze Square. It is completely linear, flat, and, to the tune of Chopin's funeral march, it
sucks into itself a great crescent of the sea with a heave of its resort-
colonial breast.

It is spread out below like a case of drawing instruments containing a compass ensconced in velvet that has just described the bay,
sketched the arched eyebrows of the hills, and closed up.

Although public life in Abkhazia has about it much that is naïvely
crude, and many abuses, one cannot help being captivated by the
administrative and economic elegance of this small maritime republic, proud of its rich soils, box-tree forests, its State Farm olive grove
at New Athos, and the high quality of its Tkvarchel coal.

Rose thorns punctured kerchiefs, and the tame bear cub with the
grey snout of some ancient Russian, of some dunce-capped Ivan the
Fool, squealed, and his squeal cut through glass. Brand-new auto-
mobiles kept rolling up straight from the sea, and their tires sliced
up the eternally green mountain . . . From underneath the bark of
the palm tree they extracted a grey fiber from which they made
theatrical wigs, and in the park the flowering agave plants, like candles weighing six poods, shot up a couple of inches every day.

Lei gave sermons on the mount on the danger of smoking and

issued fatherly reproofs to the gardener. He once asked me a question that struck me profoundly: "What was the mood of the petty bourgeoisie in Kiev in 1919?"

I think his dream was to quote Karl Marx's *Capital* in the hut of Paul and Virginie.

In my twenty-verst strolls, accompanied by silent Latvians, I developed a certain feeling for the lay of the land.

Theme: a race to the sea of gently sloping volcanic hills, joined together by a little chain—for the pedestrian.

Variation: the little green key of altitude is passed from height to height, and each new slope puts the hollow under lock.

.   .   .   .

I visited Beria, the president of the Society of the Friends of Caucasian Letters, and was close to giving him greetings for Tartarin and the gunsmith Costecalde.

A marvelous figure from Provence!

He complained of the difficulties involved in working out the Abkhazian alphabet, and spoke with respect about that Petersburg clown, Evreinov, who had been seduced in Abkhazia by the cult of the goat, and complained about not being able to obtain any serious scientific studies because of the distance from Tiflis.

The hardheaded knocking together of billiard balls is just as pleasant to men as the clicking of ivory knitting needles is to women. The bandit-cue would devastate the pyramid, and a quartet of epic heroes from Blücher's army, resembling each other like brothers, serving on the duty roster, with an air of precision about them and a bulb of laughter in their chests, exclaimed with pleasure over the charm of the game.

And the old men, Party members, didn't lag behind them.

From the balcony, through army binoculars, you could get a clear view of the track and the stands on a swampy parade ground the color of billiard cloth. Once a year there are great horse races to test the endurance of anyone who wants to compete.

A cavalcade of biblical elders would follow the boy who won.

Relatives scattered around the many versts of the ellipse would deftly pass wet towels on the end of poles to the flushed horsemen.

In a distant swamp meadow a lighthouse would keep turning like the Tate diamond.

And somehow I saw the dance of death, the wedding dance of phosphorescent insects. At first it seemed as if the tips of very thin little cigarettes that kept wandering about were being puffed to a glow, but their flourishes were too daring, free, and bold.

The devil knows where they were heading!

Coming closer: insane electrified ephemera, twitching, tracing, devouring the black hack-work in print at the present moment.

Our heavy fleshly body decays in just the same way, and our activity will turn into just such a pandemonium of signals gone amuck, if we do not leave behind us substantial proof of our existence.

It is frightening to live in a world that consists only of exclamations and interjections!

Bezymensky,[12] strong man lifting cardboard weights; round-headed, gentle, inkstained blacksmith—no, not blacksmith, bird-vender—no, not even birds—the balloons of RAPP—he was forever stooping, humming, and swacking people with his blue eyes.

An inexhaustible operatic repertoire gurgled in his throat. His open-air-concert, mineral-water heartiness never left him. A lounger, with a mandolin in his soul, he lived on the string of a ballad, and his heart's core sang under a phonograph needle.

THE FRENCH

And here I stretched my vision and sank my eye into the wide goblet
of the sea, so that every mote and tear should come out of it.

I stretched my vision like a kid glove, stretched it on a board,[13]
out onto the blue neighborhood of the sea.

I swiftly and rapaciously and with a feudal frenzy inspected the
demesnes of my eye's measure.

In such a way one puts one's eye into a wide goblet full to the
brim so that a mote will come out.

And I began to understand the binding force of color—the fervor
of sky-blue and orange T-shirts—and that color is nothing other
than a sense of the start of a race, a sense tinged by distance and
locked into its size.

Time circulated in the museum according to the hourglass. A
brick-colored trickle ran, the goblet was emptied, but then the
same golden stream of a dust storm from the upper part of the glass
into the lower.

Hello, Cézanne! Good old grandfather! Marvelous worker. Best
acorn of the forests of France.

His painting was certified on the oak table of a village notary. He
is incontestable, like a will made in sound mind and firm memory.

But what captivated me was the old man's still life. Roses that
must have been cut in the morning, full-fleshed and rolled tight, unusually young tea roses. Exactly like scoops of rich vanilla ice cream.

On the other hand, I took a dislike to Matisse, an artist for the
rich. The red paint of his canvases fizzes like soda. He is not privy
to the joy of ripening fruits. His powerful brush does not heal the
vision, but gives it the strength of an ox, so that the eyes become
bloodshot.[14]

I've had enough of this carpet chess and these odalisques!

Persian whimseys of a Parisian *maître*!

The cheap vegetable pigments of Van Gogh were bought by
calamitous accident for twenty sous.

Van Gogh spits blood like a suicide in a cheap hotel. The floor-
boards in the night café are tilted and stream like a gutter in their
electric madness. And the narrow trough of the billiard table looks
like the trough of a coffin.

I never saw such barking colors!

And his streetcar-conductor's vegetable-garden landscapes! The soot of suburban trains has just been wiped from them with a wet rag.

His canvases, smeared with the omelette of catastrophe, are as clear as visual aids, as the charts in a Berlitz school.

The visitors move about with little steps as though in church.

Each room has its own climate. In Claude Monet's room there is river air. Looking at the water painted by Renoir, you feel blisters on your palm as if you'd been rowing.

Signac invented the corn-colored sun.

The woman who explains the pictures leads the culture and education officials behind her.

To look at them, you'd say a magnet was attracting a duck.

Ozenfant worked out something surprising by using red chalk and slate-grey squirrels on a black slate background and modulating the forms of glass blowing and fragile laboratory equipment.

You would also be greeted by Picasso's dark-blue Jew and Pissarro's raspberry-grey boulevards, flowing like the wheels of an immense lottery with their little boxes of hansom cabs, their fishing-pole-whips pitched on their shoulders, and the shreds of splashed brain on the kiosks and chestnut trees.

But perhaps you've had enough?

Generalization is already waiting, bored, at the door.

To anyone recuperating from the harmless plague of naïve realism I would recommend the following method of looking at pictures.

Under no circumstances go in as if into a chapel. Don't be thrilled or chilled, and don't get glued to the canvas . . .

With a stroller's stride, as on a boulevard—straight on!

Cut through the large heat waves of the space of oil painting.

Calmly, without getting excited—the way Tatar children bathe their horses in Alushta—lower your eye into what will be for it a new material environment—and remember that the eye is a noble, but stubborn, animal.

Standing before a picture to which the body heat of your vision has still not adjusted itself, for which the crystalline lens has not yet found the single suitable accommodation, is exactly like singing a serenade in a fur coat behind a double set of windows.

When that equilibrium has been attained, and only then, begin the second stage of restoring the picture, the washing of it, removing its old peel, its outer and most recent barbaric layer, the stage that links it, as it does every work of art, to a sunny, solid reality.

With its extremely subtle acidic reactions, the eye, an organ that possesses its own acoustics, augmenting the value of the image, exaggerating its own achievements to a degree that offends the senses and then making a great fuss over it, raises the picture to its own level; for painting is much more a matter of internal secretion than of apperception, that is, of external perceiving.

The material of painting is organized in such a way that nobody altogether loses, and that is its distinction from nature. But the probability of a lottery is inversely proportional to its feasibility.

And it is only here that the third and final stage of entering a picture begins—confronting the intention behind it.

And that traveler, the eye, presents his ambassadorial credentials to the consciousness. And then a cold agreement is reached between the viewer and the picture, something rather like a state secret.

From the embassy of painting I went out into the street.

Right after having left the Frenchmen, the light seemed to me the phase of a waning eclipse, while the sun itself was wrapped in silver foil.

At the entrance of the cooperative stood a mother with her son. The boy was emaciated, respectful. Both were in mourning. The woman was sticking a bunch of radishes into her reticule.

The end of the street, as if crushed by a pair of binoculars, swerved off into a squinting lump; and all of this—distant and deceptive [*lipovyi*][15]—was stuffed into a string bag.

AROUND THE NATURALISTS

Lamarck fought sword in hand for the honor of living nature. Do you think he reconciled himself to evolution as easily as did the scientific barbarians of the nineteenth century? But I think embarrassment for nature burnt the swarthy cheeks of Lamarck. He could not forgive nature for a trifle called the variability of species.

Forward! *Aux armes!* Let us wash ourselves clean of the dishonor of evolution.

Reading the taxonomists (Linnaeus, Buffon, Pallas) has a soothing effect on the disposition, straightens out the eye, and communicates to the soul a mineral quartz tranquillity.

Russia as depicted by that remarkable naturalist Pallas: peasant women distill the dye "mariona" from a mixture of birchleaves and alum; the bark of the linden tree peels off on its own to become bast, to be woven into shoes and baskets; the peasants use a thick petroleum as medicinal oil; the Chuvash girls jingle with trinkets in their tresses.

Whoever does not love Haydn, Gluck, and Mozart will never understand a thing in Pallas.

He transformed the corporeal roundness and graciousness of German music to the Russian plains. With the white hands of a *Konzertmeister* he collects Russian mushrooms. Damp chamoisskin, decayed velvet, but when you break it open, it's a pure, deep blue.

Let us speak of the physiology of reading. It is a rich, inexhaustible, and, it would seem, forbidden theme. Out of everything material, of all physical bodies, a book is the object that inspires man with the greatest confidence. A book established on a reading stand is like a canvas stretched on a frame.

When we are completely rapt in the activity of reading, we mainly admire our generic properties, we feel a kind of exaltation at the classification of our own various stages.

But if Linnaeus, Buffon, and Pallas colored my mature years, it is the whale I thank for having awakened in me a childish astonishment at science.

In the zoological museum: drip . . . drip . . . drip . . . Practically nothing in the way of empirical experience.

Time to turn off that tap!

Enough!

I have concluded a truce with Darwin and placed him on my

imaginary bookstand next to Dickens. If they should happen to dine together, Mr. Pickwick would join them as a third. One can't help being taken by Darwin's good nature. He is an unintentional humorist. The humor of situation is habitual to him, accompanies him wherever he goes.

But is good nature a method of creative cognition, a worthy means of life-probing?

In Lamarck's reversed, descending movement down the ladder of living creatures, there is a greatness worthy of Dante. The lower forms of organic existence are the hell of humanity.

The long grey antennae of this butterfly had a bristly structure and looked just like the little branches on a French academician's collar or like the silver palm fronds placed on a coffin. The powerful thorax is shaped like a little boat. The slight head is like a kitten's.

Its wings with their big eyes were made of the fine old silk of an admiral who had been both at Cesme and Trafalgar.

And suddenly I caught myself wildly desiring to have a look at nature through the painted eyes of that monster.

Lamarck feels the gaps between species. He hears the pauses and the syncopation in the evolutionary series.

Lamarck wept his eyes out over his magnifying glass. In natural science he is the only Shakespearean figure.

Look—that blushing, semirespectable old man goes running down the staircase of living creatures like a young man who has just been treated kindly at an audience with a government minister or made happy by his mistress.

No one, not even the most inveterate mechanist, regards the growth of an organism as resulting from the variability of the external environment. That would be entirely too presumptuous. The environment merely invites the organism to grow. Its functions are expressed in a certain benevolence which is gradually and continually canceled by the severity that holds the living body together and finally rewards it with death.

So, for the environment, the organism is probability, desire, and expectancy. For the organism, the environment is a force that invites. Not so much a surrounding cover as a challenge.

When the conductor draws a theme out of the orchestra with his baton, he is not the physical cause of the sound. The sound is already there in the score of the symphony, in the spontaneous collusion of the performers, in the crowdedness of the auditorium, and in the structure of the musical instruments.

Lamarck's animals are out of fables. They adapt themselves to the conditions of life. In the manner of La Fontaine. The legs of the heron, the neck of the duck and the swan, the tongue of the ant-eater, the asymmetrical or symmetrical structure of the eyes in certain fish.

It was La Fontaine, if you wish, who prepared the way for Lamarck's doctrine. His overly clever, moralizing, judicious beasts made splendid living material for evolution. They had already apportioned its mandates among themselves.

The artiodactylous reasoning of the mammals clothes their fingers with rounded horn.

The kangaroo moves with the leaps of his logic.

This marsupial in Lamarck's description of weak forelimbs (i.e., limbs that have reconciled themselves to their own uselessness); strongly developed hind extremities (i.e., convinced of their own importance); and a powerful thesis called the tail.

Children have already settled down to play in the sand at the pedestal of the evolutionary theory of Grandfather Krylov, that is, so to speak, Lamarck–La Fontaine. Once having found a refuge in the Luxembourg Gardens, Lamarck's theory grew cluttered with balls and shuttlecocks.

And I love it when Lamarck deigns to be angry and smashes to smithereens all that Swiss pedagogical boredom. Into the concept of "nature" there bursts the Marseillaise!

Male ruminants butt foreheads. They have no horns as yet.

But an inner feeling, born of anger, directs "fluids" to the forehead, which aid in forming a substance of horn and bone.

I take off my hat. I let the teacher go first. May the youthful thunder of his eloquence never fade!

"Still" and "already" are the two bright points of Lamarckian thought, the throbbings of evolutionary glory and emblazoning, the signalmen and advance scouts of morphology. He was one of that breed of old piano-tuners who jingle with bony fingers in other people's mansions. He was permitted only chromatic notes and childish arpeggios.

Napoleon allowed him to tune up nature, because he regarded it as imperial property.

In Linnaeus' zoological descriptions, one can't miss the successive relationship to, and a certain dependence on, the menagerie of the county fair. The proprietor of the wandering show booth or the hired barker tried to show their merchandise at its best. These barkers never dreamed they would play a certain role in the origin of the style of classical natural science. There they were, lying all out, talking rot on an empty stomach; yet at the same time they couldn't resist being carried away by their own art. Some demon would save them, but also their professional experience, and the lasting tradition of their craft.

As a child in small-town Uppsala, Linnaeus could not have failed to visit the fair or listen with delight to the line of patter offered in the wandering menagerie. Like boys everywhere, he went numb and melted before the savvy bloke with the jackboots and whip, that doctor of fabulous zoology, who would shower praises on the puma as he brandished his huge red fists.

In linking the important accomplishments of the Swedish naturalist to the eloquence of the carnival loudmouth, I have not the least intention of belittling Linnaeus. I wish only to remind my reader that the naturalist, too, was a professional storyteller, a public demonstrator of new and interesting species.

The colorful portraits of animals in Linnaeus' *Systema Naturae* might well hang beside pictures of the Seven Years' War or an oleograph of the Prodigal Son.

Linnaeus painted his monkeys in the tenderest colonial colors. He would dip his brush in Chinese lacquers, and he would paint with brown and red pepper, with saffron, olive oil, and cherry juice. And he managed his task with dexterity and gaiety, like a barber shaving the *Bürgermeister*, or a Dutch housewife grinding coffee on her lap in a big-bellied coffee mill.

Delightful—the Christopher-Columbus brilliance of Linnaeus' monkey house.

It is Adam passing out certificates of merit to the mammals, aided by a Baghdad magician and a monk from China.

The Persian miniature has a slanted, frightened, graceful almond eye.

Sensual without sin, it convinces one like nothing else that life is a precious gift, inalienable.

I love the Moslem enamels and cameos!

Pursuing my simile, I would say: the beauty's burning, equine eye descends to the reader, gracious and aslant. The charred cabbage-stumps of the manuscripts crunch like Sukhum tobacco.

How much blood has been spilt on account of these touch-me-nots![16] How conquerors enjoyed them!

Leopards have the sly ears of punished schoolboys.

The weeping willow, having rolled itself up into a globe, flows and swims.

Adam and Eve hold counsel, dressed in the latest paradisial fashion.

The horizon has been abolished. There is no perspective. A charming slowness of wit. The vixen's noble ascent of the stairs, and the feeling that the gardener is leaning against the landscape and the architecture.

Yesterday I was reading Firdousi and it seemed to me that a bumblebee was sitting on the book sucking it.

In Persian poetry ambassadorial winds blow out of China bearing gifts.

It scoops up longevity with a silver ladle and endows whoever might desire it with millennia by threes and fives. That is why the rulers of the Djemdjid dynasty are as long-lived as parrots.

After having been good for an incredibly long time, Firdousi's favorites suddenly for no reason at all become scoundrels, solely in obedience to the author's luxuriously arbitrary fancy.

The earth and the sky in the book of *Shahnama* are afflicted with goiter—they are delightfully exophthalmic.

I got the Firdousi from the State Librarian of Armenia, Mamikon Artemevich Gevorkian. I was brought a whole stack of little blue volumes—eight, I think. The words of the noble prose translation —it was the French version of Von Mohl—breathed a fragrance of attar of roses. Chewing his drooping gubernatorial lip, with the unpleasant voice of a camel, Mamikon sang me a few lines in Persian.

Gevorkian is eloquent, clever, and courteous, but his erudition is altogether loud and pushy, and his speech fat, like a lawyer's.

Readers are forced to satisfy their curiosity right there in the director's office, under his personal supervision, and books that are placed on that satrap's table take on a taste of pink pheasant's meat, bitter quails, musky venison, and cunning hare.

ASHTARAK[17]

I managed to observe the clouds performing their devotions to Ararat.

It was the descending-ascending motion of cream poured into a glass of ruddy tea, dispersing in all directions like curly-puffed tubers.

And yet the sky in the land of Ararat gives little pleasure to the Lord of Sabaoth; it was invented by a titmouse in the spirit of most ancient atheism.

Coachman's Mountain,[18] glittering with snow, a small field, sown as if for some mocking purpose with stone teeth, the numbered barracks of construction sites and a tin can jammed with passengers— there you have the outskirts of Erevan.

And suddenly—a violin, divided up into gardens and houses, broken up into a system of terraced shelves, with crossbars, interceptors, dowels, and bridges.

The village of Ashtarak hung on the purling of the water as on a wire frame. The little stone baskets that were its gardens would make the finest gift for a coloratura at a charity performance.

A place to spend the night was found in a large four-bedroom house that had belonged to some dispossessed kulaks. The collective farm administration had scattered its furniture and set it up as the village guesthouse. On a terrace that might have given refuge to all the seed of Abraham a milky washstand was grieving.

The orchard was a dancing class for trees. The schoolgirl shyness of the apple trees, the vermilion competence of the cherries . . . Look at their quadrilles, their ritornelli and rondeaux.

I was listening to the purling of the kolkhoz accounts. In the mountains a drenching rain slanted through, and the abysses of the street gutters ran more swiftly than usual.

The water rang and welled up on all the floor-levels and terraced shelves of Ashtarak—permitting the camel to pass through the eye of the needle.

I have received your eighteen-page letter, completely covered in a hand straight and tall as an avenue of poplars, and to it I answer:

First sensual encounter with the material of an old Armenian church.

The eye searches for a form, an idea, expects it; but stumbles instead on the moldy bread of nature or on a stone pie.

The teeth of your vision crumble and break when you look for the first time at Armenian churches.

The Armenian language cannot be worn out; its boots are stone. Well, certainly, the thick-walled word, the layers of air in the semivowels. But is that all there is to its charm? No! Where does its traction come from? How to explain it? Make sense of it?

I felt the joy of pronouncing sounds forbidden to Russian lips, secret sounds, outcast, and perhaps, on some deep level, shameful.

There was some fine water boiling in a pewter teapot and suddenly a pinch of marvelous black tea was thrown into it.

That's how I felt about the Armenian language.

I have cultivated in myself a sixth sense, an "Ararat" sense: the sense of attraction to a mountain.

Now, no matter where I might be carried, it is already speculative and will abide with me.

The little church in Ashtarak is of the most ordinary kind and, for Armenia, submissive. It is a little church in a six-sided headdress with a rope ornament along the cornices of the roof and the same sort of stringy eyebrows over the meager mouths of its chinklike windows.

The door is quieter than water, lower than grass. I stood on tiptoe and glanced inside: but there was a cupola in there, a cupola!

A real one! Like the one in St. Peter's in Rome, above the thronged thousands, the palms, the sea of candles, and the Pope's sedan chair.

There the recessed spheres of the apses sing like seashells. There we have the four bakers: north, west, south, and east, who, their eyes plucked out, knock into the funnel-shaped niches, rummage about the hearths and the spaces between the hearths and find no place for themselves.

Whose idea was it to imprison space inside this wretched cellar, this beggars' dungeon—in order to render it there a homage worthy of the psalmist?

When the miller can't sleep, he goes out bareheaded to inspect his millstones. Sometimes I wake up at night and check on the conjugations in Marr's grammar.

The teacher Ashot is immured in his flat-walled house like the unfortunate character in Victor Hugo's novel.

Having tapped his finger on the case of his sea-captain's barometer, he would go out into the courtyard that led to the reservoir and plot the precipitation curve on a chart of graph paper.

He worked a small-scale orchard of a tenth of a hectare, a tiny garden baked into the stone-grape pie of Ashtarak, and had been excluded from the kolkhoz as an extra mouth to feed.

In a hollow space in his bureau he kept a university degree, a high-school diploma, and a wishy-washy packet of water-color sketches, innocent hallmark of his character and talent.

In him was the hum of the past imperfect.

Hard worker in a black shirt, theatrically open at the neck, with a heavy fire in his eyes, he retired into the perspective of historical painting, in the direction of the Scottish martyrs, the Stuarts.

A story has yet to be written about the tragedy of semieducation. I think the biography of the village teacher might well become the coffee-table book of our day, as *Werther* once was.

Ashtarak, a rich, snugly nested settlement, is older than many European cities. It was celebrated for its harvest festivals and for the songs of the Ashugs. People who grow up close to vineyards are fond of women, sociable, skeptical, and tend to be touchy and idle. The people of Ashtarak are no exception.

Three apples fell from heaven: the first for the one who told the tale, the second for the one who listened, and the third for the one who understood. That is the way most Armenian fairy tales end. Many of them were written down in Ashtarak. This region is the folkloric granary of Armenia.

ALAGEZ

What tense do you want to live in?

"I want to live in the imperative of the future passive participle, in the 'what ought to be.' "

That's the way I'd like to breathe. That's what pleases me. There is such a thing as mounted, bandit-band, equestrian honor. That is why I like the splendid Latin "gerundive"—that verb on horseback.

Yes, the Latin genius, when it was young and greedy, created that form of imperative verbal traction as the prototype of our whole culture, and it was not merely "that which ought to be," but "that which ought to be praised"—*laudatura est*—that which pleases . . .

Such was the talk I carried on with myself as I rode horseback among the natural boundaries, the nomads' territories and the gigantic pastures of Alagez.

In Erevan, Alagez had stuck out in front of my eyes like "hello" or "goodbye." I saw how its snowy crown melted from one day to the next and how in good weather, especially in the morning, its tinted cliffs crunched like dry toast.

And I felt drawn to it, over the mulberry trees and the earthen roofs of the houses.

A piece of Alagez lived right there with me in the hotel. For some reason, a heavy specimen of the black volcanic glasslike mineral called "obsidian" lay on the window sill. A fifty-pound calling card left behind by some geological expedition.

The approaches to Alagez are not fatiguing, and it is no trouble at all on horseback, in spite of its fourteen thousand feet above sea level. The lava is contained in earthen blisters, along which one rides easily.

From the window of my fifth-floor room in the Erevan hotel, I had formed a completely wrong notion of Alagez. I thought it was a monolithic ridge. Actually, it is a system of folds and develops gradually—proportionately to the rise, the accordion of diorite rock uncoiled itself like an alpine waltz.

And a spacious day it was that fell to my lot!

Even now, as I think back on it, my heart skips a beat. I got tangled up in it as in a long shirt extracted from one of the suitcases of my ancestor Jacob.

The village of Biurakan is known for its baby-chick hunt. They rolled about the floor like little yellow balls, doomed to be sacrificed to our cannibal appetite.

We were joined in the school by a wandering carpenter, an experienced and adroit man. Taking a swig of cognac, he told us he had no use for either artels or labor unions. He said his hands were made of gold, and he was respected and could find a place anywhere. He needed no labor exchange to find a customer: by smell and by rumor he could guess where his work was needed.

Seems he was Czech by birth, and the Pied Piper.

In Biurakan I bought a large clay saltcellar, on account of which I had a lot of trouble later.

Imagine a crude Easter-cake mold—a peasant woman in farthingale or hoop skirt, with a feline head and a big round mouth right in the middle of her robe into which you could easily thrust your whole hand.

It was a lucky find from what was, by the way, a rich family of such objects. But the symbolic power with which some primitive imagination had invested it had not escaped even the casual attention of the townsmen.

Everywhere there were peasant women with weeping faces, shuffling movements, red eyelids, and cracked lips. They had an ugly way of walking, as if they had the dropsy or had strained a tendon. They moved like hills of weary rags, stirring up the dust with their hems.

The flies eat the children, gathering in clusters at the corners of their eyes.

The smile of an elderly Armenian peasant woman is inexplicably fine—there is so much nobility in it, exhausted dignity, and a kind of solemn, married charm.

The horses walk among divans, step on the pillows, wear out the shafts. You ride along feeling you have an invitation from Tamerlane in your pocket.

I saw the tomb of a giant Kurd of fabulous dimensions and accepted it as normal.

The lead horse minted rubles with her hoofs and her prodigality knew no bounds.

From the pommel of my saddle dangled an unplucked chicken, killed that morning in Biurakan.

Once in a while my horse would bend down to the grass, and its neck expressed its allegiance to the Standpats, a people older than the Romans.

A milky quietude ensued. The whey of silence curdled. The curds of the bells and the cranberries of the harness bells of various calibers muttered and clashed. Near every wellyard the karakul committee proceeded with its meeting. It seemed as if dozens of small circus owners had pitched their tents and show booths on the louse-bitten hill and, unprepared for the full house, taken unawares, swarmed about in their camps, clattering their dairy dishes, cramming the lambs into their lair, and rushing to lock up for their night in oxrealm the world-weary, steaming damp heads of cattle, distributing them among their stalls in Bay City.

Armenian and Kurdish camps do not differ in their arrangements. They are cattle-breeders' settlements on the terraces of Alagez, stopovers for villas, laid out in carefully chosen places.

Stone markers indicate the floor plan of the tent and the small adjoining yard with its heaped wall of dung. Abandoned or unoccupied camps look as if they had been burnt out.

The guides from Biurakan were glad to stop overnight in Kamarlu: they had relatives there.

A childless old couple received us for the night into the bosom of their tent.

The old woman moved and worked with weepy, withdrawing, blessing motions as she prepared a smoky supper and some felt strips for bedding.

"Here, take the felt! Grab a blanket . . . Tell us something about Moscow."

Our hosts got ready for bed. An oil wick lit up the tent, making it seem high as a railroad station. The wife took out a coarse army nightshirt and put it on her husband.

I felt as shy as if I were in a palace.

1. The body of Arshak[19] is unwashed and his beard has run wild.

2. The king's fingernails are broken, and the wood lice crawl over his face.

3. His ears have grown dull with silence, but once they listened to Greek music.

4. His tongue is scabby from jailers' food, but there was a time when it pressed grapes against the roof of his mouth and was adroit as the tip of a flutist's tongue.

5. The seed of Arshak has withered in his scrotum and his voice is as sparse as the bleating of a sheep.

6. King Shapukh[20]—thinks Arshak—has got the better of me, and, worse than that, he has taken my air[21] for himself.

7. The Assyrian grips my heart.

8. He is the commander of my hair and my fingernails. He grows me my beard and swallows me my spit, so accustomed has he grown to the thought that I am here, in the fortress of Aniush.

9. The Kushan people rebelled against Shapukh.

10. They broke through the border at an undefended place, as through a silken cord.

11. The Kushan attack pricked and disturbed King Shapukh, like an eyelash in his eye.

12. Both the sides (enemies) squinted, so as not to see each other.

13. A certain Darmastat, the most gracious and best-educated of the eunuchs, was in the center of Shapukh's army, encouraged the commander of the cavalry, wormed his way into his master's favor, snatched him, like a chessman, out of danger, and all the while remained in full view.

14. He was governor of the province of Andekh in the days when Arshak, in his velvet voice, used to give orders.

15. Yesterday he was king but today he has fallen into a fissure, has scrunched himself into a belly like a baby, and he warms himself with lice, enjoying the itch.

16. When the time came for his reward Darmastat inserted into the Assyrian's ears a request that tickled like a feather:

17. Give me a pass to Aniush Fortress. I would like Arshak to spend one additional day, full of hearing, taste, and smell, as it was before, when he amused himself at the hunt or busied himself with the planting of trees.

Sleep is easy in nomad camps. The body, exhausted by space, grows warm, stretches out, recalls the length of the road. The paths of the mountain ridges run like shivers along the spine. The velvet meadows burden and tickle the eyelids. Bedsores of the ravines hollow out the sides. Sleep immures, walls you in. Last thought: have to ride around some ridge.

Notes

Introduction: Friends and Enemies of the Word

1. "The Word and Culture."
   The reader without Russian wishing to learn something about Mandelstam will find the following works indispensible: Clarence Brown, *Mandelstam* (Cambridge: Cambridge University Press, 1973; this is the first volume of what promises to be a two-volume critical biography of Mandelstam; it contains a number of sensitive translations and exegeses of his poems—it was Brown's intention that his book serve as an anthology as well—and some of the critical essays; unfortunately, it stops as of 1928); Brown's edition of *The Prose of Osip Mandelstam* (Princeton: Princeton University Press, 1965; contains Mandelstam's only "novella" and his fictionalized autobiographical works); Nadezhda Iakovlevna Mandelstam, *Hope against Hope*, trans. Max Hayward (New York: Atheneum, 1970) and *Hope Abandoned*, trans. Max Hayward (New York: Atheneum, 1974) (Mandelstam's widow's two books of memoirs, still the most authoritative source on his life and attitudes to life and poetry); and her single venture into interpretive criticism, *Mozart and Salieri*, trans. R. A. McLean (Ann Arbor: Ardis Press, 1973; the title is from a short play by Pushkin, on which Mandelstam himself had commented); the two volumes that I edited, with introductions and notes, published in the series Russian Literature in Translation by the State University of New York Press: *Selected Works of Nikolai S. Gumilev*, trans. Burton Raffel and Alla Burago (Albany, 1972), and *Complete Poetry of Osip Emilevich Mandelstam*, trans. Burton Raffel and Alla Burago (Albany, 1973; contains, in addition to a long interpretive essay that is the companion of the present one, two chapters from Nadezhda Mandelstam's memoirs that did not appear in the English translation cited above); a recent issue of *Soviet Studies in Literature*, 9, no. 4 (Fall 1973), which includes Soviet writing on Mandelstam, ranging from the "apologetic" introduction by Alexander Dymshits to the truncated Soviet edition of Mandelstam's poems, to the perceptive and subtle essay by Lidia Ginzburg; Arthur A. Cohen, *Osip Emilievich Mandelstam: an Essay in Antiphon* (Ann Arbor: Ardis Press, 1974), which takes up the complex question of Mandelstam's Jewishness and its relation to his Christianity.
2. Osip Mandel'shtam, *Sobranie sochinenii* [Collected works], ed. Gleb Struve and Boris Filipoff, 2d ed., 3 vols. (Washington, D.C.: Inter-

Language Library Associates, 1967–1971) (henceforth cited as Mandel'shtam), 2: 484. See also Brown, *Mandelstam*, p. 35.

3. Brown, ed., *The Prose of Osip Mandelstam*, p. 111.

4. See the essays "The Morning of Acmeism" and "About the Nature of the Word."

5. Osip Mandel'shtam, *Stikhotvoreniia* [Poems] (Leningrad: Sovetskii pisatel, 1973); see the English translation of the introduction by Alexander Dymshits, "I Enter the World . . . ," *Soviet Studies in Literature* 9, no. 4 (Fall 1973).

6. The translation in this volume first appeared as "Talking about Dante," *Delos*, no. 6 (1971): 65–107. In connection with this essay, the commentary by Mandelstam's Italian translator, A. Ripellino, "Note sulla prosa di Mandel'stam," in *La Quarta Prosa* (Bari, 1967), p. 10, is of considerable interest.

7. T. S. Eliot, *Selected Essays, 1917–1932* (London: Faber and Faber, 1932), p. 229.

8. See the essay "François Villon," p. 118.

9. N. Mandelstam, *Hope against Hope*, pp. 184–190.

10. Gaston Bachelard, *On Poetic Imagination and Reverie*, trans. Colette Grandin (Indianapolis: Bobbs-Merrill, 1971), p. xxiii. Bachelard's account of Novalis as a "poet of earth" would have pleased Mandelstam (Bachelard, *La Terre et les reveries de la volonté* [Paris: Librairie José Corti, 1948], p. 285).

11. "Pushkin and Scriabin." Neither Pushkin nor Scriabin was in any conventional sense of the word a Christian. Pushkin was an agnostic, Scriabin a kind of diabolist and practitioner of white magic. Yet Mandelstam refers to Scriabin in this tantalizing fragment—the full version of which seems to have been irretrievably lost—as both a Christian and "a raving Hellene." The reference to the curious police activities around the funeral of Pushkin as "the sun's burial by night" has many echoes in Mandelstam in the image of the "black sun." See also Iurii Ivask, "Khristianskaia poeziia Mandel'shtama" [The Christian poetry of Mandelstam], *Novyi Zhurnal* 103 (1971): 109–123.

12. "Pushkin and Scriabin."

13. "The Morning of Acmeism."

14. Mandelstam, no. 117. Throughout this volume, where Mandelstam's poems are cited, I use the numbering of the Struve-Filipoff edition (see note 2 above), which the *Complete Poetry of Osip Emilevich Mandelstam*, trans. Raffel and Burago, also follows.

15. "The Word and Culture."

16. Boris Pasternak, "Pro eti stikhi" [About these lines], in *Stikhi i poemy, 1912–1932* (Ann Arbor: University of Michigan Press, 1961), p. 4.

17. "The Word and Culture."

18. "The Nineteenth Century."

19. "Humanism and Modern Life."

20. "The Word and Culture." See the extremely interesting essay by Victor Terras, "Osip Mandel'shtam i ego filosofiia slova" [Osip Mandelstam and his philosophy of the word], in *Slavic Poetics: Essays in Honor of Kirill Taranovsky*, ed. R. Jakobson, C. van Schooneveld, and D. Worth (The Hague: Mouton, 1973), pp. 455–460; also of considerable interest, Kirill Taranovsky, "Pchely i osy v poezii Mandel'shtama" [Bees and wasps in Mandelstam's poetry], in *To Honor Roman Jakobson* (The Hague: Mouton, 1967). Basing himself on Mandelstam's remarks on the importance of knowing where a poet comes from ("Badger's Burrow"), Taranovsky makes a strong case for his "emergence" from Viacheslav Ivanov. His notion of a subtext, interesting in itself, becomes, more and more as he illustrates its meaning, somewhat academic. *Russian Literature*, no. 2 (The Hague: Mouton, 1972), a special issue devoted to the poetry of Osip Mandelstam, contains articles by Iu. Levin, D. Segal, R. Pshibylcki, and K. Taranovsky. *Russian Literature*, no. 7/8 (1974), contains articles by K. Taranovsky, "The Jewish Theme in the Poetry of Osip Mandel'shtam," idem, "Osip Mandel'shtam: 'Na rozval'njach, ulozhennych solomoj' "; N. A. Nilsson, "Mandel'shtam's Poem 'Voz'mi na rodost' "; J. van der Eng-Liedmeier, "Mandel'shtam's Poem 'V Peterburge my sojdemsja snova.' "

21. In a number of essays and poems, Mandelstam uses "Buddhist" rather curiously to denote a kind of detachment in which the observer has no participation in the scene which he observes but looks on it with the privileged eye of God. In this sense, Mandelstam viewed nineteenth-century science as Buddhist—but also the transparent realism of Flaubert (and, with more justice, the Goncourts) and anthroposophy in religion. He owes the conception to his early reading of Alexander Herzen, the father of Russian socialism and a brilliant stylist. In Herzen's book *Dilettantism in Science*, the chapter dealing with the right-Hegelians is called "Buddhism in Science." See Alexander Herzen, *Selected Philosophical Works* (Moscow, 1956), pp. 71–96.

22. "Literary Moscow."

23. Elena Tager, quoted by Brown, *Mandelstam*, p. 69.

24. William Arrowsmith, "Aristophanes' Birds: The Fantasy Politics of Eros," *Arion*, n.s. 1, no. 1 (1973): 119–167. See also the charming account of Mandelstam's attempt to learn Greek in Brown, *Mandelstam*, p. 47.

25. "About the Nature of the Word."

26. "Pushkin and Scriabin."

27. Victor Terras, "Classical Motives in the Poetry of Osip Mandelstam," *Slavic and East European Journal* 3 (1966): 251–267; Brown, *Mandelstam*, pp. 253–375.

28. Cohen, *Osip Emilievich Mandelstam*, p. 60.

29. "The Word and Culture."

30. "Storm and Stress."
31. N. Mandelstam, *Hope against Hope*, p. 264.
32. Mandel'shtam, 1: 239, no. 352.
33. Cohen, *Osip Emilievich Mandelstam*, p. 69.
34. *Journey to Armenia*. The "termenvox" was an electrical musical instrument, invented by Mandelstam's friend Lev Termen.
35. *Journey to Armenia*.
36. N. Mandelstam, *Hope Abandoned*, p. 549.

> "Before that I nonetheless have seen
> Rich Ararat draped in its Bible cloth
> And I spent 200 days in the Sabbath Land
> They call Armenia."
> (Mandelstam, no. 237)

37. *Journey to Armenia*.
38. Ibid.
39. Ibid.
40. "The Morning of Acmeism."

Conversation about Dante

Although this essay was probably the last written (1933–1934) of those included in this volume, it expresses more fully than any other the range and the focus of Mandelstam's sensibility as a critic, and so there is a certain logic in placing it first. It is not so much an attempt to characterize Dante as a literary figure as it is the elaboration of a poetics inspired by the reading of Dante, an attempt to get at the mainsprings of poetry, what poetry is and what it does, rather than an enumeration of its devices or the elaboration of a theoretical system based on a study of these devices. For Mandelstam, Dante is the archpoet, as Italy (the Mediterranean) is the home, the childhood, of modern European culture. Mandelstam is interested in the source, the basic physical impulse of poetry, and its elaboration in form—though he is no more a "Formalist" in his approach, for all his elaboration on rhyme and the *terzina*, than he is "sociological," for all the importance he attaches to Dante's social origins and the Italian class structure of his time.

During his student years at Heidelberg and the Sorbonne, long before the Revolution, Mandelstam may have spent a few weeks in Italy as a tourist. He knew the *Divine Comedy* in the superb Russian translation of his friend Lozinsky, but began to study Italian seriously only in the 1930's. In the summer of 1933, in Koktebel, in the Crimea, he read a draft of this essay aloud to Andrei Biely, whom he had previously regarded as a literary enemy, but about whom he then severely revised his opinion, and to whom he subsequently dedicated a cycle of poems. Biely may in a certain sense be taken as the gifted and highly cultivated poet, novelist, and man of letters with whom this "conversation" takes place.

1. Dante, *Inferno*, XVI, 22–24. Brown and Hughes have translated directly from Mandelstam's Russian. Dante's Italian reads:

"Qual soleano i campion far nudi ed unti,
    avvisando lor presa e lor vantaggio,
    prima che sien tra lor battuti e punti."

I would translate: "As stripped and oiled wrestlers used to do, looking for a grip and an advantage before they started hitting out at each other."

2. For a strikingly similar account of lyrical composition, see Northrop Frye, *The Anatomy of Criticism* (Princeton: Princeton University Press, 1957), pp. 275–277.

3. Dadaism was the modernist movement in the arts, originating in Switzerland during the years of the First World War, whose founders were Tristan Tzara and Kurt Schwitters. The name suggests children's word-formation, baby talk.

4. "And soothingly would speak the language
that used to delight fathers and mothers:

.   .   .   .

would tell her family tales
about the Trojans and Fiesole and Rome."

5. In Russian, *zaum*. Translated elsewhere in this volume as "metalogic." *Zaumnyi* means "metalogical." The reference is to Khlebnikov and the Futurists and their experiments with "transsense" or "metalogical" language. See Dante, *Purgatorio*, XI, 103–108.

6. The Italian reads:
"Poi si rivolse, e parve di coloro
    che corrono a Verona il drappo verde
    per la campagna; e parve di costoro
quegli che vince e non colui che perde."
Mandelstam seems to have made a slight mistake in the translation, which should read: "Then he turned back, and seemed like one of those who run through the open field at Verona for [the prize of] the green cloth; and of them he seemed like him who wins, not like him who loses."

7. "Averroës, who composed the great commentary."

8. "Turn around: what are you doing?"

9. "Io avea già il mio viso nel suo fitto;
    ed el s'ergea col petto e colla fronte,
    com' avesse l'inferno in gran dispitto."

10. " 'And if,' continuing what he had said before,
    'they have learnt that art badly,' he said,
    'it torments me more than this bed.' "

11. "O Tosco, che per la città del foco
    vivo ten vai così parlando onesto,
    piacciati di ristare in questo loco.
    La tua loquela ti fa manifesto
    di quella nobil patria natio,
    alla qual forse fui troppo molesto."
    (Inferno, X, 22–27)

12. *Raznochinets* (*razno-*, "various"; *chin*, "rank") : in the nineteenth cen-
    tury, a member of the intelligentsia who was not of noble origin. He
    could be the son of a priest or a merchant who did not follow in his
    father's footsteps, or someone of even lower social origin, who had man-
    aged to acquire an education. The term might also be used ironically in
    connection with the declassing of the old Russian nobility into a service
    class, a class in which status was more and more determined by rank in
    the civil service. Thus, a *razno-chinets* is not necessarily a "commoner"
    by origin, but he might well be. In the Russian literary tradition, the
    pathos of the "noble *raznochinets*" is exemplified in the character of
    Evgeny in Pushkin's "The Bronze Horseman," a poor clerk whose an-
    cestors were prominent nobility. In the 1860's, however, "the decade of
    the *raznochintsy*," as it was commonly called, these were men of differ-
    ent but humble class origins (sons of priests, merchants, etc.) who re-
    ceived a higher education and qualified for medium civil-service rank for
    the first time—i.e., "the newly educated," but also those of lowly or
    obscure origins hobnobbing for the first time with their social and eco-
    nomic superiors by virtue of their education. Mandelstam identified *him-
    self*, as well as Dante, as a *raznochinets*. He was not well acquainted
    with the social history of Florence, but poetic instinct suggested Dante's
    social awkwardness—in this instance, I suspect, mistakenly.

13. A reference to Pushkin's very complex relationship to the Emperor Nich-
    olas I and the St. Petersburg court. Pushkin was very proud of his ances-
    try, of what he called his "six hundred years of nobility," although pain-
    fully aware that it counted for little in the St. Petersburg of the 1830's.
    He often contrasted the position of powerful parvenus with his own. At
    the same time, he referred to himself as a *meshchanin* (that is, a bour-
    geois, but of a special kind; an artisan who peddles his own wares on the
    market)—in part ironically and in a derogatory sense, in response to a
    parvenu's slur on his ancestry; yet in part proudly, as someone who made
    his own way, who was someone in his own right, without reference to
    ancestors. At the same time, Pushkin was appalled at the low level of
    literary taste, the contempt in which Russian letters were held by snobs
    who preferred French, and in general the difficulty of being a poet in
    Russia. These feelings were exacerbated by the fact that the emperor be-

stowed on Pushkin the dubious honor of making him a Kammerjunker—an honorary court position that required attendance in uniform. It was, however, an honor normally bestowed on youths in their teens, and Pushkin was in his thirties; there was also some suspicion that either the emperor himself or persons close to him had designs on Pushkin's wife. For a number of reasons connected with the institution of autocracy and the personality of Nicholas I, as well as for reasons of economic dependence, it was impossible for Pushkin to refuse the position, in which he writhed miserably during his last years, and which contributed much to the final impasse of his life, a fatal duel.

14. "As though insulting Hell with his immense disdain." (See note 9 above.)

15. "Their eyes, which were only moist inwardly before, overflowed down to the lips . . ."
Mandelstam follows those commentators who interpret *le labbra*, "the lips," as referring to the eyelids, hence "the labial eye." But see Singleton's commentary (Dante Alighieri, *The Divine Comedy*, trans. Charles S. Singleton, Bollingen Series 80 [Princeton: Princeton University Press, 1970], 1 [pt. 2]: 588).

16. "I was already in a place where the resounding of the water that fell into the next circle could be heard like the hum beehives make."

17. Obviously those of Gustave Doré.

18. From Blok's poem "Ravenna."

19. "Two paws he had, hairy to the armpits; his back and his chest and both his sides were painted with knots and rings: With more color, groundwork, and patterning than ever Tatars or Turks made cloth; nor did Arachne ever weave such webs on her loom."

20. "Cimabue believed that in painting."

21. "Thus I cried with face uplifted."

22. The Italian text reads:

Quante 'l villan ch'al poggio si riposa,
    nel tempo che colui che 'l mondo schiara
    la faccia sua a noi tien meno ascosa,
come la mosca cede a la zanzara,
    vede lucciole giù per la vallea,
    forse colà dov' e' vendemmia e ara:
di tante fiamme tutta risplendea
    l'ottava bolgia, sì com' io m'accorsi
    tosto che fui là 've 'l fondo parea.
E qual colui che si vengiò con li orsi
    vide 'l carro d'Elia al dipartire,

quando i cavalli al cielo erti levorsi,
che nol potea sì con li occhi seguire,
　　ch'el vedesse altro che la fiamma sola,
　　sì come nuvoletta, in sù salire:
tal si move ciascuna per la gola
　　del fosso, ché nessuna mostra 'l furto,
　　e ogne fiamma un peccatore invola."

A more literal translation would read:

As many as the fireflies the peasant sees, taking his rest on the hill—
　　in the season when he who lights the world
　　least hides his face from us,
and at the hour when the fly yields to the mosquito—
　　when he looks down into the valley,
　　down there perhaps where he gathers the grapes and where he plows:
with so many flames was all aglitter
　　the eighth ditch, as I perceived
　　as soon as I came to where the bottom could be seen.
And as he who revenged himself with the help of the bears
　　saw Elijah's chariot at its departure,
　　when the horses rose straight up to heaven,
could not so follow it with his eyes
　　as to see anything except the flame alone,
　　like a little cloud ascending:
so each flame moves along the throat of the ditch,
　　not one showing its theft,
　　yet each flame concealing a sinner."

23. Mikhail Vasilevich Lomonosov (1711–1765). Russian polymath, of
peasant origin. (His father was a prosperous peasant-entrepreneur who
owned many boats and engaged in trade.) Best known for his contribu-
tion to chemistry, but also a poet, grammarian, historian, and reviver of
handicrafts. He played a vital role in the reform of Russian versification.
24. This is a very free version of *Inferno*, XXVI, 112–120. The Italian reads:

" 'O frati,' dissi, 'che per cento milia
　　perigli siete giunti all'occidente,
　　a questa tanto picciola vigilia
de' vostri sensi, ch'è del rimanente,
　　non vogliate negar l'esperïenza,
　　di retro al sol, del mondo senza gente.
Considerate la vostra semenza:
　　fatti non foste a viver come bruti,
　　ma per seguir virtute e conoscenza.' "

A literal translation would read:

" 'O brothers,' I said, 'who through a hundred thousand
dangers have reached the West,
do not deny this so brief remaining
vigil of your senses
experience of the unpeopled world
behind the sun.
Consider your origin:
you weren't made to live like brutes,
but to follow virtue and knowledge.' "

25. "We see like one who has bad light."
26. "And if it had already come to pass, it would not be too early.
So let it be, since it really must be so;
it will weigh on me the heavier as I grow older."
27. Marina Ivanovna Tsvetaeva (1892–1941). Mandelstam's friend and
contemporary, who emigrated in 1922, returned to the Soviet Union in
1938, committed suicide in 1941. The quotation is from a cycle of her
poems about Moscow, written in 1916.
28. "With which the little child runs to his mother—."
29. "Fold on fold," or "layer within layer." Literally, "skirt within skirt."
30. The Italian should read: ". . . da la Muda." Translation: "A narrow
hole in the Tower."
31. "Never did the Danube in Austria,
nor the Don away off there under its cold sky,
make so thick a veil over their current in winter
as there was here: for even if Tambernic
had fallen on it, or Pietrapana,
it would not have given, even at its edge, so much as a creak."
32. "O you who are two within one fire,
if I merited of you while I lived,
If I merited much or little of you,"
33. "All were saying: 'Benedictus qui venis,'
strewing flowers up and about,
'Manibus o date lilia plenis.' "

("Benedictus qui venis": "Blessed are you who come." "Manibus . . .":
"Oh, with full hands give lilies.")
34. "Crowned with olive over a white veil,
a lady appeared to me, clothed, under a green mantle,
in the color of living flame."
35. "Like birds which, risen from the bank,
as if rejoicing at their pasture,
make themselves now into a rounded, now into an elongated flock,

so within lights the holy creatures
  flying, sang, and made themselves
  now into a D, now into an I, now into an L in their configurations."

36. Georg Friedrich Philipp von Hardenberg (1772–1801). Romantic poet,
    mystic. Studied philosophy under Fichte and history under Schiller. Later
    studied geology, became assessor of salt mines. Catholic. Reference is to
    his unfinished novel, *Heinrich von Ofterdingen*, Ch. 5.

37. "Let the Fiesolan beasts make
    themselves into fodder, and not touch the plant,
    if any still grows on that dung heap of theirs."

38. "He took away the shade of our first parent,
    Abel his son, and Noah,
    Moses, obedient law-giver;
    Abraham the patriarch and David the king,
    Israel with his father and his children
    and with Rachel, for whom he did so much."

39. Konstantin Batiushkov (1787–1855). Pushkin's contemporary, a poet
    Mandelstam very much admired. The image is from his poem "Shadow
    of a Friend."

About Poetry

O Poezii was published in Leningrad in 1928. The collection was
chosen by Mandelstam himself, and reworked by him—but also by the
censor. I have used here the texts of the Struve-Filipoff edition,
which uses the texts of original publication, with variants in the notes.

THE WORD AND CULTURE
First published, 1921.

1. Pushkin, *The Gypsies*. In this passage the old gypsy tells Aleko an
   old legend about Ovid in Moldavia, without recalling the poet's name,
   or age. He tells it as if it happened yesterday.

2. Ovid, *Tristia*, 1.3.1–4.

   "When the gloomy memory steals upon me
   of the night that was my last time in the city,
   when I bring to mind that night on which I left so many things dear
     to me,
   even now, the teardrops fall from my eyes."

3. Jacques Louis David (1748–1825). French painter. Before the
   Revolution, leading exponent of the Classical trend in painting; court
   painter to Louis XVI. Became an ardent republican, was elected to
   the Convention, and voted for the king's death. Later, under Napoleon,

became first painter to the emperor. Under the Restoration spent his
last years in Brussels.

4. Catullus, no. 46. "Away let us fly, to the famous cities of Asia."

5. Reference is to Ovid's *Amores*, I.4.65, not to the *Tristia.*

6. See Mandelstam's essay "The Nineteenth Century," which quotes in
   full the poem referred to here. See also "About the Nature of the
   Word," note 2, concerning Derzhavin.

7. Mandelstam, no. 103.

8. Verlaine, "Art poétique," stanza 6. "Take eloquence and wring its
   neck!"

9. Mandelstam, no. 104.

10. "Listen to the tipsy song." This appears to be a misquoting of "Art
    poétique," stanza 2:

> "Rien de plus cher que la chanson grise
> Où l'Indécis au Précis se joint."

("Nothing more precious than the tipsy song [*or* gray song] in which
the Vague is joined to the Precise.")

ATTACK
First published, 1924.

1. Mikhail Alekseevich Kuzmin (1875–1936). Poet, novelist, playwright,
   composer, critic. Author of an important and influential essay, "On
   Beautiful Clarity," whence "Clarism"—the first of a series of revolts
   against the literary dominance of Symbolism. Homosexual, slightly
   decadent. A poet of the Alexandria theme, whom it might be interesting to compare with Cavafy, L. Durrell, E. M. Forster. Remained in
   the USSR, but published almost nothing after 1930.
       Vladimir Vladimirovich Mayakovsky (1893–1930). *The* poet of the
   Revolution. But a strange, complex, contradictory character. A great
   poet. Futurist. Committed suicide.
       Velemir Vladimirovich Khlebnikov (1885–1922). Futurist. Yet
   also a kind of primitive mystic. Magician with words, who broke words
   down to their primitive roots and then built them up again. Died
   in extreme poverty.
       Nikolai Aseev, or Aseyev (1889–1973). Second-string Futurist poet,
   friend and disciple of Mayakovsky, who showed more early promise than
   he later developed.
       Viacheslav Ivanovich Ivanov (1866–1949). Poet, historian, scholar,
   classicist, critic, philosopher. An outstanding Symbolist poet. Studied
   Roman history under Theodor Mommsen. Came under influence of
   Nietzsche. One of the central figures of the Silver Age. Left Russia in
   1924, but did not break completely with the Soviet Union until much
   later. Converted to Catholicism and became a Roman Catholic priest.

He was mentor to the young Mandelstam, as to many other younger poets. His book on the cult of Dionysus, especially, in the popularized form in which it appeared in *Novy Put'*, had considerable influence.

Fedor Sologub, pseudonym of Fedor Kuzmich Teternikov (1863–1927). Symbolist poet and novelist.

Anna Andreevna Akhmatova, born Gorenko (1888–1966). Acmeist poet. First wife of Gumilev, whom she divorced in 1918. Her lover, Nikolai Punin, was, like Gumilev, arrested, and he died in prison. During the period of which Mandelstam writes she was a splendid and influential poet; but in the period between the Second World War and her death she wrote her very greatest poetry, in a strikingly different mode, and her role and influence were unique.

Boris Leonidovich Pasternak (1890–1960). Probably better known to an American audience than any other Russian poet; the author of *Doctor Zhivago*.

Nikolai Stepanovich Gumilev (1886–1921). Head of the Acmeist group. Executed in August, 1921, as a conspirator. See *Selected Works of Nikolai S. Gumilev*, trans. Raffel and Burago.

Vladislav Felitsianovich Khodasevich (1886–1939). Poet, critic, essayist. Parents partly Jewish, partly Polish. Went into emigration; partly rehabilitated in the USSR in 1963, though still not published there. See the moving account of him by his former wife, Nina Berberova, in *The Italics Are Mine*, trans. Philippe Radley (New York: Harcourt, Brace, 1969).

2. *Vesy*, a journal, published by Valery Iakovlevich Briusov (1873–1924), between 1904 and 1909, as an enterprise of the publishing house of which he was the head. Although Symbolist in orientation, the journal was the most urbane, cosmopolitan, and generally sensitive literary journal in Russia.

3. One of Krylov's verse fables (I. A. Krylov, "Svin'ia pod dubom" [The pig under the oak tree], in *Basni* [Fables] [Moscow and Leningrad, 1956], p. 191). The fable is said to be based on an anecdote about Peter the Great and his courtiers.

4. Dmitry Nikolaevich Ovsianiko-Kulikovsky (1853–1920). Prominent critic and literary scholar of the period around the turn of the twentieth century. His work was characteristically sociological in its approach to literature, with a strong concern as well for the "psychology" of the author. His political views were "advanced" and "progressive." His work also reflects the strong influence of Comte and Taine.

ABOUT AN INTERLOCUTOR
First published, 1913.

1. From his long poem *The Gypsies*.
2. Evgeny Abramovich Baratynsky, or Boratynsky (1800–1844). Russian

poet, contemporary of Pushkin. One of the great Russian poets of the nineteenth century, though more appreciated in the twentieth than by his contemporaries.

3. Konstantin Dmitrievich Balmont (1867–1942). Early Russian Symbolist poet, who emigrated in 1921 and died in Paris. Recently, critics like Professor Vladimir Markov have tried to revive a certain interest in his work.

4. Nekrasov, "Poet i grazhdanin" [Poet and citizen]. See "Badger's Burrow," note 8.

5. Semen Iakovlevich Nadson (1862–1887). Melancholy poet of partly Jewish descent, who died of tuberculosis at an early age. Sentimental, diffuse, his poetry of regret and frustration nevertheless had an enormous impact on the Russian generation that came of age in the 1880's.

ABOUT THE NATURE OF THE WORD
First published, 1922.

1. Gavrila Romanovich Derzhavin (1743–1816). Greatest Russian poet of the eighteenth century. Cultivated an odd, interesting and passionate baroque style, sometimes eloquent and solemn, sometimes even grandiloquent, and sometimes "rough," unpolished and very expressive.
   Simeon Polotsky, or Simon of Polotsk (1629–1680). Monk, important church leader, writer and translator. Tutor of Tsar Aleksei's children. Experimented with Russian syllabic verse and with dramaturgy.

2. An oblique reference to the well-known essay by Kuzmin.

3. Also called *The Song of Igor's Campaign*. The title has other variants. It is often referred to briefly as the *Igor Tale*. An anonymous heroic epic dealing with the campaign of the Russian prince Igor against the Turkic Polovtsy. Believed by most scholars to have been composed in the late twelfth century. There has nevertheless been a prolonged scholarly controversy, by no means as yet resolved, as to its authenticity, with a number of scholars concluding the likelihood of an eighteenth-century forgery in the manner of Ossian. For an English version, see the translation by Sidney Monas and Burton Raffel, *Delos*, no. 6 (1971): 13.

4. In an earlier draft, cited by Struve and Filipoff in their notes, Mandelstam quotes two lines of the song:

"Bona puella fur Eulaluà
Bel anret corps bellerzonr, anima."
       (Mandel'shtam, 2: 632)

These are the first two lines of the ninth-century " 'Séquence' de Sainte Eulalie," quoted as follows by Albert Henry, ed., *Chrestomathie de la littérature en ancien français*, 3d ed. rev. (Bern: A. Francke, 1965), p. 3:

"Buona pulcella fut Eulalia:
Bel auret corps, bellezour anima."

("A virtuous maiden was Eulalia: she had a beautiful body and a more beautiful soul.")

5. Pseudonym for Boris Nikolaevich Bugaev (1880–1934). Poet, novelist, critic, mystic, literary theoretician; Symbolist, disciple in anthroposophy of Rudolf Steiner. His father was a brilliant mathematician and a well-known conservative figure in university politics. Brilliant in many fields, Biely is best known in English for his novel *St. Petersburg*, trans. John Cournos (New York: Grove Press, 1959). When Biely died in January, 1934, Mandelstam wrote a cycle of poems dedicated to him.

6. Fedor Ivanovich Tiutchev (1803–1873). One of Russia's very greatest poets. A great philosophical poet, and the poet of chaos. Lived for many years abroad, serving as a diplomat in Munich and Turin. The hero-victim of an intensive love affair late in life with his daughter's governess that resulted in an intense group of love poems. In his political views, a right-wing slavophile.

7. Peter Iakovlevich Chaadaev (1794–1856). See Mandelstam's essay "Peter Chaadaev." See also Peter Chaadaev, *Philosophical Letters and Apology of a Madman*, trans. Mary-Barbara Zeldin (Knoxville: University of Tennessee Press, 1969). After a brilliant military career and early retirement as colonel of hussars, Chaadaev began those musings on Russian culture, history, and destiny that resulted in the *Philosophical Letters*. They were never intended for publication; whether the one letter that found its way into print had been so intended by Chaadaev is not altogether clear. But it was his first and last published work, for on publication he was declared "officially insane" by the political police—the first famous instance, but unfortunately not the last. It is quite impossible to separate the intrinsic quality of Chaadaev's writings from their historical impact, which was so enormous that almost all of subsequent Russian intellectual history may be said to devolve from it.

8. Vasily Vasilevich Rozanov (1856–1919). A strange and controversial writer almost impossible to classify. A "ruminator" on all manner of subjects, whom the Formalist critic Victor Shklovsky called a "novelist" because his works are put together somewhat in the manner of fiction, though they are composed not only of narration and dialogue, but also of diary entries, aphorisms, private letters, and newspaper clippings. He exulted in the "privacy" and "intimacy" of his style.

9. Innokenty Fedorovich Annensky (1856–1909). Russian poet and critic. Headmaster of the Tsarskoe Selo lyceum, Annensky was a superb classicist and a translator from the Greek and from the French. He was one of the inspirers of the revolt against Symbolism in the direction of Acmeism.

10. Sergei Mitrofanovich Gorodetsky (b. 1884). Early Acmeist poet, who introduced notion of "Adamism." (See *Selected Works of Nikolai S. Gumilev*, trans. Raffel and Burago.) He accepted the Revolution whole-

heartedly, managed to adapt himself to Stalinism, and enjoyed considerable success as well after the thaw.

Vladimir Narbut (1888–?). Acmeist poet; joined the Communist
Party in the Ukraine during the Civil War; afterward, ran a small publishing house. He was expelled from the Party in 1928 and is rumored to
have been arrested in 1937 or 1938.

Mikhail Alexandrovich Zenkevich (b. 1891). Early Acmeist; poet
and translator. Joined Party in 1947.

11. Ernst Theodor Wilhelm Hoffmann (1776–1822). German Romantic
writer and jack-of-all-trades. Ingenious writer of macabre fantasies and
great storyteller. Substituted Amadeus for Wilhelm in his name, as homage to Mozart. The full range of his talents was most clearly displayed
in his collection of stories *Die Serapionsbrüder* (4 vols., 1819–1821)—
the name of a club of Hoffmann's more intimate friends.

12. Henry Thomas Buckle (1821–1862). English historian, author of the
History of Civilization in England, a monument to the hope for a "science" of history.

13. Antonio Salieri (1750–1825). Director of the Italian Opera at Vienna.
Beethoven, Schubert, and Liszt were his students, and they seem to have
learned from him especially in the matter of dramatic composition. His
intrigues against Mozart gave rise to the stories that he poisoned Mozart.
(See A. Della Corte, *Un italiano all'estero* [Torino: G. B. Paravia,
1936].) Pushkin uses this legend in his "little tragedy," *Mozart and
Salieri.* There, Salieri poisons Mozart to balance the equation of cosmic
justice; i.e., he feels that the musical genius that eludes him in spite of
all his incredibly hard work and perfectionist habits must not be allowed
to be seen to settle on Mozart, portrayed as a "natural," without any
effort at all. It is a play in which "hard-working talent," burdened by a
sense of cosmic injustice, avenges itself on "natural genius." Mandelstam
interpreted the poetic drama differently. For him, Salieri represented the
principle of hard, even superhuman, work and effort—the obligation imposed by genius—while Mozart represented "inspiration" alone. Nadezhda Mandelstam has pointed out that Mandelstam thought of Mozart
and Salieri as two principles, to some degree antagonistic, yet *both* essential to the creative process. He tended, however, to emphasize the importance of Salieri, regarded by other readers of Pushkin as the villain
of the piece. (See N. Mandelstam, *Mozart and Salieri.*) Mrs. Mandelstam suggests very acutely that when Mandelstam talked of Salieri the
figure he really had in mind was Bach.

NOTES ABOUT POETRY
First published, 1923.

1. Nikolai Mikhailovich Iazykov (1803–1846). A major Russian poet in
the 1820's. Pushkin thought his poetry too much champagne, not enough

water. But he was Gogol's favorite poet. *Iazyk* means "language" or "tongue," and Gogol wrote: "Not in vain was he given such a name; he is master of his language as an Arab is of his fiery steed" (quoted by D. S. Mirsky, *A History of Russian Literature* [New York: Knopf,, 1949], p. 104.)

2. The "apostles to the Slavs"; brothers. Cyril, originally named Constantine, died in 869; Methodius in 885. They were born in Thessalonica, of Greek descent, but acquainted with Slavonic. Cyril was educated at Constantinople and went on a mission to the Jewish Khazars on the Sea of Azov. Later, both brothers participated in the struggle between the native Slavic nobility of Bohemia and Moravia against the German clergy, which included a struggle over the liturgical language, the Germans commanding a monopoly of Latin. Under the patronage of Rostislav, Prince of Moravia, Cyril attempted to translate parts of the liturgy into Slavonic. What is called Cyrillic script was probably not invented by him, though it is not unjustly associated with his name. Cyril was welcomed back to Rome, where he brought the relics of Saint Clement. He is buried in the Church of San Clemente in Rome.

3. One of the first artificial international languages, like Esperanto.

4. Pillar saints; i.e., saints who practiced the ascetic discipline of sitting for prolonged periods of time on top of a pillar, flagpole-sitters of the ancient world, though of course with a very different purpose, that being to emphasize their complete separation from the world and the temptations and distractions of the world. The most famous of these was Simeon of Syria, who, in the fifth century, built himself a pillar, climbed it, and between the years 420 and 459 remained sitting there.

5. Christoph Willibald von Gluck (1714–1787). German composer from Bohemia. Strongly influenced by Handel. By lending to recitative a special weight and an effect of its own, he gave opera a new dramatic force.

6. Afanasy Afanasievich Fet (1820–1892). Illegitimate son of a Russian landowner named Shenshin and a German woman named Foeth. Great lyric poet of nature, love, and despair, at a time when major poetry seemed otherwise to have dried up in Russia.

7. Alexander Ivanovich Herzen, or Gertsen (1812–1870). Illegitimate son, or "child of the heart," of a great senatorial nobleman, Iakovlev. Author of one of the great books of memoirs of the nineteenth century (*My Past and Thoughts: The Memoirs of Alexander Herzen*, trans. Constance Garnett, rev. Humphrey Higgins, 4 vols. [New York: Knopf, 1968]). Author of an important essay, "Buddhism in Science." Early Russian socialist, and perhaps more than any other single person the intellectual "daddy" of *narodnichestvo*, or Russian populism, through his conception of the *mir*, or village commune, as a kind of primal education in socialism. Influential as a publicist, who changed the European view of Russia: before Herzen, European intellectuals tended to see

Russia as a monolith; Herzen persuaded them to make a crucial distinction between the government and the people. From London, Herzen published his Russian newspaper, *Kolokol* [The bell], which played an important role in the immediate background of the emancipation of the serfs between 1857 and 1861. In 1863, the newspaper began to lose influence, and Herzen was displaced in the minds of the radical Russian public as an important figure by more extreme and strident personalities. The scene referred to here is a vivid one from the early pages of Herzen's memoirs.

Nikolai Platonovich Ogarev (1813–1877). Interesting minor poet of melancholy reflection and unfulfilled yearning; friend and political ally of Herzen's.

THE END OF THE NOVEL
Published for the first time in the collection *About Poetry*, 1928.

BADGER'S BURROW
First published, 1922.

1. Alexander Alexandrovich Blok (1880–1921). Great Russian poet, to some degree a Symbolist, but above all schools, as Mandelstam indicates. He used the great themes—country, love, destiny—and wrote exalted verse often in the mode and form of popular songs. His long poem *The Twelve* is called by many *the* poem of the Revolution.
2. Razumnik Vasilevich Ivanov-Razumnik (1878–1946). Critic, historian, prominent figure in both Russian political and literary circles, closely associated with the left wing of the Socialist Revolutionary Party, a friend of Blok's and Biely's. Left Russia in 1943, died in a D.P. camp. Published interesting prison memoirs, *My Prisons*. It was he who, in one of his early books, called the Russian intelligentsia "a spiritual brotherhood." His literary criticism was not of a kind that Mandelstam approved.

Iuly Isaevich Aikhenvald (1872–1928). Impressionist critic, an emigré from 1921.

Wilhelm Alexandrovich Sorgenfrei (1882–1938). Critic, poet, and translator.
3. Boris Mikhailovich Eikhenbaum (1886–1959). One of the Formalist critics, author of brilliant essays on Gogol, on Tolstoy, and on poets and poetry. Later, turned more to long, scholarly-biographical works.

Victor Maksimovich Zhirmunsky (1889–1972). Distinguished scholar and critic. In his youth, he was very close to the Formalists. Still earlier, he was, with Mandelstam, a student at the Tenishev School in St. Petersburg.
4. Apollon Alexandrovich Grigoriev (1822–1864). One of the Russian

poètes maudits, author of an interesting book of memoirs, *My Literary Wanderings*, much admired by Dostoevsky. An intense slavophile, he praised the Russianness of the Moscow region called Zamoskvorech'e (the area beyond the Moscow River from the main city, populated by merchants and artisans) and placed a high poetic value on things distinctively Russian.

5. Sophie Perovsky (1853–1881). A Russian revolutionary, member of the People's Will Party (Narodnaia Volia). Born into a noble family, she joined the "Going to the People" Movement of 1872–1873. She was arrested several times. She worked very closely with A. I. Zheliabov and became his common-law wife. With him, she led the conspiracy to assassinate Alexander II, in which she played a decisive part.

6. Nikolai Ivanovich Kostomarov (1817–1885). Russian and Ukrainian historian and ethnographer, who had an early reputation as a radical. His notion of the distinctive features of Ukrainian history opposed him to "official" historians.

   Sergei Mikhailovich Soloviev (1820–1879). The founder of modern historical studies in Russia, the Russian Ranke. He was also the father of the philosopher and mystic Vladimir Soloviev.

   Vasily Osipovich Kliuchevsky (1841–1911). Historian noted for the elegance of his style in lecturing and writing as well as for his scholarship; his interest focused on the nonstate aspects of historical development, especially the *social* and the sociocultural. He emphasized the importance of geographical factors in Russian history and the shaping influence of the process of colonization.

7. Vladimir Sergeevich Soloviev (1853–1900). Theologian and philosopher, poet and mystic; tried to promote the reunion of Christendom under the leadership of the Pope. His intuition of Sacred Wisdom, or Sophia, produced three visions of the feminine embodiment of that Wisdom, the Eternal Womanly, or *Ewige Weibliche*. Both his poetry and his teachings had enormous impact on the development of Symbolism.

8. Nikolai Alekseevich Nekrasov (1821–1878). Leading Russian poet of the second half of the nineteenth century. Above all, *the* poet of Russian Populism. Many of his poems are sentimental and rhetorical; yet he probably was the most influential of *all* Russian poets and helped to shape the sensibilities of Dostoevsky, Blok, and the whole Russian radical intelligentsia. His specialty was the pathos of poverty, in a mode very close to folk traditions and resonant for Russian culture.

9. A special form of folk song, usually very short, associated with a factory or working-class milieu, usually witty, often ribald.

THE NINETEENTH CENTURY
First published, 1922.

1. Not quite. Mandelstam is using Baudelaire for his own purposes. Baude-

laire's albatross is laid out on the deck of a boat, not the earth, and is rather a different kind of bird:

"Souvent, pour s'amuser, les hommes d'équipage
Prennent des albatros, vastes oiseaux des mers,
Qui suivent, indolents compagnons de voyage,
Le navire glissant sur les gouffres amers.

A peine les ont-ils déposés sur les planches,
Que ces rois de l'azur, maladroits et honteux,
Laissent piteusement leurs grandes ailes blanches
Comme des avirons traîner à côté d'eux."
          (*Les Fleurs du mal*: "L'Albatros")

("Often, for fun, the men of the crew catch albatrosses, vast sea birds, which follow, indolent travel companions, the ship gliding over the bitter abysses. No sooner have they laid them on the planks than these kings of the blue, awkward and ashamed, woefully let their great white wings languish like oars at their sides.")
The last line concludes a comparison of the albatross "out of his element" with the poet: "Ses ailes de géant l'empêchent de marcher." ("His giant's wings prevent him from walking.")

2. See "Buddhism in Science," in Alexander Herzen's *Selected Philosophical Works* (Moscow: Foreign Language Publishing House, 1956).
3. An intricately prescribed Japanese verse form.
4. Mandelstam, no. 133.

PETER CHAADAEV
First published, 1915. For Chaadaev, see "About the Nature of the Word," note 7.

1. These are the opening lines of Ershov's well-known fairy-tale poem of the hump-backed horse ("Skazka o kon'ke-gorbunke"), which exists in many editions and many translations. The horse is a magic animal that can fly.

NOTES ABOUT CHÉNIER
First published, 1928.

1. André Chénier (1762–1794). French poet, son of a diplomat, poet of liberty. At first, he approved of the French Revolution; later, he wrote an ode to Charlotte Corday upon her assassination of Marat; he was arrested and guillotined on 8 Thermidor. Pushkin admired him.
2. Clément Marot (1496–1544). French Renaissance poet and humanist, translator of Ovid. In his poems there are traces of imitations of Villon. Marot did *not* father the line known as the Alexandrine, which takes its

name from the twelfth-century *Roman d'Alexandre*, and which Marot rarely if ever used. Ronsard, a generation later, popularized it. *Aleksandriitsa*, genitive form of *aleksandriets*, the word Mandelstam uses, is not the one normally used for the Alexandrine and causes some puzzlement.

3. "Fathers of a people, architects of the laws!
You who know how to establish with a firm, sure hand
A solemn code for man."

4. "As Latona, pregnant, almost a mother,
Victim of a jealous power,
Without refuge wandered over the earth."

5. "The oppressor is never free."

6. *Les Bucoliques* is a collection of poems by Chénier; there is no comparable work called *Idylles*, although there *is* a series of poems within the *Bucoliques* called "Idylles marines."

7. "And then in a charming way the letter inquires
What I want of you, what commands I have for you!
What do I want? you say! I want your return
To seem very slow to you; I want you to love me
Day and night (night and day, alas, I am in torment).
Present in their midst, be alone, be absent;
Sleep, thinking of me! Dream that I am near;
See only me, unceasingly, and be completely with me."

FRANÇOIS VILLON
First published, 1913.

1. "Will you leave him here, poor Villon?"

2. *Cassell's New French Dictionary* translates *pet* as "fart" and *vesse* as "silent evacuation of wind."

3. "Movement above all!" As was mentioned in the introduction, Verlaine's line (in "Art poétique") actually reads: "De la musique avant toute chose" ("Music above all").

Uncollected Essays and Fragments

PUSHKIN AND SCRIABIN (Fragments)

Published by Struve and Filipoff from an incomplete typed copy found by Nadezhda Mandelstam among Mandelstam's papers. The essay probably dates back to the time of the composer's death in 1915. According to the editors, the essay was completed in 1919 or 1920. It was submitted to a Miscellany of some sort, which never appeared. Later, Mandelstam, who apparently felt some misgivings about the essay, was unable to find it in its completed form. These fragments have appeared in the Russian emigré press, in 1963 and 1964, as well as in the Struve-Filipoff edition. The essay shows traces of a muted polemic with Mandelstam's former mentor, Viacheslav Ivanov, and Ivanov's notions of the "suffering god," the cult of Dionysus and its resemblance to Christianity. Perhaps *polemic* is too strong a word. The choice of Scriabin and Pushkin as exemplars of Christian art is odd, to put it mildly. Scriabin was a kind of demonist and Pushkin an agnostic, certainly a religious man but hardly a Christian.

1. Alexander Nikolaevich Scriabin (1872–1915). Russian modernist composer. Pasternak worshipped him and was an ardent disciple in his youth. Experimented with synesthetic effects of light and sound.
2. Having died from wounds received in a duel with a foreigner, Pushkin, in the winter of 1837, was buried secretly at night—his body was secretly removed from St. Petersburg to a monastery graveyard near Pskov, because the government of Nicholas I feared "nationalist" demonstrations.
3. The motif of the black sun, or nighttime sun, recurs many times in Mandelstam's work. George Ivask has traced it to Gérard de Nerval's poem "El Desdichado," where the poet writes of the "soleil noir de la Mélancolie" ("black sun of Melancholy"). The image has, in fact, a number of origins: *The Tale of Igor's Men* (image of the solar eclipse), Racine, Viacheslav Ivanov, the Talmud. The pun in Russian on "sun-heart" (*solntse-serdtse*), lost in English, refers to Pushkin. For a discussion of the image see the Struve-Filipoff edition (Mandel'shtam, 3: 404–411). See also George Ivask's essay in that same volume, "Ditia Evropy" [Child of Europe], especially pp. x–xi; Taranovsky, "Pchely i osy v poezii Mandel'shtama"; and Brown, *Mandelstam*, pp. 231–237.

THE MORNING OF ACMEISM

First published in 1919. But probably written much earlier, in 1912 or 1913, as a third "manifesto" of Acmeism, following those of Gumilev and Gorodetsky. For discussions of Acmeism as a movement, see my introductions to *Selected Works of Nikolai S. Gumilev* and *Complete Poetry of Osip Emilevich Mandelstam*, both trans. Raffel and Burago. The striking similarity between the tenets of Imagism (before it became, as Ezra Pound put it, "Amygism," referring to the coarse but indubitable energies of Amy Lowell) and Acmeism have been pointed out several times, most recently, and with great acumen, by Brown, *Mandelstam*. In his literary essays, Mandelstam tends to minimize the importance of "Adamism," associated with Gorodetsky. Nevertheless, he continues to emphasize the biological metaphor, the notion of the image as an "organ." It might perhaps be added that among the many meanings of Acme or Akme—peak, pinnacle, height—is that of climax, including the notion of sexual climax.

LITERARY MOSCOW
First published, 1922.

1. Fedor Iaseevich Dolidze (b. 1883), used to organize poetry readings both in Petrograd and Moscow and in the provinces. On one particular evening, according to the notes in the Struve-Filipoff edition (Mandel'shtam, 2: 647), he arranged for the election of a "King of Poetry," and Igor Severianin's followers, who packed the hall, got their favorite elected. This was in February, 1918, in Moscow. Mayakovsky, apparently, wasn't too happy about it. On another occasion, an evening of "feminine poetry" was arranged, at which Marina Tsvetaeva read.
2. Marina Ivanovna Tsvetaeva (1892–1941). A great and splendid poet. Mandelstam is most unfair to her here. In fact they were close at one time, and three of his poems are dedicated to her. Her fate was a tragic one. She emigrated and lived in Czechoslovakia for many years, isolated from the "emigration" as such. She returned to the Soviet Union after the disillusionment of Munich. Her husband was killed; her daughter was arrested, but survived. She herself committed suicide in Elabuga, not far from Kazan. She has been posthumously "rehabilitated."
3. Anna Dmitrievna Radlova, born Darmolatova (1891–1949). Poet, translator of Shakespeare and Marlowe.
4. Alexander Afanasievich Potebnia (1835–1891). Literary scholar, professor at the University of Kharkov; along with A. N. Veselovsky, one of the main proponents of Neo-Kantianism in literary and linguistic theory. In attacking him, as they did, the Formalist critics could scarcely conceal their great debt to him and Veselovsky. See Victor Erlich, *Russian Formalism*, 2d. ed. (The Hague: Mouton, 1965.)
5. Victor Borisovich Shklovsky (b. 1893). The youngest, most brilliant, and possibly also the most erratic of the Formalists. He founded the group called Opoyaz. Later, he showed great courage in honoring his friendship with the Mandelstams. See his volumes, recently translated by Richard Sheldon and published by Cornell University Press, *A Sentimental Journey* (Ithaca, 1970) and *Zoo* (Ithaca, 1971).
   For Eikhenbaum and Zhirmunsky, see "Badger's Burrow," note 3.
6. Pseudonym for Adelina Efron (b. 1900). She later converted to a standard, cheery Socialist Realist style in the 1930's.
7. Sophie Iakovlevna Parnok (1885–1933). Poet and translator. Mandelstam is, apparently, as unfair to her as to Tsvetaeva. She published some poems under the name of Andrei Polianin, but the bulk of her work remained unpublished. I have been told by scholars who are familiar with her *Nachlass* and whose judgment I trust that she is an unrecognized poet of the magnitude of Tsvetaeva or Akhmatova. The family name was originally Parnakh, and her brother, who emigrated to Paris, was known as a poet and a critic of the dance. See Brown, ed., *The Prose of Osip Mandelstam*, p. 47.
8. See "Attack," note 1.

9. MAF: Moscow Association of Futurists. The Lyrical Circle: a circle of poets whose one published *Miscellany* included poems by Mandelstam.

10. Aleksei Eliseevich Kruchenykh (1888–1973). Futurist poet who attempted to create an entirely new language. See his *Izbrannoe* [Selected works], introduced by V. Markov (Munich: Fink, 1973).

11. See "Attack," note 1.

LITERARY MOSCOW: BIRTH OF THE *Fabula*
First published, 1922.

1. Leonid Nikolaevich Andreev, or Andreyev (1871–1919). Author of *The Seven Who Were Hanged* and the play *He Who Gets Slapped*. He often moved from a Realist-Naturalist style to something approaching Surrealism. A prolific and well-known writer in his time, he has since fallen from fashion.

   Maxim Gorky, pseudonym of Aleksei Maksimovich Peshkov (1868–1936). Very well known; a gifted, if extremely uneven writer. He was, between quarrels, a friend of Lenin's. Having supported the Bolsheviks for a long time by means of his royalties, he became a prominent and important political figure at the time of the Revolution, when he criticized the Bolsheviks severely and finally, after a quarrel with Lenin, left Russia in 1921, only to return again in the late 1920's, at Stalin's urging, to become the official idol of Soviet literature and the patron saint of Socialist Realism. During the time of the Civil War, he did more than any other single man to keep writers and the literary intelligentsia alive. See the very interesting observations about him in Berberova, *The Italics Are Mine*, pp. 174–197 and passim.

   Ivan Sergeevich Shmelev (1875–1950). Prerevolutionary Russian Realist writer of the Znanie school (from the publishing house Znanie, or "Knowledge," under Gorky's tutelage). Emigrated in the early 1920's.

   Sergeev-Tsensky. Pseudonym of Sergei Nikolaevich Sergeev (1875–1958). "Realistic" writer of the sad lot of the peasant and the provincial intelligentsia. Later he did Socialist Realism.

   Evgeny Ivanovich Zamiatin (1884–1937). Author of the antiutopian novel *We;* also a brilliant essayist and critic. In 1971, he was allowed to leave the Soviet Union and go to Paris. Although one of the few gifted writers with some real understanding of Marxism as well as a commitment to the Revolution, he has never been rehabilitated.

2. Almanacs, in the publication of which Gorky played a large role. See note 1 above on the Znanie school. For the most part, the writers involved were Realists like Gorky.

3. Pseudonym for Boris Andreevich Vogau (1894–1937). Author of *The Naked Year*; a gifted and innovative writer. Got into trouble, arrested. Recently rehabilitated.

4. The Serapion Brothers, a group of ten young and talented writers and

poets, founded in the 1920's. Their manifesto tried to proclaim some sort of political and stylistic independence, and what they had in common was a commitment to craftsmanship. Their title derived from the novella by Hoffmann.

5. Nikolai Nikolaevich Nikitin (1895–1963). A member of the Serapion Brothers, but managed to adjust to the 1930's. He won the Stalin Prize in 1951 for a novel about Anglo-American intervention in Russia at the time of the Civil War (1918–1919).

   Konstantin Aleksandrovich Fedin (b. 1892). Author of *Cities and Years*.

   Mikhail Iakovlevich Kozyrev (b. 1892). A novelist of great unimportance.

   Vadim Germanovich Lidin (b. 1894). Minor writer, was a war correspondent in the Second World War; author of a moderately interesting book of memoirs published in 1957.

   Mikhail Mikhailovich Prishvin (1873–1954). A remarkably gifted nature and travel writer.

6. Nikolai Leskov (1831–1895). Storyteller and novelist. At his best, one of the greatest of Russian prose writers, but very uneven. His story "The Enchanted Wanderer" is well known.

7. Vsevolod Ivanov (b. 1895). Novelist, whose early prose showed a certain poetic sense of exotic detail. Member of the Serapion Brothers' literary circle, which tried to establish a certain independence from ideology for literature. In his youth he worked at some odd jobs, including that of fakir in Central Asia.

STORM AND STRESS

First published, 1923. The Russian title, "Buria i natisk," is the standard translation of the German *Sturm und Drang*.

1. Aleksei Nikolaevich Apukhtin (1840–1893). Sentimental poet of melancholy *Weltschmerz*; in some of his works, a civic, reform-oriented poet.

   Arseny Arkadievich Golenishchev-Kutuzov (1841–1913). Author of many long narrative poems, close to Apukhtin in spirit; mood of melancholy world-weariness.

2. Mikhail Alekseevich Kuzmin (1875–1936). Poet, novelist, critic, composer, with a decadent yellow-ninetyish flavor. Both imaginative and prolific. Wrote a novel about Cagliostro. It was he who gave Mandelstam's collection of poems, published in Berlin, the title *Tristia*. See also "Attack," note 1.

3. Evdokia Petrovna Rostopchina (1811–1858). An amateur poet. She wrote an allegorical poem about oppression in Poland which got her into trouble with the political police of Nicholas I. Khodasevich has written a splendid essay about her.

Peter Andreevich Viazemsky (1792–1878). Pushkin's friend, a minor poet and gifted critic.

4. *Balagannyi raeshnik.* At Russian fairs and carnivals, the side-show barker usually announced the attractions of his booth in rhymed lines.

5. Sergei Esenin (1895–1925). Poet of peasant origin, friend and protégé of Kliuev, though eventually more famous. Wrote elegiac poems about the Russian countryside; indulged in a desperate pose called "hooliganism"; married Isadora Duncan. Committed suicide.

Nikolai Kliuev (1885–1937). Poet of peasant origin. A mystical revolutionary, his enthusiasm began to wane as early as 1918. Arrested in 1933 and died in Siberia.

6. François Coppée (1842–1908). French poet and novelist, known as *poète des humbles*; wrote about cares, loves, and sorrows of common people. Late in life reconverted to Catholicism, became violent nationalist and anti-Dreyfusard.

HUMANISM AND MODERN LIFE
First published, 1923.

FOURTH PROSE

First published, 1966, in the first New York edition of Mandelstam. A *samizdat* version, which had been circulating for some time, was published by *Grani* [Facets] in 1967. A revised version was published by Struve and Filipoff in their edition of 1971. A section of the manuscript, apparently dealing with Mandelstam's views on socialism, was destroyed. The title "Fourth Prose," according to Nadezhda Iakovlevna, was a kind of amiable code name by which she and Mandelstam referred to the piece. However, it also signified, literally, Mandelstam's fourth piece of prose: i.e., after "The Hum of Time," "The Egyptian Stamp," and *About Poetry.* It is also a playful reference to the "fourth estate" and Mandelstam's "vow" to it (See Mandelstam, no. 140). There is also a suggestion of the "Fourth Rome" that was never to be. It is Mandelstam's "declaration of independence" and statement of solidarity with the fourth estate. It was written in 1929–1930, before the Mandelstams' trip to Armenia, and tinkered with as late as 1931. This spirited outburst against the notion of an "authorized" literature, against all the still relatively genteel but extremely ominous beginnings of totalitarian thought control, was inspired by the "Eulenspiegel affair."

The ZIF (Zemlia i Fabrika, "Land and Factory") publishing house commissioned Mandelstam to revise an edition of a translation of *Till Eulenspiegel* (*Ulenspiegel*, in the Russian transliteration) in 1928. The translation had been once revised by V. N. Kariakin in 1916, from one made in 1915 by A. G. Gornfeld under the pseudonym of Korshan. When the new edition appeared in 1928, Mandelstam alone was credited with it on the title page. Neither Mandelstam nor the original translators knew of this or had given their consent. In that world of Literature with a capital *L*, in which Mandelstam was considered a maverick, and which was itself in the process of being organized for the slaughter yard, the affair was rapidly blown up into a scandal. Mandelstam was accused of plagiarism. The bitter tone of his references to "translation" and "translators" has something of its origins here; but of course the real enemies were Literature and Totalitarianism.

Mandelstam might have used the occasion to make his amends, to conform and join the literary sheep. He refused. He answered the charges with the pledge of the entire body of his literary work. In May, 1929, Mandelstam wrote an article (not included in this volume) about the wretched current state of translation. This was answered by a crude attack. A number of writers came to his defense—among them, Boris Pasternak, Mikhail Zoshchenko, Valentin Kataev, and even such Bolshevik and proletarian stalwarts as Alexander Fadeev and Leopold Averbakh. (Zoshchenko [1895–1958] was a brilliant satirist and master of comic melancholy, much admired by Mandelstam for his sense of the "new" Soviet language and its relation to reality; see his *Scenes from the Bath-House*, trans. S. Monas [Ann Arbor: University of Michigan Press, 1961]. Kataev [b. 1897] was the author of *The Embezzlers*, trans. I. Zarine [New York: Dial Press, 1929], and the play *Squaring the Circle*; he was liberal and protective in his attitude to younger writers. Fadeev [1901–1956] was an old-fashioned "monumental" novelist, generally an orthodox Socialist Realist writer; his novel *The Young Guard*, first published in 1945, was rewritten drastically to conform to Stalin's orders. He became secretary-general of the Writers' Union. Averbakh [1903–?] was a literary critic, militant advocate of a proletarian literature, and leader of the Russian Association of Proletarian Writers [RAPP]; he was later liquidated as a Trotskyite.)

The Federation of Unions of Soviet Writers (the centralized Writers' Union had not yet been formed) resolved the "controversy" by declaring that, though Mandelstam had been unfairly attacked, he was morally to blame for having failed to draw up a contract with the original translators. The affair was not really forgotten until Bukharin intervened and arranged for Mandelstam's trip to Armenia.

"Fourth Prose" is an outburst, an anathema directed against those who defame "Mother Philology," a therapeutic release of all that Mandelstam had been holding back since the early 1920's. As therapy, it ended the writing block which had left almost a five-year gap in his poetry. It also helped him clarify to himself his own position as an outsider, for whom there could no longer be any thought of compromise or concession. It was a full-voiced assertion of his own identity as well as a denunciation of "the enemies of the word." (See N. Mandelstam, *Hope against Hope*, pp. 177–178; also, *Hope Abandoned*, pp. 526–530.)

1. Benjamin Fedorovich Kagan (1869–1953). Well-known mathematician. Professor at Moscow University since 1923. Won a Stalin Prize in 1923. Not clear why he was brought into the Mandelstam "case"; perhaps because he had himself translated numerous mathematical texts.

2. Isaiah Benediktovich Mandelstam, a namesake, but not a relative. Also a translator.

3. In Mecca, one of the highlights of the Moslem pilgrimage to Mecca, formerly a pagan shrine, then site of Mohammed's early preachments.

4. Groups of Komsomols or young Communists, organized to help the Party ostensibly in its struggle against bureaucracy and mismanagement. Their activity was greatly expanded with the conclusion of the New Economic Policy in 1928. Often, "the light cavalry" was used, as Struve and Filipoff point out, to pry into the personal life of members of the intelligentsia, people accused of retaining some sort of inner allegiance to the prerevolutionary way of life. Struve and Filipoff suggest that the assignment of cripples to such a task was not uncommon; there may have been some deliberate selection of people who could in some way be counted on to carry a grudge.

5. Commission for the Improvement of the Living Conditions of Scholars, created in 1921.

6. Pseudonym for Alexander Stepanovich Grinevsky (1880–1932), a writer with an unusual and exceptionally adventurous biography; he had been a sailor, a fisherman, a prospector for gold, a soldier, a Socialist Revolutionary, a convict in exile and in prisons. Had a considerable reputation even in the pre-Soviet period for his stories of fantasy and adventure; no less successful in the Soviet period with novels along those lines.

7. One of the charges that kept coming up against Mandelstam, associating him with the "old regime," was the one that he wore a "fur coat." Nadezhda Iakovlevna has eloquently described the poor tattered coat that was the pale spring from which this great rumor gushed forth. But she also refers to it symbolically: "In ['Fourth Prose'] he spoke of our blood-stained land, cursed the official literature, tore off the literary 'fur coat' he had momentarily donned and again stretched out his hand to the upstart intellectual, 'the first Komsomol, Akaky Akakievich' " (N. Mandelstam, *Hope against Hope*, p. 178).

8. Organized in 1920 as the Writers' Club; later the house of the Writers' Union. There is a splendid satirical description of the goings-on there in Michael Bulgakov's novel, *Master and Margarita*, trans. Mirra Ginsburg (New York: Grove Press, 1967). It is called Griboedov House there. Griboedov was also a Russian "classic," but his name means, literally, "mushroom eater," and the outstanding "cultural" feature of the house is its excellent, cheap restaurant.

9. Arkady Georgievich Gornfeld (1867–1941). A well-known scholar and critic. Before the Revolution he was a prominent contributor to the populist-oriented journal *Russian Wealth* (*Russkoe bogatstvo*) and the

author of a number of books on Russian and foreign literature.

10. This is an admittedly poor attempt to render *khaldy-baldy*, a nonsense phrase to be sure, but one that suggests a number of things. *Balda* is a blockhead, or a hammer. *Khalda* isn't anything, but suggests *khaltura*, or hack work. Since the phrase is repeated several times, my incapacity to translate it has some seriousness. Clarence Brown suggests "idiot-shmidiot." That has advantages, and disadvantages.

11. Askanaz Artemevich Mravian (1886–1929). People's Commissar of Foreign Affairs for the Republic of Armenia in 1920–1921. From 1923 until his death he was Commissar of Public Education and vice-chairman of the Armenian Sovnarkom. *Muravei* means "ant," on which Mandelstam puns the commissar's name; hence "antic," an attempt to convey Mandelstam's pun.

12. Antisemitism was part of the campaign against Mandelstam.

13. The line is from Sergei Esenin's poem, "I will not begin to deceive myself . . ." ("Ia obmanyvat' sebia ne stanu . . .") from his poem-cycle called *Taverns of Moscow* (*Moskva kabatskaia*, 1922).

14. Dmitry Dmitrievich Blagoi (b. 1893). Soviet literary scholar.

15. D'Anthès was the man who killed Pushkin in a duel. He was also, much later, a senator under Napoleon III.

16. Vladimir Galaktionovich Korolenko (1853–1921). Novelist, populist, humanitarian social reformer. Wrote many stories and novels of peasant life, somewhat sentimentalized. Interesting book of memoirs, *A History of My Contemporary.*

17. The *Stock Exchange News* (*Birzhevye Vedemosti* or *Birzhevka*) was a well-known newspaper before the Revolution and printed much more than stock-exchange news. After the Revolution, it changed its title several times, but expired in 1918; that is, it was closed. It had been owned by Stanislav Maksimovich Propper. The *Evening Red Gazette* was a popular Petrograd-Leningrad newspaper.

18. Nikolai Ivanovich Bukharin (1888–1938). An Old Bolshevik, member of the Party since 1906; Lenin, in his *Testament,* called him the Party's ablest theoretician. Later, one of Stalin's victims. He was at the time the editor of *Pravda,* the official organ of the Party. *Pravda,* of course, means "truth" (or "justice"). He was later editor of *Izvestiie.* In 1929, Stalin's noose was already beginning to tighten around Bukharin. He was finally made to participate in the Great Purge Trials and was executed in 1938. He was Mandelstam's only important official Party "protector" and benefactor. Nadezhda Iakovlevna has pointed out in her memoirs that Mandelstam and Bukharin had in common the traits of impulsiveness and honesty, of doing things without careful calculation of the cost.

19. Angelina Bosio was an Italian soprano who sang four seasons in St. Petersburg before she died there in 1859. Her death is the subject of a poem by Nikolai Nekrasov, "About the Weather" ("O pogode"). In

Mandelstam's story "The Egyptian Stamp," she plays a notable role, and Mandelstam seems to associate her with overtures and finales, beginnings and ends. See Brown, ed., *The Prose of Osip Mandelstam*, pp. 149–189; also, Brown's notes to same. Mandelstam planned to write more, perhaps a novel, about Bosio.

20. Vechnaia Pamiat'. Penultimate part of the Requiem Mass of the Russian Orthodox service, repeated three times.

21. Marie-Joseph, the younger brother of André Chénier, was a successful playwright. He is said to have remained silent when his speaking out might have saved his brother André (who had begun by welcoming the French Revolution, but later wrote in praise of Charlotte Corday) from the guillotine. He survived the Terror and was lavishly successful under Napoleon. So much for "literature"!

22. Dante is very much on Mandelstam's mind. It is not too fanciful to assume that something like a darkly modern *Divine Comedy* is beginning to stir.

23. Central figure of Gogol's short story "The Overcoat."

24. "Hey, Ivan"—from a poem by Nikolai Nekrasov of that title. Many of Nekrasov's poems deal with and are dedicated to outcasts and the suffering poor. Moiseich means "son of Moses." Nekrasov's figure is also called Ivan Moiseich.

25. A *bublika* in the original, which is almost a cross between a doughnut and a pretzel.

26. The well-known statue of the great Russian fabulist, which depicts all around and below him the animals that were the characters of his verse fables. The linking of Zoshchenko and Krylov is, in my opinion, a flash of critical inspiration.

27. Moscow Union of Consumer Associations.

28. *Viy*—from Gogol's story of that name. A gnomelike creature, whose eyelids reach to the ground, and who therefore cannot see. Once his eyelids have been raised with outside help, however, he can point to the source of evil.

29. See Mandelstam, no. 354.

Journey to Armenia

First published, 1933. I have relied basically on the text in the Struve-Filipoff edition (Mandel'shtam, 2: 137–176) but have collated this with the text published in *Literaturnaia Armenia* 167, no. 3: 83–99, to which is added an interesting postscript by Nadezhda Mandelstam.

Armenia appealed to both the Christian and the Hellene in Mandelstam. The journey was at once a reprieve, a symbolic journey, and an apocalypse. The essay on Dante is also closely linked with the journey. Mandelstam took it at a time when Soviet writers were in the habit of

visiting far corners of the USSR to report back on the strides of progress
made by the first five-year plan and the collectivization of agriculture—
two revolutions within the Revolution, with more drastically far-reach-
ing effects than the October Revolution itself, for it was these that actually "Sovietized" or, rather, Stalinized the Soviet Union. A number of
talented writers at this time were singing the praises of the White Sea
Canal, built with slave labor. This is one of the themes of Solzhenitsyn's
richly orchestrated *Gulag Archipelago*. Of course, Mandelstam's "travel
piece" turned out altogether differently.

While others celebrated the organization of time and place into a
totalitarian knot through the minutely detailed and severely imposed
five-year plans, Mandelstam sang timelessness, or rather a different kind
of time; time linked to the "all-human" world of the Mediterranean,
Classical and Christian. He sang Bergsonian time and the power of the
word and of "building."

The *Journey* is also a vision of the end; Mandelstam's own end certainly. He identifies very closely with the captured Armenian king at the
end of his account. Yet the survival of Armenia encourages him to ride
on. It is not likely he hoped much for his own physical survival; but the
journey taught him something of *his* place in time; and that was heart-
ening.

A considerable role in Mandelstam's life in Armenia belongs to B. S.
Kuzin (the biologist B. S. K.), who, at a time when literary people were
shunning Mandelstam, spoke to him long and earnestly about evolutionary theory, and who also prompted him, through his interest in German
literature, to reread many of the German writers who were close to him.

1. From *On Guard* (*Na Postu*), the journal of RAPP (Russian Association
   of Proletarian Writers). A militantly proletarian tendency in pre-1934
   Soviet literary life.
2. Reference is probably to Pushkin's Mazepa (*Poltava*) rather than
   Byron's. I use Byron's spelling, assuming it more familiar to the English
   reader.
3. Khlysty: a religious sect. The meaning is literally "flagellants," but they
   were not known for their dour ascetic self-scourging as much as for their
   ritualized joyous responses to the divine; they were "ecstatics."
4. Another religious sect. Literally means "milk-drinker."
5. "Official" language. The charge was often leveled against Mandelstam.
6. Nikolai Iakovlevich Marr (1864–1934). Gifted linguist; Marxist. Persuaded Stalin of the truth or at least the usefulness of his theory of the
   class origins of language. For a time, he occupied a place in linguistics
   almost equivalent to that of Lysenko in genetics. After his death, he and
   his work were denounced by Stalin himself, in Stalin's last major theoretical pronouncement, in 1952, his essay on linguistics.
7. That part of Moscow beyond the Moscow River from the main city, as-

sociated with the playwright Ostrovsky and with Apollon Grigoriev, a place inhabited by merchants and artisans, and redolent of the spirit of old, traditional Russia.

8. Paul Signac, *D'Eugène Delacroix au néo-impressionisme* (Paris, 1911).

9. The Russian word *obyvateli*, which means literally "the inhabitants, those who live there," also carries the connotation of "philistines."

10. Boris Godunov, regent during the reign of Tsar Fedor I (1584–1598), Fedor's brother-in-law, and one of the last close companions of Fedor's father, Ivan the Terrible. Later himself elected Tsar (1598–1605) by the Zemsky Sobor. His reign inaugurated the Time of Troubles. Godunov was the descendant of a minor boyar family that was Tatar in origin, and it was sometimes said that the Tatar shone through.

11. To my query, Clarence Brown responded: "The termenvox is the well-known musical instrument named after its inventor, the immortal Lev Termen (b. 1896)," to which he added, "of course."

12. Alexander Ilyich Bezymensky (b. 1898). Poet, member of the Party since 1916. During the period 1923–1936, he had been an active member of RAPP (Russian Association of Proletarian Writers) and one of the basic contributors to its journal *On Guard (Na Postu)*.

13. The Russian says literally "shoe tree." It did not strike me as correct to stretch a glove on a shoe tree. However, the play of words in Russian justifies the usage: *na kolodku,* "on a shoe tree"; *okolodok,* "neighborhood."

14. In Russian, fruits ripen and eyes become bloodshot by means of the same verb: *nalivaiushchikhsia plodov,* "ripening fruits"; *glaza nalivaiutsia krov'iu,* "eyes become bloodshot."

15. *Lipovyi* means "deceptive," but also suggests *lipa,* a linden or lime tree; i.e., "linden-lined."

16. *Nedotroga* may mean either the flower or an especially touchy person.

17. One of the oldest settlements in Armenia, at one time an important cultural center. It is about twenty miles from Erevan and contains a number of ancient ruins, some going back as far as the fifth century.

18. A suburb of Erevan, on the way to Ashtarak.

19. King of the Arshakide dynasty, which ruled Armenia from 63 to 428 A.D. In the fourth century the kingdom was divided into Roman and Iranian spheres of influence.

20. Shapur, or Sapores (Greek), or Pahlavi Shahpur II (310–379), defeated the Romans in 363 (death of Julian), and overran Armenia; made some attempt to impose Zoroastrianism on Christian Armenia. Shapur imprisoned the Parthian King Arshak (Arsaces III) in a fortress, where the latter committed suicide. In spite of the political unrest that characterized it, the fifth century that followed these events was the Golden Age of Armenian culture.

21. Mandelstam works in the "stolen air" theme, central to "Fourth Prose."

Index of Names